I HATE PCS,

SECOND EDITION

Bryan Pfaffenberger

I Hate PCs, Second Edition

Library of Congress Catalog No.: 94-66725

ISBN: 1-56529-827-6

96 95 94 3 2 1

Interpretation of the printing code: the rightmost double-digit number is the year of the book's printing; the rightmost single-digit number, the number of the book's printing. For example, a printing code of 94-1 shows that the first printing of the book occurred in 1994.

Publisher: David P. Ewing

Associate Publisher: Corrine Walls

Publishing Director: Lisa A. Bucki

Managing Editor: Anne Owen

Product Marketing Manager: Greg Weigand

Dedication

To Suzanne, always

Credits

Acquisitions Editor:
Nancy Stevenson

Product Director:
Steve Schafer

Production Editor:
Noelle Gasco

Copy Editors:
Elsa Bell
Danielle Bird
Lori Lyons
Lynn Northrup

Technical Editor:
Michael Watson

Book Designer:
Amy Peppler-Adams

Cover Designer:
Sandra Stevenson

Production Team:
Stephen Adams
Stephen Carlin
Jenny Chung
Kim Cofer
Karen Dodson
Angela Judy
Bob LaRoche
Beth Lewis
Steph Mineart
Shelly Palma
Chad Poore
Linda Quigley
Bobbi Satterfield
Nanci Sears Perry
Susan Shepard
Ann Sippel
Tina Trettin
Dennis Wesner
Donna Winter
Lillian Yates

Indexer:
Charlotte Clapp

Editorial Assistants:
Ruth Slates
Theresa Mathias

Composed in *Goudy* and MCP*digital* by Que Corporation.

About the Author

Bryan Pfaffenberger got his first computer in the Stone Age of personal computing—1981, to be exact. Since then, he has written more than 40 books that help people learn how to use PCs. The author of Que's best-selling *Que's Computer User's Dictionary*, he has taught computing and computing applications at a variety of colleges and universities. When he's not trying to explain how to use computers, he teaches the sociology, history, and ethics of technology at the University of Virginia's School of Engineering and Applied Sciences. All these serious things aside, he enjoys backpacking, mountain biking, and cracking jokes. He lives with his wife, kids, and cats in the country near Charlottesville, Virginia.

Acknowledgments

A lot of people contributed to this book. But I'd like to start by thanking the department store employee who, while trying to demonstrate how to start a computer, picked up the mouse and attempted to turn on the computer by using it like a TV remote control—you know, pointing it at the screen and clicking the button. (I am not making this up.) From this, I concluded that millions of people would probably benefit from having "All The Basic Stuff" explained to them in a way that wasn't socially embarrassing.

We've worked hard on this second edition of *I Hate PCs* to make sure that this book meets your needs and deals with the latest developments in personal computing, such as sound boards, CD-ROM discs, and the Internet. (If you don't know what these are, don't worry—that's what this book is for!).

Writing a book such as this one isn't a lonely, personal thing—it's the product of active, creative collaboration by lots of talented people. Thanks to them all, but I'd like to single out Lisa Bucki, this project's Publishing Director, for her concept of the revision's scope; Steven Schafer (Product Director), for many helpful (and sometimes hilarious) comments on the manuscript; Michael Watson (Technical Editor), for the best technical editing job that I've seen in writing more than 40 books; and Noelle Gasco, Danielle Bird, Lynn Northrup, and Elsa Bell for a very diligent editing job, always with the reader's needs in mind. Nancy Stevenson (Acquisitions Editor) helped to keep us all in touch—as did the Internet and CompuServe! In fact, this book was written in spite of the fact that the Atlantic Ocean had positioned itself between your author and Que Corporation.

Most of all, I'd like to thank readers like you who not only want computer technology explained to them, but want to have fun doing it. You've taught all of us to lighten up a bit!

Trademark Acknowledgments

PCs!

Contents at a Glance

	Introduction	3
I	Up and Running!	10
II	Let's Get Physical (Hardware)	80
III	Software	244
IV	Save Me!	342
V	Quick and Dirty Dozens	374
	Index	395

Table of Contents

Introduction 3

About This Book 4
Part I: Up and Running! 4
Part II: Let's Get Physical (Hardware) 5
Part III: Software 7
Part IV: Save Me! 8
Quick & Dirty Dozens 8
About This Book's Icons 9

I Up and Running! 10

1 Learn the Minimum — and Love It 13

Computers Scare Me! 14
You Need To Become Computer Literate—NOT 15
What This Book Is About 16
What's a PC? 17
A *Clone*? Is It Illegal? 17
But I Still Don't Understand What a Computer Is! 18
What Can You Do with a Computer? 19
What's All This Junk on My Desk? 21
Introducing a Desktop PC System 22
Do I Have To Know How All This Stuff Works? 27
The World of Computer Programs (Software) 27
Where Do I Go from Here? 31

2 On Your Mark, Engage 33

Setting Up Your System 34
Ouch, My Back Hurts! 35
Front Panel Stuff 36
Turn On, Tune In, Get Confused 39
How To Start Your Computer 39
Well, Did It Start? 40

What You See 41
  The BIOS Message 41
  Say Aaahh, and Let's Check Those Memory Chips 42
  Hello, Drive A? 43
  Loading DOS 43
What Now? 44

3 Read This If You See C:\... 47

The DOS Prompt, Beloved by Millions—Not! 48
Invoking (Er, Running) a Program 49
In Search of the Missing Program: Changing Directories 50
The DIR Command 53
Making a Graceful Exit 55
Turning Off Your Computer 56
Restarting the Computer 57

4 Read This If You See a Box That Says "Program Manager" 59

What is Windows? 61
Why Windows? 62
What Do You Mean, This Is Gooey? 62
Handy Guide to the Basic Mouse Maneuvers 65
Windows Calisthenics 65
Pull-Down Menu Basics 67
Dialog Box Basics 69
I Hate Using the Mouse! 70
And Now Back to Program Manager,
  Already in Progress 71
Opening a Program Group Window
  within Program Manager 72
Tile and Cascade 73
Launching Programs 75
Switching Back to Program Manager 76
Exiting a Windows Application 77
Quitting Microsoft Windows 79

II Let's Get Physical (Hardware) 80

5 Inside the Big Box 83

The Parts of a Typical System 84
The Really Important Parts 85
Forgettable Stuff Inside the System Unit 86
Can I Really Forget the "Forgettable" Stuff? 87
486? Pentium? Huh? 88
8088 89
286s or ATs 90
386—The Bare Minimum 90
486—Now We're Cookin' 91
Pentium 91
What's a "Power PC?" 92
Is My Computer Fast? 93
Hard Disk 97
What Does "200MB" Mean? 98
Help! I'm Out of Space on My Hard Disk! 99
Memory—It Isn't Storage 100
Do I Have Enough Memory? 101
What is "Memory Management," and Do I Have To Do It? 103
This Game I Just Bought Requires "Expanded Memory"! What's That? 103
Ports 103
We Wouldn't Want Things To be Too Simple, Would We? 104

6 Disks and Disk Drives 107

Floppy Disks vs. Hard Disks 108
Buying the Right Floppies for Your System 110
What Size Drive Do You Have? 110
Density and Capacity 111
360KB 5.25-inch disks 113
1.2MB 5.25-inch disks 113
720KB 3.5-inch disks 113
1.4MB 3.5-inch disks 114
The Floppy Disk Match Up 114

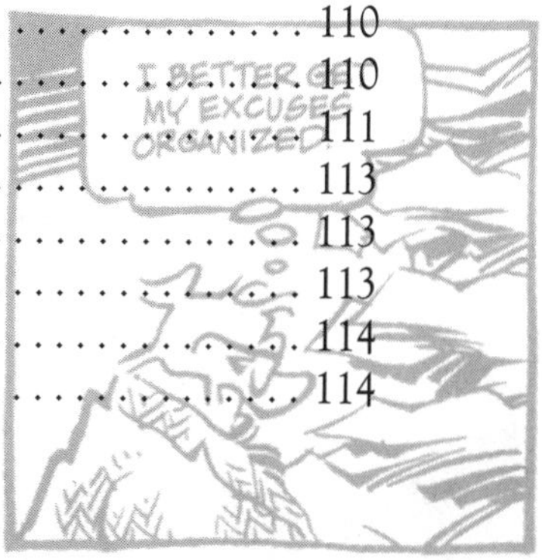

Buying Disks 115
Inserting and Removing Floppy Disks 116
Don't Mess with This Disk 118
Keeping Your Disks and Disk Drives Happy 118
Dire Warnings Concerning Things Not To Do With Disks 119
Does My Drive Need To Be Cleaned? 120
Formatting Floppies 120
Formatting with DOS 120
Formatting with Windows 122
Did Everything Go Smoothly? 123
What's On This Disk? 124

7 Monitors **127**

The Monitor and the Adapter 128
The Acronym-Collector's Guide to Computer Monitors 129
Do I Need a Video Accelerator? 131
What's a "Local Bus"? 132
And What Adapter Do You Have? 134
Monitors Are Pretty Simple 134
Screen Sizes 135
What's the Difference Between an Analog and a Digital Monitor? 136
What is Interlacing and Dot Pitch? 136
What Is This Resolution Number All About? 137
Monochrome or Color? 138
What Are Those Funny Knobs? 139
Cleaning the Screen 139
The Joy of Screen Savers 139
Are These Things Safe? 140
It Says It's an "Energy Star Monitor"! 141

8 Keyboards, Mice, and More **143**

The Computer Keyboard 144
Those Highly Irritating Toggle Keys 145
Decoding All Those Keys with Arrows on Them 147
The Cursor Won't Move! 148

Weird Keys That Typewriters Never Had . . . 148
It Tells Me to Type Ctrl+A, but I Can't Get It To Work! . . . 150
What to Do If You Hear a Beep While Typing Really Fast . . . 151
I Spilled My Pepsi On It! . . . 151
Keyboard Styles of the Rich and Famous . . . 152
What's That Funny Numb Feeling . . . 154
Mice Are Nice . . . 155
How Do I Hook This Thing Up? . . . 158
It Says I'm Not Using the Right Mouse Software! . . . 159
There's No Pointer! . . . 159
Trackballs . . . 160
Handwriting Recognition . . . 161
Speech Recognition . . . 161

9 Nobody Loves Printers, But We Do Need Them **165**

Types of Printers . . . 166
What About Color? . . . 168
So, What's the Best? . . . 168
Will It Work with My Programs? . . . 170
What Is a "Page Description Language?" . . . 171
What Are Those Funny Buttons? . . . 172
The Joy and Confusion of Printer Fonts . . . 172
Fonts with DOS . . . 174
What is TrueType and Why Do Font Lovers Prefer Windows? . . . 174
I Paid *Thousands* For This System. How Come I Get Courier On the Printouts? . . . 175
It says, "24 Points." Huh? . . . 176
What Are "Soft Fonts?" . . . 176
Hah hah! She Has to Install Her Printer . . . 176
What Does "LPT1" Mean? . . . 176
Making the Physical Connection . . . 177
Test Your Printer . . . 178
Testing, Testing, 1, 2, 3.... . . . 178
It Won't Respond! . . . 178
Setting Up Your Printer with Windows . . . 179

The Pain and Heartbreak of Printing Problems 180

10 Sound! Action! Multimedia! 183

Why Bother? 185
But Isn't All This Just Hype? 187
What Do I Need for Multimedia? 188
Sound Boards 189
My Notebook Doesn't Have Any Expansion Slots! Can I Get Sound? 191
I Can't Hear Anything! 191
What Is MIDI? 191
CD-ROM Drives 192
This Drive Is Only $99! 193
Can I Play My Audio CDs? 194
It Says It Comes with a Caddy! 194
Do I Need a Drive That Can Play More Than One Disc? 194
Speakers 195
Digital Photography 196

11 You've Got Your Modem (or Fax Board) Working! 199

What is a Modem—and, for That Matter, a Fax/Modem? 200
Why Are Modems Needed? 200
9600 Baud? Huh? v.32 bis! What? 201
Hooking Up Your Modem 202
You'll Need Communication Software 203
Things to Do with Your Modem 204
Sharing Data with a Friend or Coworker 204
Electronic Mail 204
Calling On-Line Services 204
Having Fun with Local Bulletin Boards 206
Using the Internet 207
What is the Internet for? 207
How Do You Get Connected to the Internet? 208
Fax It to the Max! 209
If I Had a Scanner 210
This Hand-Held Scanner Is Cheap! 211

Local Area Networks (LANs) 211
Why a Network? 211
It Says I Have a Drive Called "F!" 213
Questions To Ask Your Network Administrator 213

12 Take It With You... And Work All the Time! 217

From Luggable to Palmtop 218
There are Notebooks, and Then There Are Notebooks... 221
What Does "PCMCIA" Stand For? 223
Can I Take It to the Beach? 223
My Battery's Dead! 224
No, It Isn't a Bomb! It's a Computer! 225
Please, Give Me My Mouse Back! 225
Making Connections 226
No Keyboard? It's a PDA! 228

13 Them Ol' System Software Blues 231

What's An Operating System? 232
What Are System Utilities? 234
Back It Up (Or Else...) 234
Doubling Your Disk Space 236
Restoring Your Hard Disk's Peak Performance 236
The Great Virus Hunt 236
Managing Memory 237
Undelete 238
Cache Software 238
Disk Repair Utilities 238
So, Where Do I Get All These Cool Utilities? 239
Do I Have To Use MS-DOS? 241
What's PC-DOS? 241
What's Novell DOS 7? 242
What's OS/2? 242
What's UNIX? 243

III Software 244

14 Grunt-Level Operating System Facts 247

Files 248
Why Directories, Anyway? 250
Why Can't I Put Everything In One Big Directory? 250
Why Do They Call It a "Tree"? 251
One Directory at a Time 253
What is the "Current Directory"? 253
Path Names 254
Those Wacky Wild Cards 255
The Horror of System Files 257
Where Do I Go From Here? 258

15 All You Really Need To Know About DOS 261

What Is a "Command-Line Operating System?" 262
Changing Drives 264
How Do I Access The Disk In My Floppy Drive? 264
I Can't Access This Drive! 264
I've Had a General Failure! 264
Changing Directories 265
Clearing the Screen of Inflammatory or Embarrassing Messages 266
Peeking at a File's Contents 266
More Rather Painful Information about Path Names 267
Making Directories 268
Deleting a File 268
Deleting a Group of Files 270
Recovering from an Accidental Deletion 271
Making a Copy of a File 272
Copying a File to a Different Drive or Directory 273
Copying a Group of Files 274
Moving Files 274
Renaming Files 275
The Quest for the Missing File 276
Copying a Whole Disk 276

I Only Have One Drive! ... 277
It Says "Write Protect Error!" ... 277
My File! My File! It's Gone! (Sob!) ... 278
Learning More About DOS ... 278

16 Picture Yourself in a World Full of Icons **281**

Why You Can't Completely Ignore DOS Yet ... 282
Taking a Look at File Manager ... 282
Displaying the Files Stored on a Floppy Disk ... 284
It Says Error Selecting Drive! ... 285
Displaying Directories ... 285
Displaying Files ... 286
There's Too Many Files! I Can't Find My Novel! ... 287
Where's That File I Saved Yesterday? ... 287
I Want MORE Information! ... 287
I Want My Pretty Fonts! ... 288
Using File Manager's Windows ... 288
Selecting Files ... 288
Deleting Files ... 289
Copying and Moving Files ... 290
Copying Files by Using the Mouse ... 290
Moving Files by Using the Mouse ... 291
Duplicate File Name? Huh? ... 292
Renaming Files ... 292
Finding a Missing File ... 292
It says `No matching files were found!` ... 294
Running Programs by Using File Manager ... 294
Undeleting Files ... 294
It Says, File Destroyed! ... 296
Creating a New Directory ... 297
Deleting a Directory ... 298
Exiting File Manager ... 298

17 Finally, Programs That Actually Do Things for You **301**

About Application Software ... 302
Word Processing Programs ... 305
Spreadsheet Programs ... 306
Database Programs ... 307

A Suite Deal 308
Is Software Integration for You? 309
Beyond the Big Three 309
Fun and Games 309
What's "Shareware?" 310

18 Buying, Installing, and Starting Programs **312**

Buying Software 314
Why Shouldn't I Just Copy My Friend's Program? 315
Will It Run on My Computer? 316
Before You Open the Package... 316
Listing Your Computer's Capabilities 316
What the Program Needs 318
Help! This Program Needs 51MB of Disk Space! 319
Installing a Program with DOS 319
Installing a Windows Application 322
What Might Happen during Installation 323
Starting the Program 324
Starting a Program by Using DOS 324
Starting a Windows Program 325
Learning How To Use Your Software 325
Keeping Your Software Happy 326
Should You Upgrade? 327
What Do You Expect? This Is Version 1.0 327
How Can I Tell the Difference Between a Maintenance Upgrade and a Real New Version? 328

19 You Too Can Become a Global Village Idiot **331**

What Is the Internet? 332
That's Great, But, What Can You Do with the Internet? . . . 334
Getting Connected to the Internet 335
Cracking the Code: E-Mail Addresses 337
Beyond E-Mail: FTP, Gopher, and More 338

IV Save Me! 342

20 Gosh, It's Not Working 345

I Can't Turn It On! 346
Worst Case Scenario 1: Dead Power Supply 347
It Started, But I See an Error Message 347
Worst Case Scenario 2: Your Memory Has Gone Bad . . . 348
Worst Case Scenario 3: Your Hard Disk Has Gone Bad 349
Why Does It Always Try To Read Drive A? 349
The Power Just Went Off! 349
The Computer Won't Respond 350
My Program Won't Start! 352
Worst Case Scenario 4: You Erased the Program 353
Where's My Mouse? 353
The Time and Date Are Wrong! 354
Worst Case Scenario 5: The Battery Is Dead 355
I Can't Copy This File! 355
My File's Gone! 356
I Just Reformatted My Floppy Disk! 357
I Just Reformatted My Hard Disk! 357
This Floppy Isn't Working! 358
Worst Case Scenario 6: The File Allocation Table (What?) Is Bad 359
I Can't Access My Hard Disk! 359
My Printer Won't Print! 360
Worst Case Scenario 7: The Printer Isn't Installed Correctly 361
Still Giving You Trouble? 361
Are You in over Your Head? 362

21 Help! 365

Try These Tricks before Hitting the Panic Button 366
Describing Your System 368
Describing the Problem 369
Calling the Technical Support Hotline 370
Getting Your System Repaired 371

V Quick & Dirty Dozens 374

12 Minor But Embarrassing Beginner's Boo-Boos 377
12 Good Things You Should Always Do 381
12 Acronyms People Expect You To Know 385
12 Most Common DOS Error Messages 388
12 More Cool Things To Get for Your Computer 391

Index 395

Introduction

Unlike some of those geeks who walk around boasting about how much memory they have, you're not in love with PCs. My congratulations—you've resisted all the computer hype, and that says good things about you: Sensible. Skeptical. And sane. After all, if someone fell in love with a microwave oven, we'd haul them off to the looney bin, wouldn't we?

You don't love PCs, but you have to use one. Perhaps, in your bosses' infinite wisdom, he has seen fit to deposit one on your desk, and maybe you've been given "an afternoon or two" to learn DOS (he says, of course, "That's all the time it took *me* to learn it!" Never mind the fact that he can't remember where he left his car keys.) Or maybe you've bought one out of fear that you would be left behind in the coming computer revolution (an unpleasant prospect).

So, that's my assumption about you—you don't love PCs, you've got one staring at you, and you've got to learn how to use it. A little more: Given the fact that you have a life, you'd like to learn just the minimum that's needed to use your PC successfully. And, you wouldn't mind having fun while you're doing it.

This book has a simple, irreverent, and probably dangerous premise: There is nothing to be gained by learning everything there is to know about computers. Most people just need to know enough to turn the darned things on and get their work done as quickly as possible. You should learn the Least Possible Knowledge (LPK) that will help you do this. And that's exactly what you'll find in this book.

About This Book

Part I: Up and Running!

This is a mini-course in personal computing. If you're in a huge hurry, you can get started just by reading the first four chapters.

- ✔ Chapter 1, "Learn the Minimum—And Love It," is for people who have never used a computer before. It contains some very basic facts about your computer, including what the various parts are called.

- ✔ Chapter 2, "On Your Mark, Engage (Starting Your System)!" deals with the practicalities of starting your computer, and understanding what's happening as this occurs. You'll find lots of practical information that nobody takes the time to explain to beginners.

- Chapter 3, "Read This If You See C:\...," is for people whose computers are set up to run the MS-DOS operating system—DOS, for short. This chapter tells you how to deal with DOS basics, including how to start a program (which you need in order to do something useful with the computer). Skip this chapter if your computer is set up to run Microsoft Windows. (If you're not sure, ask the person who sold you the computer.)

- Chapter 4, "Read This If You See a Box That Says 'Program Manager,'" is for those lucky individuals whose computers are set up to run Microsoft Windows automatically. You'll learn how to perform basic Windows tasks, including starting Windows applications. Skip this chapter if your computer is set up to run DOS only.

Part II: Let's Get Physical (Hardware)

This part of *I Hate PCs* contains information about the physical part of your computer system—the parts that could break glass if you threw them hard enough. You don't have to read all of this, or even any of this. Just look up the information you need, when and if you need it.

- Chapter 5, "Inside the Big Box (Forgettable System Unit Mysteries)," goes into your computer's internal parts in more detail. Here, you'll find simple explanations of what people are talking about when they say, "I've got a 486DX2 running at 33 megahertz with 16 megs of RAM."

- Chapter 6, "Disks and Disk Drives," deals with floppy disks—how to prepare them, how to use them, and what to do if they're being uncooperative.

- Chapter 7, "Monitors (Get the Picture)," explores computer monitors and the internal thing—called a display adapter—that generates the picture. You'll learn what people are talking about when they say things like "Super VGA."

- Chapter 8, "Keyboards, Mice, and More," contains useful information and tips for using the computer keyboard (what are all those funny keys?) and the mouse (click? drag? huh?).

- Chapter 9, "Nobody Loves Printers, But We Do Need Them," helps you understand how to get your printer to work, including dealing with common printing problems. You'll also learn about those cool fonts (typefaces) that everyone's using.

- Chapter 10, "Sound! Action! Multimedia! (Sound Boards and CD-ROM)" introduces the accessory stuff you'll need to hear digital sound when you use your computer, see movies and animations, and play those CD-ROM disks you've been hearing about. This isn't just for education; sound and CD-ROM disks are on their way to becoming standard parts of computer systems. You'll find simple, clear explanations of these parts (and what they do) in this chapter.

- Chapter 11, "You've Got Your Modem (or Fax Board) Working!" introduces the parts (hardware) you need to link your computer with other computers, as well as turn it into a fax machine. This chapter also introduces on-line serves such as CompuServe, which millions of computer users really enjoy using.

- Chapter 12, "Take it with You—And Work All the Time (Notebooks and Personal Digital Assistants)!," introduces those cool notebook computers and their smaller cousins, such as Apple's Newton. Notebook computers can be a real alternative to a big, bulky desktop—I wrote this book on a little tiny Compaq Contura (less than 8 lbs).

- Chapter 13, "Them Ol' System Software Blues," introduces the basic concepts of system software, the programs that are needed to keep your computer running happily. You'll learn what MS-DOS is and what it does.

Part III: Software

This part of *I Hate PCs* deals with software, the instructions that tell your PC what to do (distinct from your instructions to the PC, which tell it where to go). As with Part II, you don't have to read all or any of these; just look at the information you need to know.

- ✔ Chapter 14, "Grunt-Level Operating System Facts: Files and Directories," introduces important concepts of file storage and disk organization that everyone needs to know—whether you're using DOS or Windows.
- ✔ Chapter 15, "All You Really Needed To Know About DOS (You Learned at the C:\> Prompt)," takes up where Chapter 3 left off. You'll learn more basic DOS procedures, such as how to copy and move files.
- ✔ Chapter 16, "Picture Yourself in a World Full of Icons (Managing Files with File Manager)," deals with file-management tasks with Windows. It takes up where Chapter 4 left off, conveying additional Windows knowledge that you'll need for day-to-day work with the computer.
- ✔ Chapter 17, "Finally, Programs That Actually Do Things for You (Application Software)," surveys the programs that can help you get your work done at the computer. You'll find mini-reviews of popular (and recommended) computer software. By the way, it's not all so serious—there's a section on games.
- ✔ Chapter 18, "Buying, Installing, and Starting Programs," deals with the practicalities of equipping your system with software, including the often time-consuming and confusing task of installing programs (transferring them from disks to your computer).
- ✔ Chapter 19, "You Too Can Become a Global Village Idiot: Electronic Mail and Internet," introduces the world's fastest-growing communication system, which you can access with your PC and a modem. You'll learn what all the fuss is about, and you'll find practical information about how to send electronic mail to the Internet and how to get access to neat things like Gopher and Usenet discussion groups.

Part IV: Save Me!

Look here if you're having trouble with your computer.

- ✔ Chapter 20, "Gosh, It's Not Working," surveys the many things that go wrong while you're working with a computer, and tells you what to do. You'll also find six Worst Case Scenarios, those (fortunately rare) disasters where something bad has really happened and you need expert help.
- ✔ Chapter 21, "Help!" gives you tips and tricks to try when you're computer isn't cooperating with you.

Quick & Dirty Dozens

These are lists of miscellaneous things that didn't really fit into any of the other chapters. Take a look to see if there's anything of interest to you.

- ✔ "12 Minor But Embarrassing Beginner's Boo-Boos," such as mispronouncing computer terms that everyone else seems to know.
- ✔ "12 Good Things You Should Always Do," such as backing up your work.
- ✔ "12 Acronyms People Expect You to Know," such as ASCII and CPU.
- ✔ "12 Most Common DOS Error Messages," and what to do when you see one of them.
- ✔ "12 More Cool Things To Get for Your Computer"—get out your VISA card!

About This Book's Icons

Flip through the book. Do you notice those pictures in the margins? These pictures signal to you the type of information contained next to the icon. If you're not interested in this type of information, skip it. Here's what the icons mean:

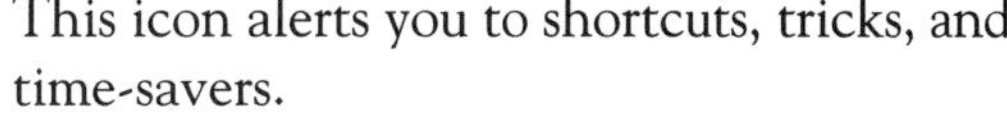

This icon alerts you to shortcuts, tricks, and time-savers.

EXPERTS ONLY

This icon flags skippable technical stuff that I couldn't resist including. I am, after all, a nerd, although I now understand, after a painful process of self-examination, that most of the rest of the world does not share my enthusiasm for technology.

CAUTION

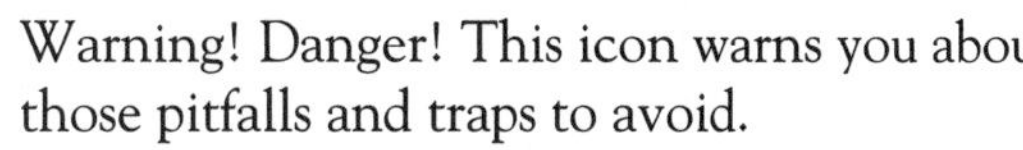

Warning! Danger! This icon warns you about those pitfalls and traps to avoid.

BUZZWORDS

This icon warns you that you're about to learn technospeak—some nifty word or phrase like *byte* or *bit* or *bit* or *blurp*.

PART I

Up and Running!

Includes:

1: Learn the Minimum—and Love It

2: On Your Mark, Engage (Starting Your System)!

3: Read This If You See C:\...

4: Read This If You See a Box That Says "Program Manager"

Shoe®
By Jeff MacNelly
THIS COMPUTER HAS CHANGED MY LIFE...

I FINALLY HAVE A SWIVEL CHAIR.

I BET THIS COMPUTER HAS REVOLUTIONIZED THE WAY YOU DO YOUR JOB.
NO, NOT REALLY.

WHAT?!
I NEVER USE IT.

BUT THE COMPUTER HAS TOTALLY CHANGED LIFE FOR MILLIONS...
RIGHT.

IS THERE SOMETHING WRONG WITH IT?
SHOULDN'T BE. IT'S BRAND-NEW.

THEN MAYBE IT'S THE SOFTWARE.

DO YOU HAVE TROUBLE WITH THE MEMORY FUNCTION?
ALL THE TIME.

YOU MEAN THE COMPUTER NEEDS MORE CAPACITY?
NO.
I MEAN I CAN'T REMEMBER HOW TO TURN IT ON.

Top Ten

Uses for an Unplugged Computer

10. Large, flat surface of system unit ideal for stacking correspondence that you really do plan to answer some day

9. Screen a great place to put Post-It notes

8. Use floppy disk drive to stash wafer-thin chocolate snack when fellow dieters stop by to chat

7. Rub keyboard over neck and back for relaxing, Dozens-O-Fingers massage

6. Hang mouse from doorknob to make hilarious cat toy

5. Use 12-foot printer cable to practice lasso techniques

4. Printer paper tray provides secure, yet accessible, storage for current issue of *Soap Opera Digest*

3. Bulky system components are easily arranged so that entire desktop is covered, leaving no room for additional work

2. Stack the system unit, monitor, and computer manuals so that Philodendron, African violet has sufficient light from window

1. Position computer so that boss cannot see you reading romance or science fiction novels

CHAPTER 1

Learn the Minimum —and Love It

IN A NUTSHELL

- Why computers scare people—and how to get over it fast
- Why it's actually a great idea to learn the minimum about computers
- What this book is about
- What a PC is (hint: not a Macintosh)
- What a "clone" is and why it's OK
- What the difference between "hardware" and "software" is
- What you can do with a computer (that's worth doing)
- A quick, guided tour of a desktop PC system
- A quick rundown of those software program things
- What DOS and Windows are
- Why you need to choose between DOS and Windows

Computers Scare Me!

Today, more than 100 million personal computers exist worldwide. For many people, that's 100 million reasons for anxious emotions, ranging from a vague sense of disquiet to outright panic.

A lot of people won't use computers because they're afraid of looking dumb—like the hapless salesperson at a Sears store, who was asked to turn on a computer for a demonstration. In a hilarious attempt to switch the machine on, he pointed the little mouse thing at the screen and tried to start the computer by clicking the mouse button (as if the mouse was a TV remote control). Of course, this was witnessed with delight by a crowd of snickering 9-year-old computer jockeys, who knew perfectly well that you can't start a computer that way.

Chances are you'll never do anything *this* dumb. But, even if you do (or think you did), just remember this: mistakes are part of learning. If you're too afraid of mistakes, you'll never learn. *That's* the biggest mistake you can make.

So, you've decided to learn how to use a PC. Maybe you've concluded that you need PC skills to keep up with the job market. Or maybe your company, in its infinite wisdom, just stuck a PC on your desk (your boss probably came by and said, "Learn how to use it? A snap! I taught myself in one afternoon!"). So, let's start by tackling these fears head-on.

Ways to talk yourself out of computer anxiety

- ✔ **I'm afraid I'll ruin something.** You can't hurt the computer by pressing the wrong key. To really do some damage, try putting the system unit through a plate glass window, or leave the mouse on a railroad track.

- ✔ **I'm afraid I won't know what to do.** Relax, I'll *tell* you what to do. And after that, you'll know how to look up the information you need.

- ✔ **I'm afraid I'll work all day and then lose my work due to a computer malfunction.** People *do* lose their work with computers—I'm sure you've heard the anguished moans of your coworkers when this has happened. But, read on—in this book, you'll learn how to make *sure* this doesn't happen to you.

- ✔ **I'm afraid everyone will laugh at me when I press the wrong key and the thing goes "beep."** Close your door so your coworkers can't hear, if possible. And remember, their computers go beep too. Into every life, a little beep must fall.

- ✔ **I'm afraid I'm going to have to read those big, thick computer books and memorize everything.** Don't worry. Those big, thick books—like Que's *Using* books—are mostly for *reference*. I mean, *nobody* actually reads those things cover to cover, except the poor, suffering souls on the editorial staff. You just look stuff up when you need to.

- ✔ **I'm afraid my kid knows more than I do.** If this is true—and it probably is—then get him or her to help you!

- ✔ **I'm afraid that using the computer will transform me from a warm, cuddly people-person into a cold, unfeeling technoweenie.** Admittedly, there are lots of cold, unfeeling technoweenies in the world. But, they were cold, unfeeling weenies before they became cold, unfeeling *techno*weenies. Computers don't change people, except maybe to make them swear a lot more.

You Need To Become Computer Literate—NOT

For years, well-meaning (but deluded) educators have repeatedly stressed the need for something called Computer Literacy. They think that learning about bits and bytes, and RAM and ROM, somehow prepares one for full citizenship in the Information Society. The people who don't learn these things, they warn, will be left behind.

This is a crock. Sure, it's wise to pick up some PC skills. Surveys show that people who know how to use PCs find jobs faster and make more money. But, learning about PCs isn't going to help you participate more effectively in the Information Society. You'd be much better off in the public library, learning how our government and economy work.

The worst thing about the "computer literacy" talk is that it puts unnecessary pressure on people who are trying to learn computers. You feel this terrible pressure to learn *everything there is to know* about personal computing, as if this was part of being a good citizen.

Some unfortunate beginners fall into the hands of what I call the Used Knowledge Salesmen. Here's one example that I find particularly sad:

A friend of mine decided that she needed to learn Microsoft Windows, so she enrolled in a course at a local community college. For an *entire semester*, every Tuesday and Thursday night, the instructor mercilessly drilled the class in every last-minute bit of information about Microsoft Windows, forced them to memorize this information, and required them to regurgitate it back on the final examination! A sample: "Describe the steps necessary to transform the button shadow from the default gray to pitch black." This would be hilarious, if it wasn't so pathetic—you just don't need to learn that much about Windows to use it effectively. There are some excellent courses at community colleges, but this wasn't one of them.

Let's start, then, with a simple, irreverent premise: *there's nothing about personal computing that's worth memorizing*. You should learn the *minimum* needed to get your work done. As for the rest, you can just look it up, if you need to. Just repeat that a couple of times. Feels nice, doesn't it?

What This Book Is About

You probably noticed that this isn't one of those big, thick computer books. That's deliberate. Oh, I know, you have this book in one hand, and in the other, you're weighing the 1,400-page tome entitled *More Than You Ever Wanted To Know About PCs*. But, for you, this book is better. And well, heck, it's cheaper.

This book contains the *minimum* stuff you need to read to get started with PCs. I've cut out anything you didn't absolutely need to know.

This includes a lot of stuff that the Used Knowledge Salespeople are trying to stuff down your throat.

What's a PC?

A PC is a *personal computer*—a computer that's designed for an individual's use. But these days, people usually mean something more specific when they say "PC." They're referring to an "IBM or IBM-compatible" personal computer (this might also be called a "DOS system" or a "Windows system"). That's what this book is about—IBM and IBM-compatible personal computers.

BUZZWORDS

IBM-COMPATIBLE

A computer that's designed to run any of the programs made for genuine IBM personal computers. These are also called *clones*.

Incidentally, I have absolutely nothing against Macintoshes, so no hate mail, please. I have a Macintosh myself. It is cute and friendly and it shows me a little happy face when I start it. I like to use my Macintosh while watching Barney on the television.

A *Clone*? Is It Illegal?

If you're using an IBM compatible, instead of a true-blue IBM computer, don't worry about the FBI showing up and dragging you off kicking and screaming. It's all perfectly legit. Originally, IBM actually *wanted* people to be able to copy the basic design of their personal computers, thinking that if everyone joined the act, the IBM design would become *the* standard in personal computing, and everyone would profit. They've since sort of regretted this—the clones got so good that there just wasn't any advantage to getting a "real IBM computer"—but, it's too late. Anyway, it *did* work, in that the IBM standard is *the* standard (too bad, Macintosh). But, "clone" doesn't mean "cheap imitation." Some of the best-performing and most reliable personal computers today are made by so-called "clone" manufacturers, such as Zeos, Compaq, and Dell.

But I Still Don't Understand What a Computer Is!

A computer is a "generic" electronic gizmo that can be turned into lots of different kinds of machines, depending on which program you start. That's exactly why they're so popular. Instead of going out and buying a fax machine, a word processing system, an expensive scientific calculator, and a Sega Genesis or Super Nintendo system, you can just buy a PC and a bunch of programs.

BUZZWORDS

COMPUTER

A marriage of inconvenience between a television and a typewriter. The result is an electronic device that costs a great deal, but does absolutely nothing—until, that is, you start a program.

BUZZWORDS

PROGRAM

A list of instructions that tell the computer what to do. A word processing program, for example, tells the computer how to help you write, edit, and print. Programs are written by bossy people called *programmers*. You don't have to write your own programs.

So, there's a basic distinction between the computer—good for nothing by itself—and the programs that make the machine do something. Computer people, addicted as they are to *technobabble*, like to speak of this distinction using the terms *hardware* and *software*. Since you'll hear these terms so much, you'd better know what they mean.

HARDWARE

The computer and all of its physical parts. These just sit there like bumps on a log without a program to tell them what to do. "Hardware," incidentally, is an abstract noun. A computer is hardware. (You're not supposed to say "the computer is a hardware," unless you like getting funny looks.)

SOFTWARE

The programs that tell the computer what to do. This is also an abstract noun. You don't say, "I'm buying a software"; you say, "I'm buying software."

TECHNOBABBLE

A strange, seemingly meaningless form of communication obsessively employed by members of the computer tribe. If you can read the following example of technobabble, you can get a good job translating it into plain English: "This new-generation support platform integrates client-server modules in a coherent application integration strategy."

What Can You Do with a Computer?

Computers are versatile machines, but they can't do everything. A couple of supposedly sure-fire winners—like tracking your recipes or controlling all the lights in your house—haven't panned out, largely because it just isn't worth the trouble to computerize these things. But, there are still lots of tasks that millions of people are learning how to perform with computers, as the following Checklist suggests. Some of these require additional equipment—but, we'll get to that in Part II, "Let's Get Physical Hardware."

Some things people are doing with computers

- ✔ **Writing**. This is the top computer application, folks. A world is fast approaching in which *everyone* will have written a bad novel.

- ✔ **Playing**. Sure, you can get your Segas and Nintendos, but PC games take full advantage of the computer's sharper screen, faster processing, larger storage, and better sound. You get smoother action, more features, and even spoken dialogue. May the Force be with you.

- ✔ **Taxes**. A winner, here. Did you ever work out all those forms, only to find that you had forgotten to put down a charitable contribution? You had to re-do all the forms by hand, a wicked ordeal. With tax software, you just plug in anything that's missing, and the program automatically recalculates all the forms. When you're finished, it prints out the forms using IRS-accepted formatting. This doesn't exactly make doing your taxes a pleasure, but it's better than doing them by hand.

- ✔ **Photography**. The century-old art of taking and processing pictures is going from chemical to digital. Already, you can buy cameras that record the image on a disk, which you can use in a specially-designed player within your computer. You can display the images on the screen, in beautiful, high-resolution color. And if they don't come out right, you can use "computer darkroom" programs to change the color balance, crop the image, and add special effects. If you want a printed copy, you can print it right on your desktop with a color printer.

- ✔ **Composing music**. The computer is perfect for musical composition: with some special equipment and the right software, you can compose right on the screen. Then, the computer plays what you've written so you can hear what it sounds like.

- ✔ **Faxing**. If you have a computer, you're close to having a fax. All you need is a relatively inexpensive accessory called a *fax modem*, and fax software. With these, you can *receive* any kind of fax. But, here's the catch: You can only *send* faxes of stuff you create within the computer. (To be able to send something that's already written or printed, you need an expensive accessory called a *scanner*, but this isn't worth buying if you only use it for faxing.) Still, if you already have a computer, this is a great way to get a home fax machine at very low cost.
- ✔ **Edutainment.** Equipped with a CD-ROM drive (essentially a compact disc player that hooks up to your computer) and full digital stereo sound, your computer becomes the perfect vehicle for *multimedia*—a new way of presenting information that combines text, stunning color images, full-motion animation, segments from videos or movies, and stereophonic sound. But, this is better than TV, because it's *interactive*—you can jump around in the presentation. Plus, with some multimedia presentations, you can even create and save your own versions of the material.

Do you have to learn to do all of these things to justify buying or learning about a PC? Absolutely not. If a personal computer can make your life simpler in just one of these areas, such as writing or creating illustrations, then your investment of time and money is well spent. I use my computer mostly for writing, but I also use it for electronic mail and, well, games. Of course, playing games is a waste of time. You're a serious person with definite goals in life, so I'm sure you don't want to entertain the idea of such a frivolous use of the computer. Incidentally, I recommend *Privateer* and *Myst*.

What's All This Junk on My Desk?

You see computers everywhere: a box, with a humongous TV thing on top; a keyboard; that little mouse thing; and, probably, a printer.

Properly speaking, these things make up a computer *system*. And what is a "system?"

SYSTEM

A collection of hardware components that has been specially designed to work together harmoniously. The television thing, for example, has to be matched to a gizmo inside the computer called a *video adapter*, or the computer won't work.

The need to match the parts to one another makes it a bit challenging to put together a system yourself. Leave that to the salespeople or the computer specialists where you work.

Introducing a Desktop PC System

Here's a quick overview of a desktop PC system. This guide also serves as a guide to the chapters in Part II, "Let's Get Physical (Hardware)."

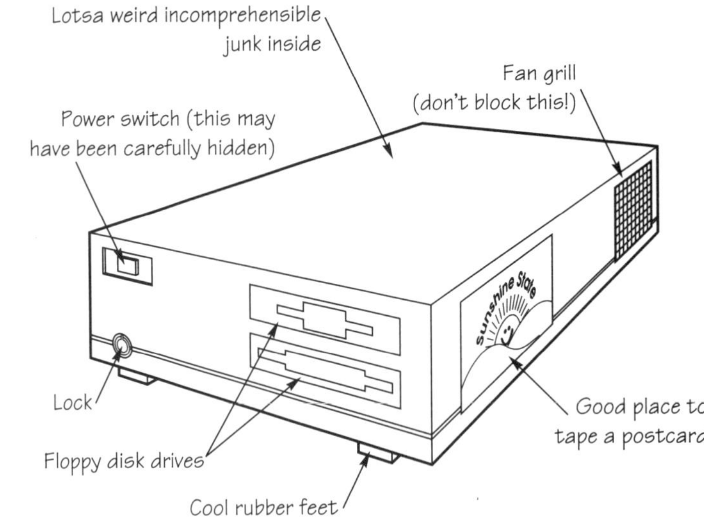

This is the cabinet that houses the computer's electronic inside parts. On the front, you see one or two slot-like openings for those computer disk things. Coming out of the back are just tons of cables. The power switch is usually located on the right side, although some computers put the switch on the back panel. Chapters 5 and 6 tell you all you really need to know about what's inside this thing.

SuperVGA Display.

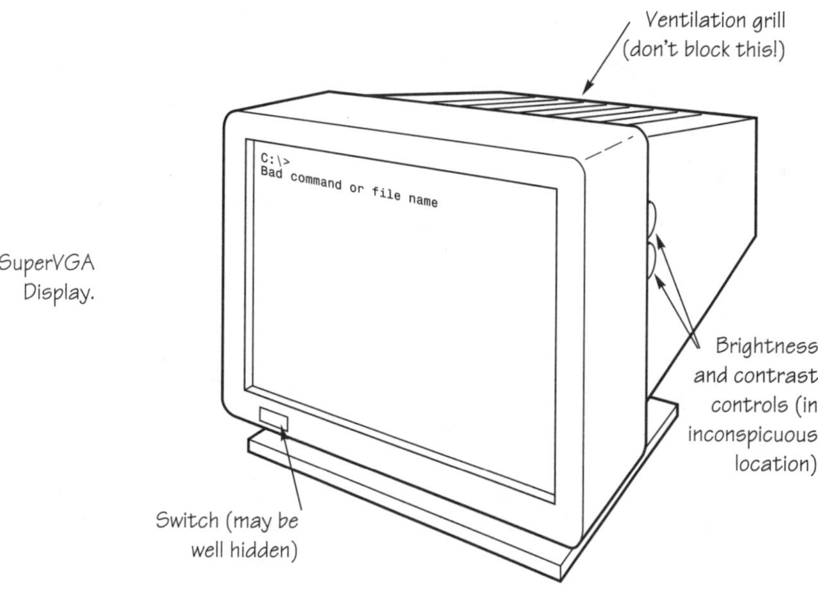

This resembles a television, but instead of seeing Oprah, you see your work. It has its own power switch, as well as brightness and contrast knobs. Monitors are the subject of Chapter 7.

Extended Keyboard.

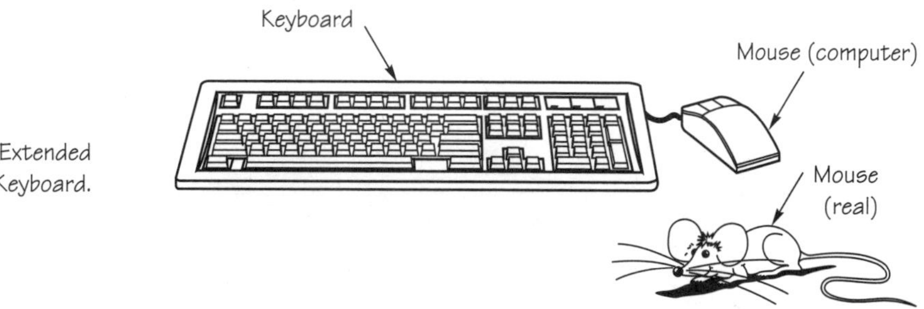

The computer keyboard lets you do two things: give commands to the computer, and do your work. There are lots of funny keys (like Ctrl and Alt) that you don't find on a typewriter; these do specific, computery things and are discussed in Chapter 8.

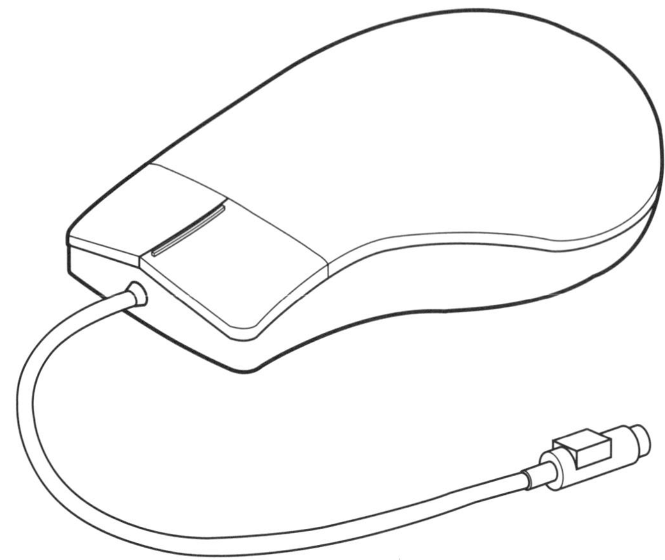

Latest Microsoft Mouse.

A mouse is a little box the size of a bar of soap. When you move this thing, it spins a little ball on the bottom of the mouse, causing a pointer to move on-screen. With some applications, you can do things by pointing the mouse pointer at them and clicking the mouse button (this does things like choosing options from on-screen lists called *menus*). Some people really like this capability and other people hate it (especially ten-finger typists, who dislike taking their fingers away from the keyboard). Chapter 8 tells you more about the mouse and when it's wise to use one.

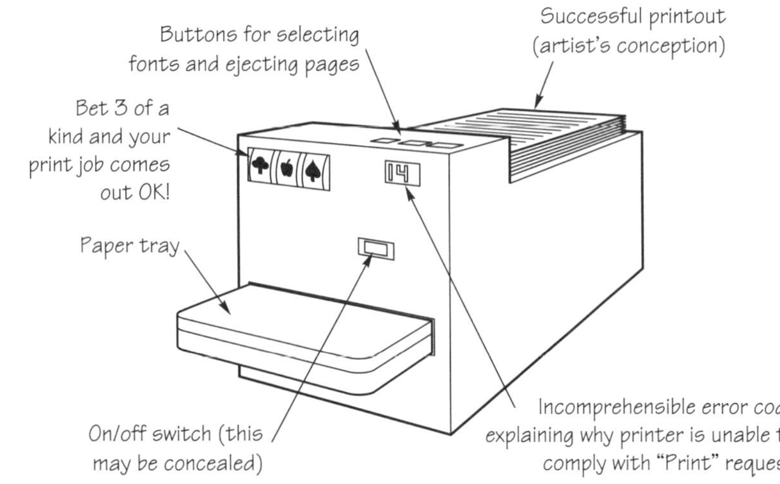

Entry-level laser printer, such as HP IIIp.

This probably looks like a little photocopying machine without the glass part, although there's a large variety—there are zillions of different printers available for PCs. The computer sends your document to the printer, which prints it. Chapter 9 surveys the often confusing world of printers.

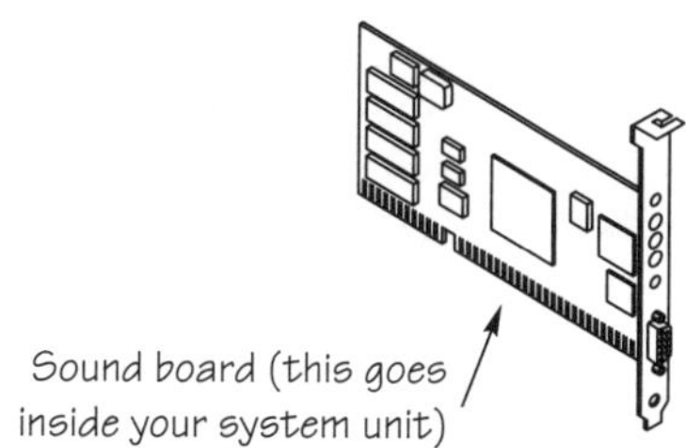

Multimedia upgrade kit, showing speakers, CD-ROM drive, and sound card.

These neat accessories are on their way to becoming standard features of PC systems. With a CD-ROM drive, you can use computer disks that contain an encyclopedia's worth of information, but with a twist—you can hear sounds and see animations, too. For full-stereo sound, your system needs a *sound board* (an internal accessory that powers the speakers) and speakers designed to work near a computer (so you don't hear any of the interference that computers pour out).

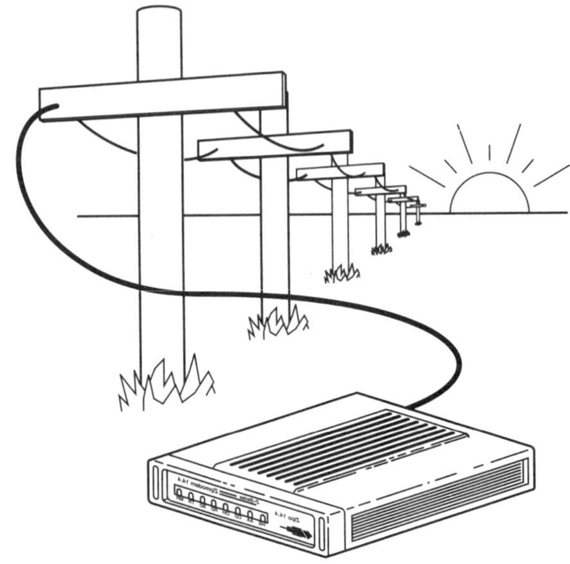

External Hayes modem.

This accessory lets your computer exchange messages with other computers via the telephone system. With a modem, you can exchange electronic mail, get files from computer bulletin board systems, check the latest news and weather, and explore the wonders of the world-wide Internet computer network. Nowadays, most modems are fax modems, meaning they can send and receive faxes, as well as computer signals. Chapter 11 covers modems and the neat things you can do with them.

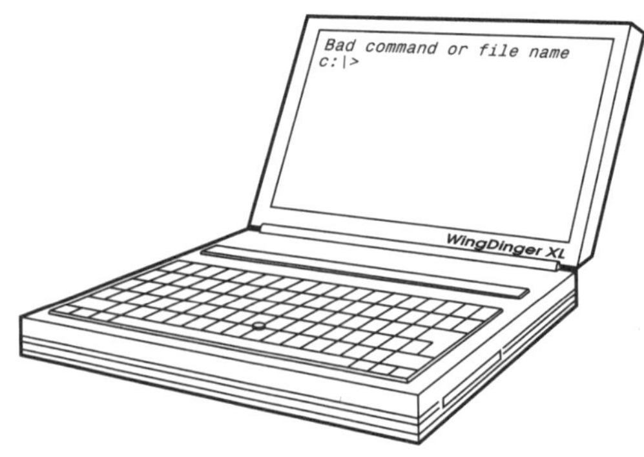

Notebook Computer.

This isn't part of a desktop computer system. It's a fully portable, battery-powered computer that you can put into a briefcase. Some people use notebooks *instead* of desktop computers. Notebook computers have all the stuff you need to do most of your work, and you can even equip them with modems. These days, a lot of people have notebook computers in addition to desktop computers. Find out why in Chapter 12.

Do I Have To Know How All This Stuff Works?

Nope. Not knowing how your car engine works doesn't stop you from driving, does it? In the early days of motoring, you had to be an amateur mechanic to keep your car running; but, those days are gone. Similarly, in the early days of personal computing, you had to be pretty knowledge-able to get a PC running—but, today, that's no longer true. You just need a general idea of what each part does. If you're really curious to know how a modem works, you can find out; but, it won't help you use electronic mail more effectively. Leave it to the electrical engineers!

The World of Computer Programs (Software)

According to one recent estimate, there are well over 100,000 programs available for IBM and IBM-compatible personal computers. Fortunately, they fall into just two categories, *system software* and *application software*.

BUZZWORDS

SYSTEM SOFTWARE

Collectively, all the programs that are required or useful for keeping the computer running happily.

BUZZWORDS

APPLICATION SOFTWARE

All the computer programs that transform the computer into a tool you can apply to a specific task, such as writing a poem, composing a sonata, or calculating the profits from an after-Christmas sale. Examples are programs such as word processing programs (like WordPerfect) and checkbook programs (like Quicken).

System software falls into two categories:

BUZZWORDS

OPERATING SYSTEM

A program that the computer requires in order to keep its parts working together in a useful way. The operating system also provides the *user interface*. This provides commands you can use to operate your computer. The operating system for IBM and IBM-compatible PCs is called MS-DOS.

BUZZWORDS

UTILITIES

Programs you use to maintain your computer and disks, as well as improve the system's performance.

Probably the worst thing about IBM and IBM-compatible computers is their operating system, MS-DOS (or just "DOS" for short). It's a throwback to the computers of ten or fifteen years ago, which were designed for use by computer experts rather than ordinary people. To get the computer to do things, you have to memorize a lot of weird things and type them at the keyboard.

LEARN THE MINIMUM—AND LOVE IT

Because DOS can be a real pain to learn, Microsoft Windows has become very popular. Unlike DOS, Windows is optional. Your computer doesn't need Windows to run the way it needs DOS. But, when you start Microsoft Windows, DOS is hidden. In its place, you get a computer that looks and works a lot more like the Macintosh. Instead of typing most commands with the keyboard, you just use the mouse to point at something you want to do, and click the mouse button. Windows makes PCs easy to learn about and fun to use.

BUZZWORDS

MICROSOFT WINDOWS

A program for IBM Personal Computers and compatibles that hides DOS and makes your computer easier to use. Windows takes over the computer and lets you control computer operations using easy-to-learn controls, such as pull-down menus, buttons, and dialog boxes. Windows makes your PC much more like a Macintosh. People say "Windows" for short.

Chances are good that your computer has both DOS and Windows. This means you could just use DOS, or you could use Windows. But which should you learn?

Reasons to use DOS

✔ **You have an older PC that can't run Windows**. If you have a PC that employs an obsolete 8088 or 80286 chip as its "electronic brain," you can't take full advantage of Windows on your computer. For more information on whether or not your PC can run Windows, see Chapter 5. If it can't run Windows, you might consider upgrading your system—or getting a new one that can run Windows—rather than learning DOS. Windows is much easier to learn and use.

✔ **The program you want to use is a DOS application**. Although you can run DOS applications from Windows, they run a lot faster

continues

Reasons to use DOS, continued

if you skip Windows and run them with DOS. For example, suppose everyone in your company is using WordPerfect 5.1 for DOS. They expect you to learn this too. Since WordPerfect 5.1 runs best under DOS, you'd better learn DOS (sorry).

- ✔ You want to use your computer to play PC games. Most PC games require DOS because Windows is just too slow for them. Since your decision to spend your valuable time playing games is so obviously frivolous, don't ask me to feel sorry for you for having to learn DOS. Incidentally, I recommend Privateer and Myst.

BUZZWORDS

DOS APPLICATION

A program designed to work with DOS. DOS applications do not require Microsoft Windows. You can start them from Windows, although they run more slowly this way.

BUZZWORDS

WINDOWS APPLICATION

A program designed to work with Microsoft Windows. Windows applications don't work with DOS. To use a Windows application, you need to learn how to use Windows.

Lots of good reasons to learn Microsoft Windows

- ✔ **It's the wave of the future**. The software publishers are putting most of their money on Windows. The best new programs will require Windows, and you won't be able to use them unless you know how to use Windows.

- ✔ **It's easy to learn**. Windows isn't as easy to learn as the Macintosh, but it's easier than learning DOS. Mostly, you just use the mouse to point at what you want to do, and click.
- ✔ **Your programs all work the same way**. In DOS, most programs use their own, unique controls for things like showing the next page of the screen. With Windows, programmers don't have this freedom. They have to use the Windows standards for doing things. You benefit because once you've learned how to do some basic task, like opening a file, it works in all Windows programs.
- ✔ **It's fun**. In the screen's background, you can put a picture of a mountain, a cat, the Starship Enterprise. If you have a sound board in your computer, you can even assign recorded sounds to on-screen events. Just imagine Porky Pig saying, "T-t-that's all, folks," when you exit Windows, and you'll have the idea.
- ✔ **Printing is simpler**. What you see on the screen, you get on your printer. And, although you can get those pretty fonts with DOS programs, it's much easier with Windows.
- ✔ **You can use more than one program at a time**. Windows lets you switch from one program to another without having to quit the first one. This is convenient and fun.

Where Do I Go from Here?

It's time to turn on the computer, and see what happens. Chapter 2 goes into the basics of starting your system and deciphering what you see.

If your computer is set up to run DOS, you'll see the notorious C:\> prompt; turn to Chapter 3 for counseling, solace, and guidance.

If your computer is set up to run Microsoft Windows, count your blessings, and turn to Chapter 4.

Top Ten

Least Popular Startup Error Messages

10. Disk destroyed. Destroy another (Y/N)?

9. Qualified user not found. Find qualified user and press any key when ready.

8. System tired of reading drive C; drive no longer valid.

7. Go ahead. Make my day (Y/N)?

6. Self-destruct sequence initiated. Two minutes to detonation. Counting.

5. Fatal error. Job killed. Authorities notified.

4. Wrong disk; error reading drive A. Insert finger in disk drive for punishment.

3. System configuration error. Spend more money on expensive accessories and press any key when ready.

2. Whole world unfair to computers. System on strike.

1. Hi. This is a computer virus. I've erased all your work. Have fun retyping it. Bye, now!

CHAPTER 2

On Your Mark, Engage (Starting Your System)!

IN A NUTSHELL

- How to work contentedly with this frustrating thing
- What's contained on the computer's front panel
- How to find the power switch and turn on the computer
- What to do if the system doesn't start
- What goes by on-screen after you start the computer
- What to do after the computer finishes its startup ordeal

Computers can be vexing things to get started—it's tough to find the switches. Worse, the computer won't start if there's a disk in the disk drive, and incomprehensible things happen onscreen for a while until the darned thing settles down. This chapter examines the computer startup procedure, reassures you about things that would otherwise scare you to death, and helps you avoid those little pitfalls that computers like to throw in your way. You also learn what to do if something really does go seriously wrong, which happens every once in a while.

TIP

Don't Go It Alone!

There are lots of people around who will be happy to help you get through your first few adventures with the computer. Try this: "I know you're busy, but since you are, like, so *incredible* with the computer, I was just wondering if you could walk me through this..." You will find that there are very few people who can resist such flattery.

Setting Up Your System

Just got your new PC? Use the following checklist to guide you through the process.

Setting up your computer

- ✔ Pick a place for your computer where you won't get glare from a window.
- ✔ Open the box containing the system unit first. Unpack it and put it on your desk. Plug it in, but don't turn it on yet.
- ✔ Open the keyboard box and plug the keyboard into the round port with 5 pins. If you have a mouse, plug this into the port with 9 pins. Don't force the cable into the plug; you may have to rotate it

so that the little notch lines up before it will go in. (For more information on these plug thingies, see the section titled, "Ports (What We Would Call a Socket)," in Chapter 5.)

- ✔ Open the monitor box and put the monitor on top of the system unit. Plug the monitor cable into the monitor port (the socket with 15 pins). Note that this cable has little screw thingies that are used to affix the cable to the socket. Don't skip doing this. You may need a little regular (non-Phillips) screwdriver.
- ✔ Your system unit may have a switched outlet plug in the back. If so, plug the monitor into this. That way, you can turn on the computer and the monitor with just one switch.
- ✔ Your printer doesn't need to be right next to your computer, but it has to be close enough for the cord to reach. Take out the cord, see how long it is, and figure out where you want to put your printer.
- ✔ Consult your printer's directions for information on how to assemble the various components, such as the paper tray, etc. Then connect the printer cable to the 25-pin socket on the back of your computer. If there are two 25-pin sockets (rare), look for one that says "Printer" or "LPT1." If it doesn't say anything, look in the computer's instruction book to find out which port is LPT1. Plug your printer into this port.

Ouch, My Back Hurts!

Before you turn on your computer, take a moment to check out the furniture and learn some good habits.

Computers aren't worth risking your health!

- ✔ **Adjust your chair**. You should be able to sit up straight, with your arms and shoulders relaxed. Your upper arms should hang straight down alongside your chest. This will help prevent back strain and backaches.

continues

Computers aren't worth risking your health!, continued

- ✔ **Lower the keyboard.** Your forearms should be angled slightly down as your fingers reach out to touch the keyboard. If your computer is on a desk, get a keyboard drawer or a computer table so you can get the keyboard low enough. This will help you avoid repetitive strain injuries (RSI), such as Carpal Tunnel Syndrome (an injury to the nerves of the hand). These injuries stem from using the computer too much or using the keyboard improperly. Don't take RSI lightly—these injuries can be extremely painful and may even require surgery to correct.
- ✔ **Position your monitor.** You should be looking down toward the monitor at a slight angle.
- ✔ **Avoid glare.** Reduce eyestrain by turning your monitor away from brightly-lit windows and lamps.
- ✔ **Take regular breaks.** Don't work for more than an hour without getting up and doing some stretching.

Front Panel Stuff

Most computers have things on their front panels—switches, buttons, indicators, coffee stains, and user-affixed oddities (often, cartoon clippings showing someone attacking a computer with a large, blunt object). You can ignore most of this stuff; but, here's a quick rundown of the things that might be useful.

Things you'll find on the computer's front panel

- ✔ **Power Switch.** Sometimes this is conveniently on the front panel. But it might be on the back panel or one of the sides.
- ✔ **Locking Switch.** Some computers come with a roundish looking locking switch that lets you lock the computer (with a roundish-looking key). That funny diagram right next to the locking switch is supposed to be a lock, get it? If it's open, the computer is

unlocked and you can start it. If it's closed, the computer is locked, and you can't start it.

- **Reset Button.**You push this button to *reboot* your computer. Rebooting (restarting) may be necessary after a computer crash—that unpleasant, but unfortunately inevitable moment when your computer freezes up and won't respond to your commands (yes, crashes do happen). Chapter 20 fills you in on the unpleasant topic of computer crashes.
- **Turbo Button.** Your computer may not have this, but if it does, leave it on. It makes your computer run at its highest speed. In other computers, there's just a little indicator light—if so, make sure it's on.
- **Speed Indicator.** On some computers the computer's speed setting (regular or Turbo) is indicated by a number in a little calculator-like display. With these computers, the higher the number, the better. After turning on the computer, push the Turbo button until the highest number appears.
- **Floppy Disk Drive.** You might have one or two of these. You put floppy disks into these for special purposes, such as adding new programs to your computer or backing up your work. For everyday work, you just use your hard disk.
- **Floppy Disk Activity Light.** This little light tells you when the floppy disk is working with the disk that's in the drive.
- **Hard Disk Activity Light.** This light comes on when the hard disk is doing something important, like saving your work. This light doesn't really give you any useful information except that the drive's alive and kicking, which is sometimes reassuring to know. On some computers, this light has a symbol next to it that looks like an oil drum. For computer people, oil drums powerfully conjure up an image of a hard disk. Don't ask why.
- **Power Light.** This little light just shows you that the computer is turned on. But you can tell anyway because that noisy fan is going inside.

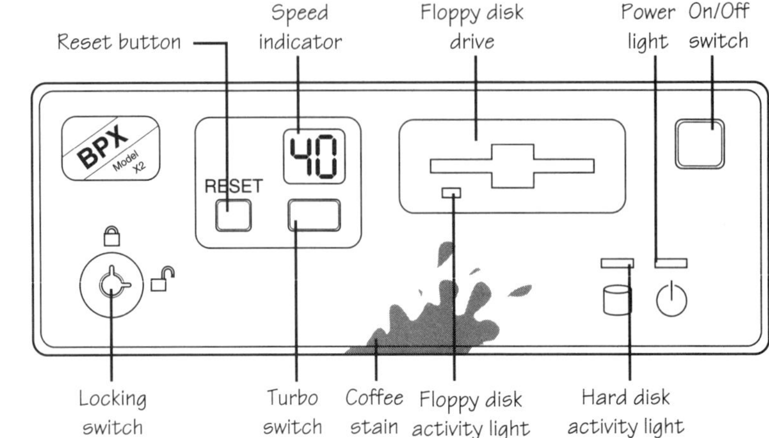

Front panel stuff (your computer may not have all of these).

Things to remember about the stuff on the front panel

- ✔ If your computer has a Turbo switch, make sure it's turned on—unless you love watching the screen take five minutes to *update* (reflect the last change you made).
- ✔ When the floppy disk activity light is on, leave the disk in the drive. If you try to remove it, the disk drive might "smear" data across the disk surface, totally wrecking the data stored on it. Wait for the light to go off, and then take out the disk.
- ✔ If you want to use the lock but can't find the key, look on the back of the computer. A lot of clone manufacturers tie the keys to the fan grill grating.
- ✔ Whatever you do, don't press the Reset button unless you're absolutely sure your computer has crashed. This restarts the computer and you might lose some or all of your work. Sometimes the computer only seems to have crashed. Check out Chapter 20 before hitting the panic button.

CHAPTER 2

ON YOUR MARK, ENGAGE

Turn On, Tune In, Get Confused

The big moment is here: it's you and the PC. You're ready to boot your computer.

No, I'm serious. I *know* this thing cost a lot of money and I'm *not* suggesting that you "boot" it until dead. That comes later.

BUZZWORDS

BOOT

To start the computer fresh, with a clear memory and a positive attitude. Computer nuts like myself distinguish between a *cold boot* (you turn the system on after it has been off for a while) and a *warm boot* (you restart the system after it has been on, for example, by pressing the Reset button). *Hot boots* are legal in certain states.

Just one more little thing before you get going. It would be too simple to put words like "off " and "on" next to the power switches on your computer. Plus, this wouldn't be cool. So, computer designers use the following symbols:

0 This means "off."

1 This means "on."

How To Start Your Computer

To start your computer, follow these simple steps:

1. Make sure there's no disk in drive A.

   Your computer won't start correctly if there's a disk in drive A (which is usually the top one, if you have two drives). If drive A has a latch that covers the drive door, you can remove the disk by flipping the latch up so the disk pops out. If drive A has a little button instead of a latch, just push the button; the disk pops out.

2. Find the switch and turn on the computer.

   If you're lucky, your system is hooked up to a *power center*—an electrical strip with several outlets. (You have to buy the power strip; it doesn't come with the computer.) If so, it's pretty easy to turn on the system: just flip the switch on the power strip. This one switch probably turns on everything—the CPU, monitor, printer, and so on.

   If there isn't a power center, you have to hunt down the switches for each component. Start with the computer (the box thing) and monitor (the TV thing).

   Look for an on/off button or switch on the front of the computer; or, failing that, look for a big red switch on the right side of the computer. Be forewarned: some system designers place the switch on the back panel where (1) you fear you'll be electrocuted if you stick your finger in the wrong hole and (2) you may jar loose some of the data cables, resulting in (even more) bizarre system behavior. As you carefully (but blindly) explore the back panel looking for the switch, be careful to avoid the cables, power cords, and the large, poisonous bugs and snakes that creep back there seeking warmth and darkness.

3. Turn on the monitor (the TV thing).

   Monitor switches are even harder to find. Look on the front, back, right side, left side, bottom, and top of the monitor. After that, kick it.

Well, Did It Start?

If you found both switches, you'll know it. The computer hums, buzzes, clicks, and whirs. These are happy noises. A great deal of information also flashes past on the screen, much faster than you can read it. Ignore it—or, if you insist, read the next section, "What You See."

If nothing happens, make sure that all the stuff is plugged in. If it *still* won't start, make sure that there's power going to the plugs where the computer stuff is plugged in; plug in a little desk lamp and try turning it on. If it won't work, call an electrician.

What You See

(But may not get)

When your computer starts, many things happen—probably too quickly to see and definitely acceptable to ignore. Here's a handy guide, in case you're curious about what's going on. If you're not curious, skip this entire section.

Can't see a thing!

If you hear something, but nothing appears on-screen, make sure that you turned on the monitor. Also, check the brightness and contrast control; somebody may have turned off the brightness all the way.

The BIOS Message

The very first thing to appear on-screen is the BIOS message. You see something like this:

```
Turbo 386 Chipset ROM BIOS Version 8.91©1992 Technology
Enterprises, Ltd.
```

BIOS is short for *basic input-output system*. It's a mini-program that's loaded into your computer at the start of every operating session. This program comes from a little chip called ROM (short for *read-only memory*). This ROM chip contains a permanently encoded program. What's BIOS for? When you turn on your computer, its memory is cleared. Blank. Zilch. Nada. Zero. It can't remember its own name. It can't remember what town it's in. It can't even find its fingers and toes.

In other words, it wakes up like we do. BIOS tells it very basic stuff which you don't need to learn about.

BUZZWORDS

ROM

This is really a forgettable term; but, because people keep trying to throw it at you in computer literacy classes, you'd better know what it is. Basically, it's a little chip which has some permanently-recorded programs on it that are needed to get the computer started.

Say Aaahh, and Let's Check Those Memory Chips

The next on-screen event is the *memory check*. Your computer might scramble your data if the memory isn't working perfectly. So, your computer runs this check every time you switch on the power. If the numbers zoom up to a certain figure and then stop, and the computer keeps going, the memory check has been successful. (Displaying a message like `Your memory is fine` would be too simple.)

TIP

It says `Parity error`! What is "parity?"

If the memory check finds a mistake, you may see a message such as `Parity error` or `Memory error`; then, the system shuts down. Obviously, this is bad news, but don't panic—one of those little memory chips is bad, and fixing it is not going to be too expensive. Look at the screen; you probably see a code that combines letters and numbers in a weird way. Write it down. This will help the computer repair technician find and replace the faulty memory chip. Then, turn off your computer, and it's off to the repair shop.

Hello, Drive A?

The next startup event is the computer's attempt to read a disk in drive A. But, there is no disk in drive A, remember? You were supposed to remove any disk in this drive. So, you hear a lot of pathetic gronking and grakking until the computer gives up, and goes hunting for your hard disk instead. This is weird and noisy, even repulsive, but normal. (Normal for computers, that is.)

Why does the computer try to look at the disk in drive A first? This is in case something goes wrong with your hard disk (gasp). The technician can start your computer by putting a DOS disk in drive A and then running a diagnostic program to figure out what's wrong.

TIP

It says, `Non-system disk or disk error`!
Congratulations. Despite my having harped on this repeatedly, you left a disk in drive A, didn't you? Bad, bad. But, never mind that, I do it all the time too. Remove the disk, and restart your system by pressing any key.

Loading DOS

Assuming all has gone well, your computer now finds DOS on your hard disk (which is called *drive* C), and you may see the message `Starting MS-DOS`. This goes pretty smoothly and automatically; but then, all hell breaks loose on-screen and dozens of incomprehensible messages flash by. These messages come from the *system configuration files*, or things that DOS wizards create to set up your system for the best possible operation. They're pretty techy, and you can ignore them.

BUZZWORDS

LOAD

To take a program from the disk and put it in the computer's memory, where you can work with it.

If you're gonna have a crash, here's where it might just happen. Any errors in these system configuration file things will cause problems, including causing your system to crash. If your computer goes comatose at this point, get help—it's too much for you to try to fix yourself.

Note: A little `C>` or `C:\>` on-screen is normal; it doesn't signal that your system is comatose, only that the computer designers were. This tells you that DOS is ready to do what you want. If you see this, all has gone well, sort of.

What Now?

There are hundreds of ways to configure a system, so I can't tell you exactly what will appear on-screen. I can make a couple of guesses, though.

BUZZWORDS

CONFIGURE

To customize a computer system or program so that certain options are in effect. For example, you can configure a computer so that Microsoft Windows starts automatically when you switch on the power.

What might happen after you start the system

- ✔ Probably, you'll see a tiny `C>` or `C:\>` on an otherwise-blank screen. This means that your computer has been configured to run DOS. Turn to Chapter 3.
- ✔ A real possibility: After a *lot* of grinding of the disk, you may see a pretty picture showing some house-type windows, lots of color (assuming you have a color monitor, of course), and, finally, a box called Program Manager. This means your computer has been configured to run Microsoft Windows. Skip the next chapter and dive right into Chapter 4.

- ✔ Less likely: A program may start. If so, find out how to exit the program and return to DOS. Ask coworkers, call someone who can help you, or in an extreme situation, pull out the program's manual.
- ✔ Even less likely: You might see something called the DOS Shell. (This is a program that is supposed to make DOS easier to use, although opinion on that claim is divided.) If so, press the F3 key (that's one of those funny function keys that runs along the top of the keyboard). This takes you back to DOS; now turn to Chapter 3 to find out how to whip DOS into shape.
- ✔ You might see a menu that tells you which key(s) to press to start a program. This is good. You're lucky. Someone has set up the system to make things easy for you. Just press the indicated number or letter to start a program.

Top Ten

Reasons for Calling the Technical Support Hotline

10. Computer manual further away than telephone; prefer to let fingers do the walking

9. Computer manual too hard to read; not as interesting as *National Enquirer*

8. Manual buried under three pounds of memos outlining new office efficiencies

7. Unable to start program

6. Unable to exit program

5. Program? What's a program?

4. Error beep too loud; audible by coworkers

3. Heard moaning sound from disk drive after installing program

2. Lonely; "just wanted to chat"

1. Apology demanded for insulting error message

CHAPTER 3

Read This If You See C:\...

IN A NUTSHELL

- What the DOS prompt is
- How to start a program
- What to do if the program doesn't start
- How to tell what's on a disk
- How to exit a program
- How to turn off the computer
- How to restart your computer

NOW WHAT
DOES IT WANT
ME TO DO?

If you've started your computer and see a C>, C:\>, or some variation on-screen, your computer has been set up to start DOS. DOS is one of the necessary evils of computing. This chapter shows you how to pull off the very basic maneuvers of using DOS and DOS programs. For more on DOS, skip ahead to Chapter 15.

The DOS Prompt, Beloved by Millions—Not!

It's cryptic. It's incomprehensible. It's the DOS prompt!

BUZZWORDS

DOS PROMPT (C:\>)

This C:\> thing is called the *DOS prompt*. It means that DOS is telling you, "We've finished all of our business inside the computer, here. What do you want to do next?" To make something happen, you type a few characters and press Enter.

DOS prompt facts, ranging from useful to stupid

- ✔ Instead of the DOS prompt, you might see a menu that tells you which key(s) to press to start a program. This is good. You're lucky. Someone has set up the system to make things easy for you. Just press the indicated number or letter to start a program.

- ✔ Your prompt might say something like `Hey, Babe. DOS geniuses know how to change the prompt to say anything they like.` It could even be something silly like `I must obey my master`, or `What is thy bidding?`

  If you're dying to make DOS prompt you with some goofy message, type **PROMPT**, press the space bar, and then type the message that you want DOS to display. Then press Enter. Your change will only affect the current session—DOS forgets it when you switch off the computer or reboot. That's good, because you'll probably get sick of it pretty fast.

✔ If your mouse doesn't seem to be working, don't panic. Some DOS applications use the mouse, but the DOS prompt doesn't. If you move the mouse while the DOS prompt is visible, nothing good happens. On the plus side, though, nothing bad happens.

Invoking (Er, Running) a Program

You've started your computer, and you see the DOS prompt. So, what do you do now? You *run a program*. (Computer people don't agree on what this should be called. You may hear the term *start*, which is simple enough, but you may run into *launch*, or even *invoke*. Personally, I like the term *invoke*, because it makes it sound as if you are about to bring down one of the gods of the Vikings to wreak havoc on your enemies.)

Here's how to start a program: type the program's name and press Enter. It doesn't matter whether you use uppercase or lowercase letters. It *does* matter that you spell it correctly.

For example, to start Lotus 1-2-3, you type:

```
123
```

and press Enter. (Pressing Enter confirms what you've typed, and sends it to the computer's "brain.") The Enter key is usually the biggest key on the keyboard, so it's hard to miss. It's where the Return key is on a typewriter.

If you make a typing mistake, like this:

```
132
```

and press Enter, you see the most beloved (not!) of all DOS error messages,

```
Bad command or file name
```

This does not mean that you, personally, are bad, or that Lotus 1-2-3 no longer exists on the computer, or any number of other catastrophic things; you probably just made a typing error. You should type

```
123
```

and press Enter, to start Lotus 1-2-3.

What do you type to start your program? If you're using WordPerfect, you type **wp** and press Enter. If you're using some other program, check the manual or ask around.

TIP

Can I correct a typing error?

Before you press Enter, you can correct a typing mistake by pressing the Backspace key. (Look for the Backspace key above the big Enter key. Sometimes the Backspace key isn't labeled Backspace; instead, it has a left arrow on it.) Pressing Backspace rubs out what you've typed—one character at a time—so that you can correct the error by retyping.

In Search of the Missing Program: Changing Directories

You typed your program's name or initials and you pressed Enter. You typed it *correctly*, darn it. And what do you get for following instructions? You still get:

```
Bad command or file name
```

Are you *absolutely* sure you typed the program name correctly? Yes? Well, let's try something else. We'll do a little *hacking*—specifically, changing directories—to see if *that* works.

BUZZWORDS

HACKING

The most basic and useful of all computer skills, based on the principles, "If at first you don't succeed, try, try again," and "Where there's a will, there's a way." This leads to exploring the computer's possibilities and learning a heck of a lot.

READ THIS IF YOU SEE C:\...

If you still can't start the program even after typing its name correctly, you may have to change to the program's directory before you can start the program.

DIRECTORY

A *directory* is a section of your disk that has been set aside to store a group of related files, such as the WordPerfect program and your WordPerfect files.

The program you want to run may be tucked away in its own, little directory. That's all very nice, but the problem is, DOS may not be able to start the program unless you switch to it first. When you switch to a directory, you make it *current*.

CURRENT DIRECTORY

The directory that DOS looks in as it tries to carry out your commands. If you type **WP** and press Enter, DOS looks in the current directory. Only one directory can be current at a time.

To make your program's directory current, you need to know its name. Ask the person who set up the computer. If no one's around who can help, you can use the DIR command to discover the name of the directory, as explained in the next section. If you're using WordPerfect 5.1, for example, you'll probably find it in a directory called WP51.

When you know the name of the directory, you can use the CD command (short for Change Directory) to make that directory current. Suppose that you want to start WordPerfect 5.1, and you learn that this program is in the WP51 directory. Here's what you type:

CD WP51

Then press Enter. Note that there's a space between the CD part and the WP51 part.

Your computer may have been set up so that the DOS prompt shows the name of the directory that's currently active. If so, the prompt now looks like this:

```
C:\WP51>
```

But, if no one has set up your system to do this, it might just look like this:

```
C>
```

You're in the WP51 directory no matter what the prompt says—provided that you typed the directory name correctly. So, you should be able to start your program now.

More tantalizing information about changing directories

- ✔ If you see the message `Invalid directory`, make sure that you've typed the directory name correctly, and try again. Don't leave out the backslash!
- ✔ If your prompt doesn't show the name of the current directory, get your local computer friend to modify it so that it does.
- ✔ Computer people love to make up odd words for things, as you may have already discovered. Here's one: "I'm logged on to WordPerfect's directory." This means, "WordPerfect's directory is current." You might also hear this as a command: "Log on to WordPerfect's directory, will ya?" This means, "Switch to WordPerfect's directory." You don't really want to know where they get the *log* part, do you?
- ✔ If you have to change directories before you can start your program, get your local computer friend to modify your system. The modification is pretty simple. It involves adding something called a PATH command to one of those files DOS consults when you start your system, and it will only take one or two minutes to do. Don't try to do it yourself, though, unless you really want to spend the next 48 hours wading through DOS manuals.

The DIR Command

(What's on this disk?)

When you don't know the name of a program or a directory and can't find out easily any other way, use the DIR command. DIR is one of the DOS commands that you'll use frequently. It lists the files and directories that are in the current directory.

BUZZWORDS

FILE

A collection of related stuff stored on disk, such as a program like WordPerfect or Chapter 12 of your latest novel. Every file has its own, unique name, which must conform to DOS's strict regulations about length (eight characters maximum, plus an optional three letter extension) and which characters you can include. Chapter 14 covers the fascinating topic of files.

To see what's on a disk, type **DIR** and press Enter. You'll see something like this on-screen:

```
Volume in drive C is HOT_STUFF
Volume Serial Number is 0D57-1500
Directory of C:\

WP51              <DIR>       08-09-94     8:37p
LOTUS             <DIR>       07-30-94    12:19p
COMMAND  COM      54,619      09-30-93     6:20a
CONFIG   SYS      1536        07-04-94     5:36p
MOUSE    SYS      30733       03-10-92    11:36a
AUTOEXEC BAT      1876        07-04-94     8:31p
```

Don't worry about most of the stuff you see here. You can learn more about it later, if you want. For now, just notice that this command lists the names of the files and directories that are found in the currently active directory. You can tell that something in the list is a directory because `<DIR>` appears after the name. This listing shows two directories: `WP51` and `LOTUS`.

When you first turn on the computer, the *root directory* is usually the current directory.

BUZZWORDS

ROOT DIRECTORY

The top-level directory on a disk. Think of the root directory as if it were a country that contains lots of states (other directories).

If you want to see a list of subdirectories only, type **DIR *.** (an asterisk followed by a period) and press Enter.

Suppose that you're trying to hunt down a program's name or initials so that you can start it. You know that the program is stored in the \123 directory. So you switch to this directory by typing **CD 123** and pressing Enter. \123 is now the current directory.

Now type **DIR *.EXE** and press Enter. (That's DIR, followed by a space, an asterisk, a period, and EXE. Don't put a space in the *.EXE part.) Most program files have the extension or last name EXE. (More on file names and their parts in Chapter 14.)

You see the program files stored in the \123 directory. You'll probably see several programs, and one of them will probably be the one you're after. To start the program, type the part of the name that comes before the period—like the **123** in 123.EXE—and then press Enter.

Making a Graceful Exit

Let's assume all has gone well and that you've started your program successfully. (Granted, this might be a pretty big assumption.) The question now arises: how to get out?

Quit properly!

Don't quit a program by just switching off the computer, tempting though it may be. It's much better to exit the program and return to the DOS prompt. There's less risk of losing your work or screwing up the choices you've made about the way the program runs.

It would be nice if you could exit every program the same way. Naturally, you can't. This was decided at a conference titled "Let's Make Things as Difficult as Possible for Our Users," held in the dawning years of the computer industry.

To exit, try one of the following:

- ✔ If the program has a bar across the top of the screen with names of menus like **F**ile and **E**dit, you can probably exit by holding down the Alt key (one of those funny extra keys on the keyboard) and pressing F. This command opens the **F**ile menu. Tap the down-arrow key until you highlight the command that gets you out of the program—**E**xit, **Q**uit, **D**ie, and so on. If you don't see such a bar, press F10 and see whether one appears.
- ✔ In Lotus 1-2-3, press the slash key (/) and then tap the right-arrow key until you move the highlight to the command called **Q**uit. Then press Enter, followed by **Y** for **Y**es.
- ✔ To quit Quattro Pro, hold down the Ctrl key and press X.
- ✔ To quit Q & A, press X at the main menu to choose X—Exit.

- Some programs give you a list of keys you can press to do various things. Usually, this list is at the bottom of the screen. In one program, the list says `F3=Quit`. If you press F3, you exit the program.

- If the program is WordPerfect, press F7. You are asked whether you want to save the document. Press N if you don't or Y if you do. Then press Y when asked whether you're really serious about leaving the program. No other program uses this key to exit, though, which is one of WordPerfect's most beloved little peculiarities.

Turning Off Your Computer

Now that you've exited your program gracefully and returned to the DOS prompt, you may want to turn off your computer. To turn off your computer, remove any floppy disks you may have inserted, and then flip off the power strip, if you have one. If you don't, flip off the power switches for the computer, monitor, and printer.

TIP

Turn it off!

In the old days, computer chips got stressed by the shock of new, fresh power flowing through them, and so the myth arose that you should keep your computer on all the time. This just isn't true anymore. Today's chips can take the heat. You save money, and you cut down on power bills. To be sure, some manufacturers still claim that switching on the power stresses components such as hard drives—while at the same time claiming that these things can run 15,000 hours without failing. I switch mine off.

Restarting the Computer

You may want to restart your computer—to take it back to that magic moment when its memory is cleared and DOS is loaded for a new, fresh computing session. You can do so without switching the power off and on. Hold down the Ctrl and Alt keys and press Del. Alternatively, press your computer's Reset button—if your computer has one. (If it does, you might find it on the computer's front panel.)

When to restart your computer with Ctrl+Alt+Del

- ✔ When a software installation program instructs you to do so. Installation programs change your computer's setup, and the new setup won't take place until you restart.
- ✔ If your system *crashes*, *hangs*, or *freezes* (something has gone haywire so that the computer no longer responds to your keyboard input). But, be sure that your computer really *is* frozen. Some operations can take a minute or two to finish, so it appears that your computer is hanging, when really it's just working more slowly than you expected. If any light on the computer is flashing, the computer is still busy. If you hear any computer-related noises, it's probably still working. Go have a cup of cappuccino and come back. If the system's still comatose, restart it.

When you restart your system, you lose any work that you haven't yet saved. Use Ctrl+Alt+Del only as a last-ditch measure, after you've exhausted all other possibilities—including getting your local computer guru to help. And be sure to remove any floppy disks before you restart. (If a disk is left in the drive, you'll probably get an error message when you restart.)

Top Ten
Pet Peeves of Computer Mice

10. Choked by own cord

9. When they drag you across that sticky spilled Pepsi

8. Not getting your ball cleaned for *months*

7. When you're left hanging off the desk by your tail

6. Having to roll around your whole life on that same old mouse pad with the stupid picture of the Starship Enterprise on it

5. That awful old keyboard that thinks it can do *anything* a mouse can do

4. Being held all day by that big hot hand

3. Cup of hot coffee teetering precariously close to you

2. When they eat buttered popcorn and then use you without washing their hands

1. Underbelly burn from kid frantically trying to shoot down Imperial TIE fighters

CHAPTER 4

Read This If You See a Box That Says "Program Manager"

IN A NUTSHELL

- What Windows is and why so many people like it
- What Program Manager does
- What a GUI is
- How to use a mouse
- How to handle basic Windows maneuvers
- How to run a Windows application
- How to switch from one application to another
- How to exit a Windows application
- How to quit Microsoft Windows

If you see a box on-screen labeled Program Manager your system has been configured to run Microsoft Windows automatically. (Your screen may not look exactly like this—Windows displays the choices made the last time Windows was used. The key point is this: If you see a box that says "Program Manager," you've got Windows.)

It's good news if you have Windows. Unlike those poor, struggling DOS users, you'll be able to choose options by moving the mouse pointer to little pictures on-screen and clicking the mouse button. As you work with your applications, you'll see your document on-screen just as it will appear when printed.

If you see something like this, your computer is set up to run Microsoft Windows.

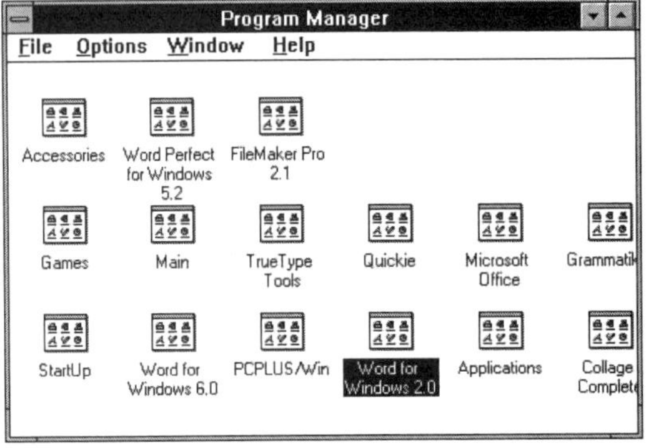

Chapter 16 discusses the ins and outs of managing files with Windows. Here, you learn how to get your program started, switch from your program to other programs, and exit Windows in one piece.

TIP

You may have Windows, but not see it. If you've been told your computer has Windows, but you don't see Program Manager after turning on your system, just type WIN and press Enter. If this doesn't work, ask the person who set up your computer to help you.

READ THIS IF YOU SEE A BOX THAT SAYS "PROGRAM MANAGER"

What Is Windows?

In case you've spent the last five years in the wilderness of the Northwest Territories, here's a tip: Windows is sweeping personal computerdom off its C> prompt. Windows makes PCs easier to use.

Windows is a program that requires DOS. What thrills people about Windows is that it makes DOS disappear—almost. Actually, DOS is still lurking around underneath Windows, and occasionally causes you to have to do things in a non-Windows way (but, more about that later).

After taking over the computer, Windows makes your computer look and work more like a Macintosh. You can make things happen just by using the mouse. As you roll the mouse around the desk, a pointer moves on-screen. To do things, you just point at what you want to do and click the left mouse button. (There are two mouse buttons. Mostly, you'll use the left one, but the right one is also being used more in growing numbers of applications.)

Windows lets you run *Windows applications*. A Windows application is a program that's designed to be used with Microsoft Windows. These programs won't run without Microsoft Windows. They're pretty cool programs, too. With almost all of them, what you see on the screen—including all those neat fonts and graphics—is normally what you get on your printer. Incidentally, "what you see is what you get" gives us what is probably the ugliest acronym ever invented, *WYSIWYG* (pronounced—can you believe this?—"whissey-whig").

Why is it called "Windows"? You'll see when you start it. The screen contains lots of boxes—called *windows*—that you can independently move and size. You can hide them or display them, stack them on top of each other, make some big and some small—whatever you want. You can have lots of windows on-screen at the same time, so that you can switch quickly from one type of activity to another. For example, in one window you can schedule a meeting on your daily calendar, and then quickly switch to a calculator in another window so that you can balance your checkbook.

Why Windows?

Windows does all the stuff DOS does, but it does it better. Windows is easier to use. And it's easier to learn. It's even easier to learn Windows programs, because they all work the same way.

TIP

So where *is* Windows? I see something called "Program Manager."

When Windows starts, you don't see anything labeled Windows, apart from some cool opening graphics. Instead, you see a big window labeled Program Manager. Program Manager is the most important part of Microsoft Windows.

Program Manager starts automatically when Windows starts. Basically, *Program Manager* is a tool or assistant that you can use to start and organize your Windows applications. Program Manager is like Windows' Grand Central Station: It's the starting point for working with Windows, and you come back to it when you want to start other applications or quit Windows. Program Manager's main function is to help you start application programs.

What Do You Mean, This Is Gooey?

If this is the first time you've seen Program Manager, congratulations! You've had your first encounter with the Brave New World of the *graphical user interface*.

BUZZWORDS

GRAPHICAL USER INTERFACE (GUI)

This term refers to a way of designing computer programs so that they're easier to use. The program uses on-screen pictures (*icons*) to represent commonly used computer procedures. Believe it or not, this acronym really is pronounced "gooey."

READ THIS IF YOU SEE A BOX THAT SAYS "PROGRAM MANAGER"

BUZZWORDS

ICON

An icon is a picture that represents something you can do with the computer, such as a program for writing or making an illustration. To select what you want to do, you just click or double-click the icon.

Going GUI (basic stuff about the Windows screen).

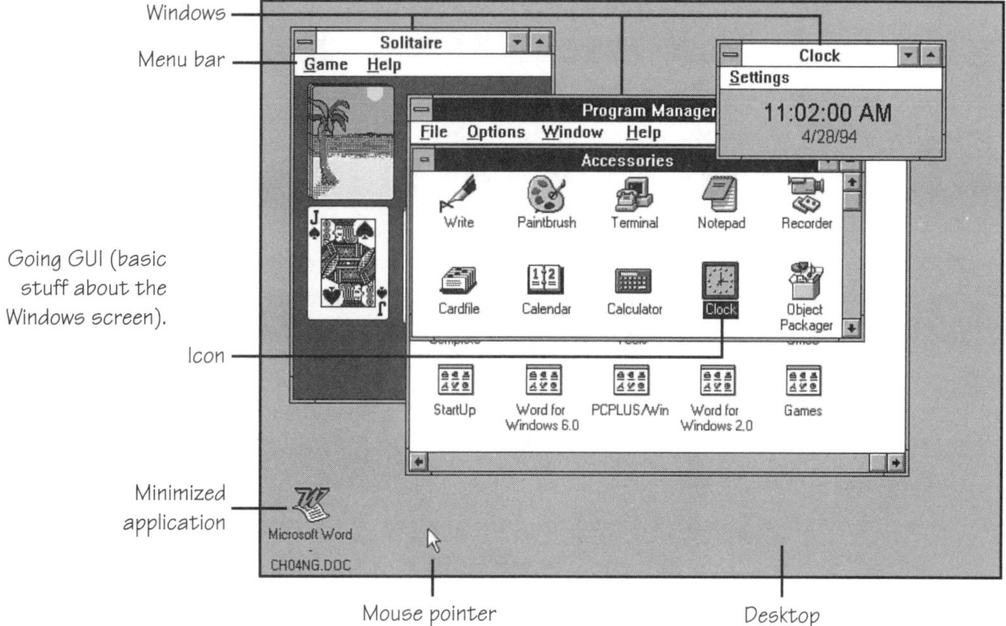

Basic stuff about the Program Manager screen

- ✔ You see windows in a GUI program. (Hey, I bet that's where they got the name for Microsoft Windows!) There are three windows in this figure: Solitaire (the game), Clock (darn, it's not even lunch time yet), and Program Manager. With Windows, you can work with more than one window at a time.

- ✔ Only one window is *active* at a time. The active window is the one with the dark *title bar* (the bar running across the top). You can

continues

Basic stuff about the Program Manager screen, continued

make a different window active just by moving the mouse pointer to another window and clicking the left button.

- ✔ Within the Program Manager window, you see icons of various applications. An *icon* is a picture that shows you what will happen if you click the icon.
- ✔ Behind the window(s) is the *desktop*, or the background of the screen. The windows are positioned on the desktop.
- ✔ The mouse pointer looks like an arrow on the screen. When you move the mouse on the table, the pointer moves too. You can use the mouse to do things, like choose options or manipulate the windows.
- ✔ At the lower left of the figure, you see an icon of a minimized application named Microsoft Word. A *minimized application* is one that has been "shrunk" down to an icon. It's nice to minimize an application when you get tired of working with it. If you point to one of the minimized applications and press the mouse button twice (this is called *double-clicking*), you see the application's window appear.
- ✔ Below the title bar in each window, you see a *menu bar*. These contain the names of *menus*. When you click one of these, the menu appears with a list of options. You can choose the option you want with the mouse.

This list pretty much sums up the basics of using Windows: working with the different parts of the window, manipulating a mouse, and using pull-down menus. That's all you really need to know to use Windows. The next sections go into the specifics.

Handy Guide to the Basic Mouse Maneuvers

After you have the hang of the basic mouse maneuvers, you'll feel right at home in Windows. These are the basics:

Name	Maneuver
Point	Move the mouse so that the on-screen pointer moves to something, like an icon. The tip (point) of the mouse pointer needs to be positioned on the item.
Click	Point to something and click the left mouse button. (Some programs also employ the right mouse button to do special, fancy things.)
Double-click	Point to something and press the left mouse button twice in rapid succession.
Drag	Point to something, hold down the left mouse button, and move the mouse. You move (or *drag*) the item around on the screen. When you've dragged the item to where you want it, release the mouse button.

Windows Calisthenics

(Go for the burn!)

With Program Manager on-screen, you're looking at a window just like the ones in the previous figure. The Program Manager window is like all the other windows you'll see in Windows applications. They all have the same parts, so let's take a closer look.

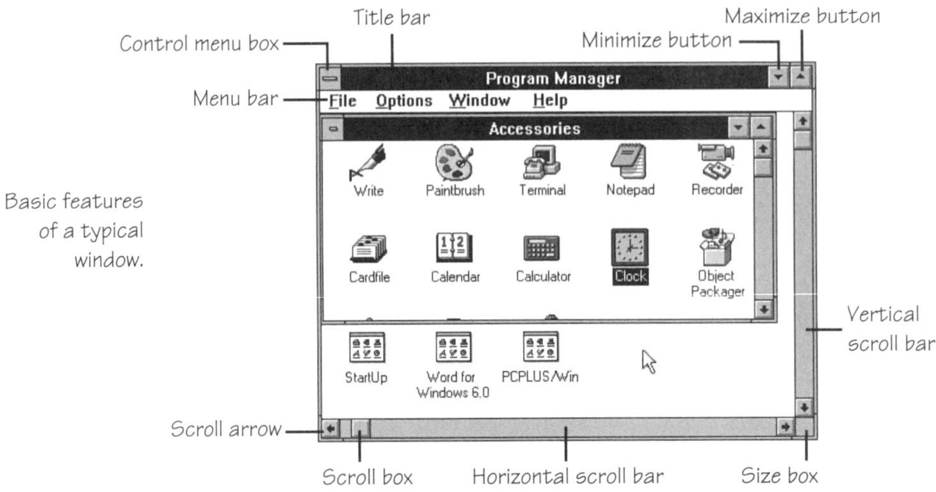

Basic features of a typical window.

Basics of manipulating Windows

- ✔ The *title bar* tells you the name of the application (here, Program Manager).
- ✔ To move a window, drag it by the title bar. You might want to move a window so that you can make room for another window next to it. (I *do* so much like to keep a game of Solitaire going.)
- ✔ To resize a window, just move the mouse pointer to any of the borders or corners (or to the size box in the lower right corner). The mouse pointer then changes shape to show you how you can move the window border (up, down, left, right, or diagonally). To move the border, just hold down the left button and drag the mouse.
- ✔ To close a window, double-click on the Control menu box. You do this if you want to quit working with an application. (If you do this to Program Manager, though, you quit Windows, so you should only do this at the end of a Windows session.)
- ✔ Note the two little arrow thingies at the top right corner of the window. If you click the "up" arrow, Windows *maximizes* this window so that it fills the screen. This is the normal thing to do if you're working with one application— make it fill the screen.

READ THIS IF YOU SEE A BOX THAT SAYS "PROGRAM MANAGER"

- After you maximize an application, the maximize arrow changes shape to one that points both up and down; if you click this again, Windows *restores* the window to its previous size. Then you can see your pretty wallpaper again, if you have any.
- If you click the "down" arrow, Windows *minimizes* the window down to an icon. This is good to do if you'd like to take a break from working with something for a while, but plan to come back to it later. (When my boss comes in, I minimize the Solitaire window.)
- When there's more stuff in the window than you can see, *scroll bars* appear.
- Click one of the *scroll arrows* to scroll the window gradually in the direction indicated. These arrows are useful if you just need to scroll a little to bring something into view.
- Drag one of the *scroll boxes* to scroll bigger distances. Dragging the scroll box is useful if you want to scroll all the way to the top or bottom of a window (or to the left or right).

To use a menu, see the next section, "Pull-Down Menu Basics."

Pull-Down Menu Basics

(What will you have?)

Most Windows applications have dozens, or even hundreds, of command options. To keep the screen uncluttered, they're hidden. To see the commands, you *pull down* a *menu* (a list of command options) by clicking on the menu.

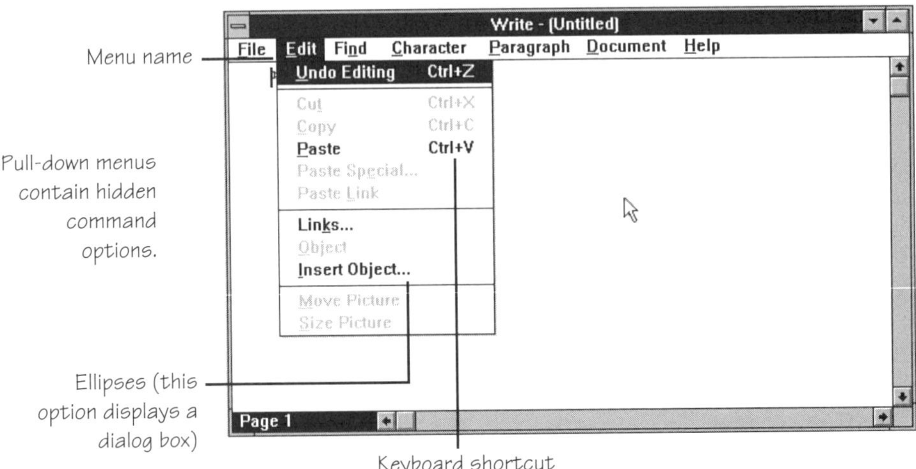

What's on the menu?

- ✔ Click the menu name again to close the menu.
- ✔ You can use the keyboard to choose a menu option. Press and hold down the Alt key, and then press the underlined letter in the command name. To close the menu without choosing anything, press Esc. You may have to press Esc more than once.
- ✔ Some menu options list keyboard shortcuts for command options, like Shift+F5. This means, "Hold down the Shift key and press the F5 key."
- ✔ Some menu options are followed by three dots, called *ellipses*. These indicate that choosing the option will reveal a dialog box. A *dialog box* is a window that requests even more information from you.

READ THIS IF YOU SEE A BOX THAT SAYS "PROGRAM MANAGER"

Dialog Box Basics

(How to have a conversation with your computer)

Dialog boxes pop up on the screen when Windows or a Windows application needs more information from you. To supply the needed information, you use the standard features shown in the figure below (this dialog box appears when you want to print something with Microsoft Word, a word processing program).

BUZZWORDS

DIALOG BOX

A special window that appears when your computer needs some information from you.

The print dialog box.

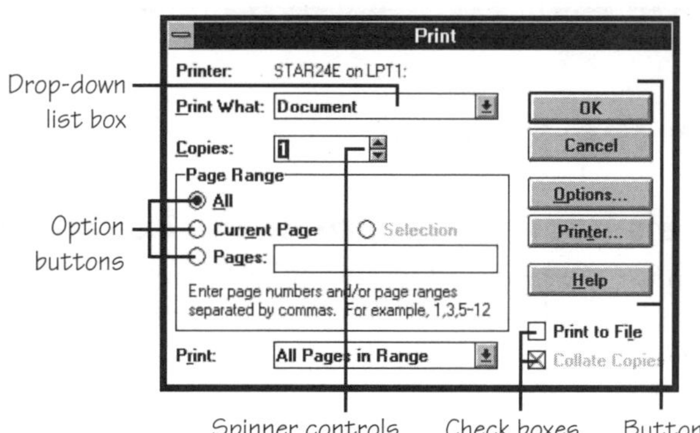

Using dialog boxes (talking back to your computer)

- ✔ In a drop-down list box, you click the down arrow to choose what you want. A menu appears that lets you click the desired option. After this, you see your choice in the box.
- ✔ Spinner controls let you increase or decrease a number by clicking the up or down arrow. If you like, you can just type the number you want.

continues

Using dialog boxes (talking back to your computer), continued

- ✔ Option buttons are like the buttons found on old 1950 and 1960 car radios—you can only "press" one of them at a time. To activate an option button, just click the circle. The one you've chosen has a black dot. If you want to de-activate the option, you click a different one.
- ✔ When you see check boxes, you can choose as many options as you like. To activate a check box, click within the box. You see an "X." If you want to deactivate the option, click it again so that the "X" disappears.
- ✔ Buttons do things. OK confirms your choices and carries out the action. The Cancel button tells the program to ignore everything you've done in the dialog box. Buttons that have ellipses display additional dialog boxes with additional options. To choose a button, just click it.

I Hate Using the Mouse!

(There's hope if you prefer the keyboard)

You can use the keyboard for lots of Windows actions. Unlike the Macintosh, which was originally designed to make you use the mouse, Windows lets you use the keyboard for almost everything. You can use keyboard shortcuts instead of the mouse, as shown in the table below. If you like using the mouse, there's no need to learn the shortcuts.

Key or key combo	What the key or combo does
Alt or F10	Activates the menu bar
Arrow keys	Moves the highlight to next item
Enter	Chooses whatever is highlighted
Esc	Closes the menu or dialog box without choosing anything

Key or key combo	What the key or combo does
Alt+Tab	Switches applications
Ctrl+Esc	Displays the Task List for task switching
Alt+space bar	Displays the Control menu for the current window
Ctrl+F4	Closes the current window
F1	Gets help
Alt+F4	Quits the current application

TIP

I punched both keys at once, but it doesn't work!

A lot of beginning users make mistakes with keyboard commands, like Alt+Esc, because they try to press both keys at once. The correct maneuver is a kind of rolling motion, beginning by pressing Alt and, while still holding it down, sweeping up to press Esc. It's all in the wrist!

And Now Back to Program Manager, Already in Progress

Program Manager gives you tools for organizing programs. Since some people have a lot of programs on their computers, Program Manager lets you put them in their own little cubbyholes, called *program groups*. A program group icon is hard to miss—it has a title and the icon shows six little program icons.

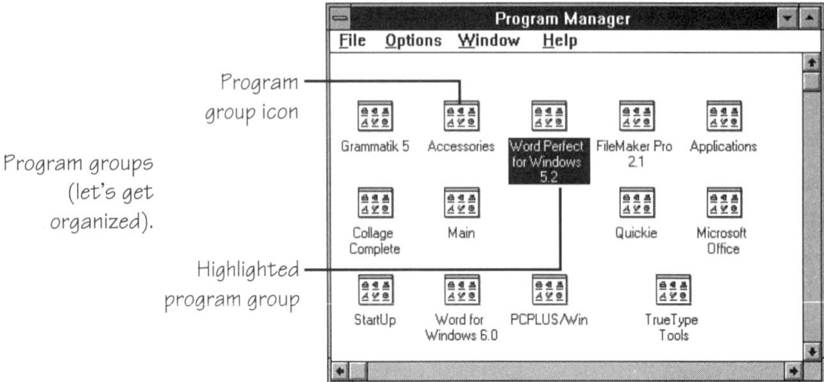

Program groups (let's get organized).

Opening a Program Group Window within Program Manager

Program Manager basics

- ✔ One of the program groups is highlighted (selected). To open this one, you can just press Enter.
- ✔ If you like using the keyboard, note that you can't use the arrow keys to move to another program group icon. You have to press Ctrl+F6—and this jumps the selection around in the order the windows are listed in the Windows menu, which is pretty frustrating if you're just trying to select the next one to the left. Use the mouse.
- ✔ To open a program group window, just double-click it. You'll see the *program items* (icons for individual programs) that it contains.
- ✔ To close a program group window, click the window's Control menu box or the minimize button—both of these do the same thing ("shrink" the window back down to a program group icon).
- ✔ You also can choose program group windows by using the Window menu.

Tile and Cascade

(These are not detergents)

Every application gives you an *application workspace*. Within this area, you can do tasks such as writing, working with numbers, or playing solitaire. With Program Manager, you can organize your programs.

Most applications let you open more than one window within the application workspace. With a word processing program, for example, you can open a window containing a poem, another containing a letter, and a third containing a memo. With Program Manager, you can open more than one program group.

When you get a lot of windows on-screen, it's hard to see the ones underneath. For this reason, Windows provides a couple of features called *tiling* and *cascading*.

To try tiling and cascading, open lots of program group windows by clicking on all the minimized icons at the bottom of the Program Group workspace. Move open windows up and out of the way, if necessary, so that you can click even more icons. (Remember, to move a window, drag the title bar.)

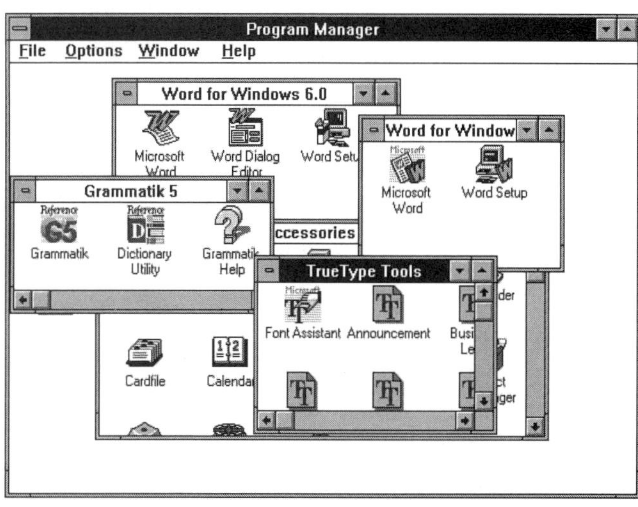

Too many windows clutter the screen!

Now click on the **W**indow menu name, and from the pull-down menu, click on **C**ascade. (As a shortcut to this rather lengthy procedure, just press Shift+F5.) As you can see, the windows are nicely "cascaded" so that you can see each window's title bar. With all the title bars in view, you can quickly choose the window you want.

Choose Cascade so that you can see each window's title bar.

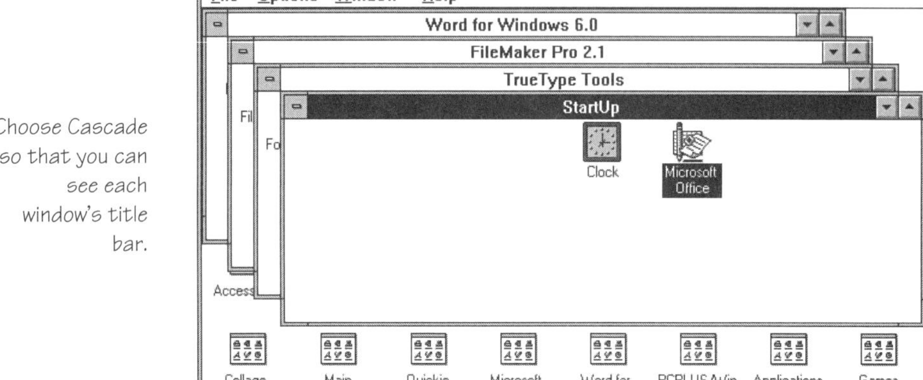

Now choose the **T**ile option from the **W**indow menu, or press Shift+F4. Now you get little bitty windows, all jammed together, side-by-side. But, at least you can see each one clearly. What's the point of this? If you click the window's Maximize button, it zooms to fill up the application workspace, hiding the others. When you click the same window's Restore button, though, it shrinks back down to its place in the tiled scheme of things. So, this is also a convenient way to work with more than one window at a time.

READ THIS IF YOU SEE A BOX THAT SAYS "PROGRAM MANAGER"

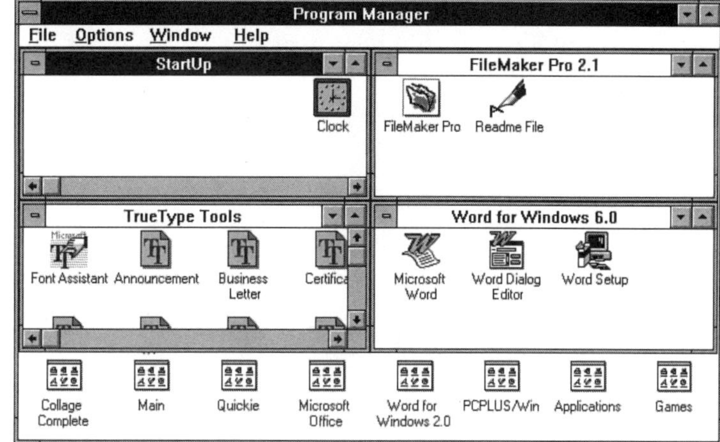

Choose Tile if you want to see all the windows.

Launching Programs

(5, 4, 3, 2, 1, liftoff!)

In Windows, you don't just start an application. That wouldn't be dramatic enough. You *launch* it. Or *run* it. Or *invoke* it. (These terms all mean the same thing.) You can launch Windows applications. But, you also can launch DOS applications. When a DOS application starts, it takes over the screen, and from then on, you never know that you're working with Windows—until you quit the DOS application, and Program Manager pops back on-screen.

To run an application, you need to display the program group window that contains the icon of the application. For example, Write, a mini word processing program, is in the Accessories program group. To open a program group, just double-click the Accessories program window.

TIP

I can't find the Accessories program group!

It's probably hidden under the program group window that's open. To close this window, just double-click the window's Control menu box (the little dash thingie in the upper-left corner).

To run Write, just double-click on the Write program icon, and Write starts. Try launching Write now.

When your application is on-screen, a whole new set of capabilities becomes available. If you start Ami Pro for Windows or Word for Windows, for example, you can write, edit, format, and print your work. If you start Quattro Pro for Windows, you can work with numbers and produce handsomely printed reports. These and other software options are covered in Chapter 18.

Even if this is the first time you've laid eyes on your application, you see the familiar window features that you've already learned, such as the pull-down menus, the scroll bars, and more. That's why people like Windows—they already know a little bit about how to use this program!

Switching Back to Program Manager

What happens to Program Manager when you start an application? It's still there. You can switch back to Program Manager without losing your work in the application that's running.

To switch back to Program Manager, click on the Control menu box to display the Control menu, and then choose the Switch To option, or press Ctrl+Esc. You then see the Task List dialog box. To switch back to Program Manager, just double-click on Program Manager in the task list.

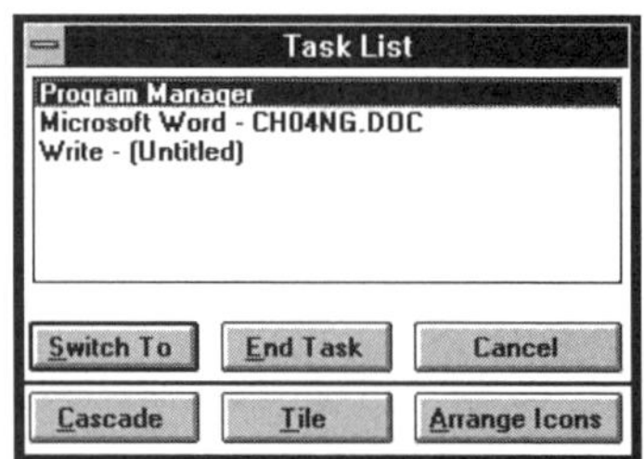

The Task List dialog box lets you switch to other applications, or back to Program Manager.

Now Program Manager pops up over the application you're running. (If the Program Manager window isn't maximized, you can probably see parts of your application in the background.) To switch back to your application, use the Control menu again and choose Switch To; but this time, double-click on the application's name in the Task List.

There are lots of cool shortcuts for switching windows. Try pressing Alt+Tab (hold down the Alt key and press Tab). Keep holding down the Alt key; each time you press Tab, you see a box giving the name of one of the active applications. To choose one, just let go of the Alt key.

Reasons for running multiple applications

- ✔ One of the nicest things about running two or more applications at once is that you can easily copy or move text or graphics from one application to another. Suppose you have an address in Cardfile; rather than retyping it, you can copy it from Cardfile and insert the copy (this is called *pasting*) into a Write document.

- ✔ You can start a time-consuming operation, like printing a lengthy document, and then switch to another application and continue working. The printing keeps going while you do other work.

- ✔ You can keep Solitaire running in the background and switch to it when you get bored. When your boss comes in, just switch back to your application and maximize it. (Now don't tell me I didn't give you any *useful* information.)

Exiting a Windows Application

(Get me outta here!)

Now that you've gotten into Windows and explored a bit, it's time to learn how to quit a Windows application gracefully. You can do so lots of different ways, but the fastest method is to double-click on the Control menu box for the program window.

TIP

It's asking me whether I want to save changes!

If you do any "experimental" typing in an application, you see a dialog box like the one shown below. This box warns you that your work will be lost unless you save a copy of it to a disk. To do so, click on **Y**es, and type a file name (the file name can be up to 8 letters and numbers). Then, click on the big Save button, or press Enter. To abandon your work (let it disappear into the computer equivalent of the Long Dark Night), just click on the **N**o button. To give up the whole thing and go back to your application, click on Cancel. Since you've probably just been fooling around, click **N**o.

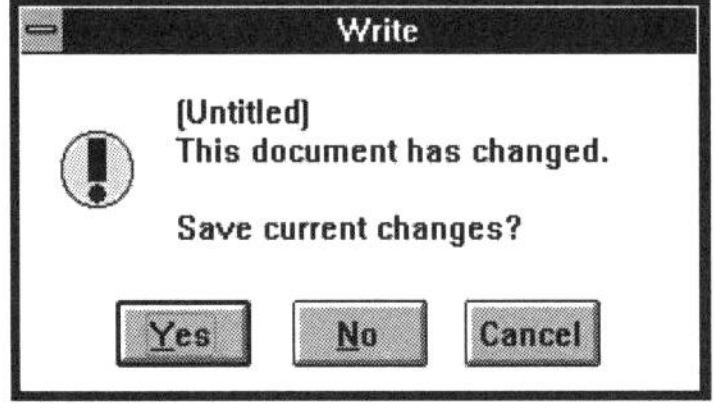

This dialog box is warning you that you'll lose the work you've done unless you save it.

TIP

How come some of the letters are underlined?

To let you know that you can choose a button just by typing the letter. It doesn't matter whether you type lowercase or uppercase.

EXPERTS ONLY

Other ways to quit (for those gotta-know-it-all type)

You also can exit by clicking on **F**ile and then clicking on the E**x**it option. Or you can press and hold down the Alt key, and then type FX. Or press Alt+F4. You can really go nuts trying to remember all these options. Pick one way you like and stick to it.

TIP

This thing has gone dead on me!

In Windows, it's easy to get stuck and to think a program has crashed when it really hasn't. A common cause: you accidentally pressed Alt or F10, which activates the menu bar. The program hasn't crashed; it's just waiting for you to select a menu name. To return to your document, press Esc.

Quitting Microsoft Windows

Even if your system starts Windows automatically, you should still exit Windows and return to that DOS prompt before switching off your computer. Why? This is the only way of saving the various working choices you've made since you've been using Windows, such as window size and location. It's a pain, but you really should do it every time you want to quit working—don't just switch off your computer with poor, helpless Windows left on-screen.

To quit Windows, exit all your applications, as described in the previous section. Now click on **F**ile, and then click on the E**x**it Windows command. You also can hold down the Alt key and press F4. You see a dialog box informing you that you're about to exit Windows. Click on the OK button, or just press Enter. You see the DOS prompt. *Now* it's safe to shut off your system.

PART II

Let's Get Physical (Hardware)

Includes:

5: Inside the Big Box (Forgettable System Unit Mysteries)

6: Disks and Disk Drives

7: Monitors (Get the Picture)

8: Keyboards, Mice, and More

9: Nobody Loves Printers, But We Do Need Them

10: Sound! Action! Multimedia! Sound Boards and CD-ROM

11: You've Got My Modem (or Fax Board) Working!

12: Take It With You… And Work All the Time (Notebooks and Personal Digital Assistants)!

13: Them Ol' System Software Blues

Shoe
By Jeff MacNelly

STOP LOOKING AT ME THAT WAY...

ACK!! I CAN'T GET THIS STUPID COMPUTER TO WORK RIGHT!!

MUST BE THE HARD DRIVE.
WHAT AM I SAYING?! I WOULDN'T KNOW A HARD DRIVE IF IT FELL IN MY COFFEE...

I'VE TRIED EVERYTHING.

I'VE PUNCHED EVERY KEY.

EVERY COMBINATION OF KEYS...

THERE'S ONLY ONE THING LEFT TO DO.

THE LAST RESORT:

READ THE DIRECTIONS.
MacNelly
6-23

Top Ten
Things Overheard in a Hardware Design Lab

10. "Awesome! They'll *never* figure this out!"

9. "So what if it takes up the whole desk? They're gonna do all their work with the computer now, anyway."

8. "Gosh, that's funny—it stops working when you pull out the plug."

7. "Who cares if it'll be obsolete in six months, then we can sell them another one."

6. "If it's good enough to run my model train, it's good enough to power this computer."

5. "Why don't we put the power switch under the case? That way, there's no chance they'll shut off the power by accident."

4. "Is it still crashing? Let's just call that an energy-saving feature."

3. "I don't get it. Is this one the female plug, or the male plug?"

2. "So what if 'TurboDrive' doesn't mean anything? It *sounds* cool, doesn't it?"

1. "Oh, *that* speed rating? We just made it up."

CHAPTER 5

Inside the Big Box (Forgettable System Unit Mysteries)

IN A NUTSHELL

- Brief, relatively painless introduction to the parts of a computer system
- What's in the system unit
- Explanation of all that 80286, 80386, 80486, and "Pentium" chatter
- Why you need a faster computer than you'd think
- Why there's never enough disk space
- How much memory you have vs. how much you need (there's never enough of this, either)
- What ports are and how to tell which is which
- How to put your system together

Hardware is the physical part of the computer: all the drives, screens, boxes, chips, and wires. If it hurts when you drop it on yourself, it's hardware. If you drop it and it doesn't hurt, it could be software. If you drop it and then it walks off in a huff, it's your cat.

The other part of the computer is *software,* which really just means programs. Different programs are designed for different tasks. There are programs for serious tasks, like balancing your checkbook or calculating a mortgage. And, yes, there are programs for even more serious tasks, like writing a will. And, as you might have surmised, there are programs for still more serious tasks, such as defending Earth from alien invaders, or helping the King on his latest Quest (highly recommended).

But, our concern here is with hardware—the vexing and troublesome stuff which, when working right, makes all these wonders possible. You take a closer look at programs in Part III of this book.

This isn't the only chapter in the book that discusses hardware. All the chapters in Part II deal with hardware, in one way or another. This chapter delves into the *system unit,* which is the computer's main box, letting all kinds of technical verbiage spew forth.

Fortunately, you need to understand only a few basic terms and concepts to understand whether a given PC is a hopped-up screamer or a deadbeat slowpoke. The rest, thank heavens, you can forget.

The Parts of a Typical System

You can divide a typical PC into two parts: the ones you can see and the ones you can't. You can also divide accessories into two parts—the ones you can afford and the ones you can't—but, that's another story.

TIP

For a quick review of the stuff you can see, check out the Chapter 1 section titled, "What's All This Junk on My Desk?"

The system's capabilities, wouldn't you know it, are determined largely by the stuff you can't see. It's sort of like the fine print in that "Spend Four Days and Three Nights in Cancun for $19.95" brochure.

The Really Important Parts

(The ones that make a difference in your computer's performance)

Name	Description
Microprocessor	A tiny, complex plug-in thingie that contains the computer's information-handling circuitry. Also called *CPU*, short for *central processing unit*. The "brain" of the computer. Stored inside the system unit. You learn more about these things in this chapter.
Hard Disk	A disk that stores DOS, your programs, and your data when you're not using them or when the computer is off. The hard disk is stored inside the system unit and can hold lots and lots of data.
Memory (RAM)	The place where your programs and data are kept while the microprocessor is working on them. RAM can only be used when the computer is on, which is why the hard disk is necessary. At the beginning of a work session, you load programs into memory (that's what happens when you start them).

This chapter gives you the lowdown on this stuff, keeping to our theme of "the less you have to learn, the better."

TIP

Your computer has a little battery, which can cause havoc if it runs down. It's used to keep track of technical information, as well as the correct time and date, when the power is off. The loss of the technical information could make it impossible to use the computer until the battery is replaced. Plus, the technical information has to be manually added, which can be a gigantic hassle. If your computer is more than 3 years old, take it to the dealer and ask to have the battery replaced. (It should be possible for you to do this yourself, right? Have you got an engineering degree?)

Forgettable Stuff Inside the System Unit

Name	Description
Motherboard	The mother of all circuit boards inside your computer; contains microprocessor and memory (RAM). Again, this is inside the system unit. It holds the memory, the microprocessor, the expansion slots, and other fancy stuff.
ROM	This stands for *read-only memory*. In brief, it's a little computer chip which stores very simple programs that help the computer get going. This includes the computer's *BIOS* program (*basic input-output system*). BIOS comes into play when you turn on your system, as you learned about in Chapter 2. You can forget about this.
Expansion Boards	Plug-in circuit boards (also called *adapters*) that add capabilities, such as sound, to your computer system. There are probably several of these already installed to handle stuff like your monitor.

Name	Description
Expansion Slots	Receptacles for the expansion boards. These are on the motherboard. Chances are that you have several empty slots inside your computer's case. These slots can be used for nifty accessories such as sound boards (see Chapter 10).
Bus	The wiring grid to which the computer's internal components are attached. The faster the bus, the faster the computer.
Power Supply	Converts electrical current into a form the computer can use. The power supply is tucked away inside the system unit. A power supply should have enough muscle to handle your system. A 200-watt power supply is generally considered about right. Really loaded systems might require a 250-watt power supply. The power supply includes a fan, which might be really noisy and irritating. Such big power supplies wouldn't be needed if PCs were designed with conservation in mind.

WHAT'S IT SAYING?

TIP

If you're ecology-conscious, look for a computer with the Environmental Protection Agency's *Energy Star* label. These systems are designed to use less power. They go into a "sleep mode" when they're inactive. If everyone used an Energy Star computer, we could save $1 billion in electric bills and keep more than 20 million tons of junk out of the air we breathe.

Can I Really Forget the "Forgettable" Stuff?

Yup. You need to think about things like which bus you want if you're going out to buy a new system, but that's not what this book is about.

Whatever bus you have, you're stuck with, for now. Actually, it doesn't matter, because none of the programs you want to run care about which bus you have. They all work, and they work pretty good. 'Nuff said.

What determines your system's capabilities are the following: the microprocessor and its clock speed, the capacity of its hard disk, and the amount of memory that's installed. The rest of this chapter goes into these points as painlessly as possible, followed by a brief look at the back of the computer (those "port" things).

Don't block the fan! If you stack stuff up against the back of your computer so that it can't breathe, you raise the possibility that the fan won't operate efficiently enough to cool critical components. This can lead to computer failures and some very expensive repairs.

486? Pentium? Huh?

(Why knowing a little about microprocessors is a good thing)

You've probably seen that cool Intel ad on TV where the camera is like a tiny spaceship, going in through the disk drive door and zooming around until it finds, first, the motherboard, and then whirls in to land on the *microprocessor*. The ad is correct in placing so much emphasis on the microprocessor. That one little thingie, more than all the other little thingies inside the system unit, determines your computer's capabilities, such as how fast it can work and what kind of software it can run.

One of the most confusing things about PCs for beginners is that there are so many different microprocessor model numbers. Intel gives each microprocessor a distinctive model number, the way Boeing numbers its airplanes. As time goes on, the Intel Corporation, which makes the microprocessors used in IBM and IBM-compatible computers, keeps making improvements. Basically, the larger the number, the greater the capabilities. An 80486 is better than an 80386.

The Pentium, incidentally, would have been called the 80586, but Intel got tired of competitors copying their numbering system (which they can do, more or less legally). So they called it "Pentium," which is supposed to suggest "5" (as in pentangle, Pentagon... get it?). Dumb, huh?

Here's a quick guide to the microprocessors that drive the PCs you're likely to encounter. You'll notice that these microprocessors are evaluated in terms of how well they run Microsoft Windows, which is discussed in Chapters 4 and 16.

If you'd like to skip this, the main point is that you need at least a 486 and preferably a Pentium to run Microsoft Windows really, really well. No hate mail, please. I know some of you are running Windows just fine on 386s, but the new programs they're writing these days assume you have more horsepower than that. Lots of people are content to stick with slower computers and keep using old programs, which is just fine with me.

EXPERTS ONLY

How Do You Pronounce These Numbers?

"Eight-oh-three-eight-six" is hard to say, so people just say "three-eighty-six" or "four-eighty-six." The cool way to write this is 386 or 486. Nobody talks about 8088s or 8086s, though, out of respect for the dead (see the next section). Incidentally, it is considered an extreme social faux pas to enter a computer store and loudly announce, "Please show me an eighty-thousand-four-hundred-eighty-six, if you don't mind." But, try it anyway—just to see how they react.

8088

(It rhymes with "out of date")

This is the original (circa 1981) microprocessor of the IBM PC. It's very slow and won't run Microsoft Windows. A slightly newer version of the 8088, called the 8086, is still woefully clunky by today's standards. A more recent low-power version called the 80C86 is found in some cheap notebook or subnotebook computers. (Flip to Chapter 12 for more information about portable computers.)

These computers might be OK for some things, like running an old copy of WordPerfect (a word processing program), but don't run out and buy one.

286s or ATs

The next step up from the original IBM Personal Computer was 1984's IBM PC AT, which stands for Advanced Technology. The AT uses the 80286 microprocessor, which runs faster and can use more memory than its 8088 and 8086 predecessors. However, it has technical limitations that prevent it from taking full advantage of Microsoft Windows and Windows programs. 286-based machines are considered obsolete. The other day, some company in my town placed an ad in the classified section for fifty 286s (including a monitor) for $140 each—which is about what they're worth.

386—The Bare Minimum

PCs based on the 80386 family of microprocessors abound these days; they're available for less than $1000 (which kind of burns me up, since I paid $2000 for mine). They're considered "entry-level systems" now. (An *entry level system* is what you buy when you're getting Your First Computer.) But, that's not such a bad thing. Heck, I wrote this book on a 386 system.

You need to distinguish between the 386DX and 386SX. "DX" is a lot better, but it's more expensive. The "SX" chip is missing some parts that would help it run faster, but it's cheaper. The price difference isn't all that great anymore, so if you're shopping around, go for the DX.

In notebook computers, you'll run across 386SL microprocessors. These are like the 386SX, except they're designed for low power consumption.

486—Now We're Cookin'

Faster and more powerful than the 386, the 80486 (or 486 for short) is where the action is these days. This baby has more than a million *transistors* (*switches*) packed into its tiny confines. It's a good choice if you're planning to run Microsoft Windows.

As with 386s, you can get 486SX and 486DX computers—with DX being the better choice. You can also get a DX2, which runs at super-fast speeds, and the 486SL, a version of the 486SX chip designed for notebook computers.

Pentium

(It would have been called 80586)

This is Intel's newest and snazziest chip. It's expensive, but it will quickly become a standard. It has twice the computing power of the 486DX2. It packs an incredible 3.1 million transistors—more than twice as many as the 486 chip, and all on a little flake of silicon that's about 1/16th square inch in size.

Prices will fall as Intel "ramps up" Pentium production. By the time this book is out, Pentium systems will probably cost what 486DX2 systems do right now.

TIP

If you're a 386 user shopping for a computer system, don't make the mistake I keep making and buy a computer that isn't powerful enough. Those dratted programmers just keep making more and more complicated programs that require faster and faster computers. It's best to buy *ahead* of this process—and since the programmers think you (should) have a 486, you'd better get a Pentium. The alternative is to have to buy a new computer every couple of years, going up one jump at a time.

BUZZWORDS

MATH COPROCESSOR

An additional circuit that helps the computer work with numbers more quickly. If you plan to do a lot of number crunching, you might want to add a math coprocessor to your system. This can be done when you order your computer, or later. 486DX and Pentium systems have a built-in math coprocessor.

What's a "Power PC?"

For Intel, trouble. This microprocessor was jointly developed by Motorola, IBM, and Apple to power a new generation of very fast personal computers. How can an upstart consortium like this pose a threat to the world's largest microprocessor corporation (Intel)?

The answer to this question is complicated, but here's the quick answer. To keep all those new chips compatible with software dating back to the 8088 days, Intel has to make complex microprocessors. But, it's been known for some time now that making less complicated microprocessors and farming out some of the operations, to other chips or software, actually makes the computer run faster. The PowerPC microprocessor is based on this idea. The new PowerPC Macintoshes are faster than Pentium machines—and this is the first generation of PowerPC chips. Worse (for Intel) is the fact that it's going to be very difficult and very expensive for Intel to wring more performance out of the Pentium's descendants, while it's going to be relatively cheap and easy to get better performance out of the PowerPC chip.

If you conclude from this that you'd better get a PowerPC-based system, wait just a sec, OK? A new microprocessor requires *compatible* software—software that's designed to run with it. And, there are, as yet, very few programs that are specifically designed to take full advantage of the PowerPC's capabilities. On the other hand, there is a large (and growing) mountain of Windows applications, and that argues for going the Pentium route.

BUZZWORDS

COMPATIBLE

Able to work with a given computer system without modification. To run on your IBM PC, programs must be compatible with the IBM standard. These programs won't run on a Macintosh.

You'll be told, "Oh, this PowerPC system can run ordinary Windows, DOS, and Macintosh programs just fine." But, don't believe it until you see it. This is being done through a horrible thing called *emulation*. A program tricks the computer into thinking it's another machine. But, your programs might run like molasses—thick molasses. That's because a computer doing emulation not only has to run your program, but also another program that tricks the computer into thinking it's a different kind of computer. For our silicon friends, this is the equivalent of patting your head and rubbing your hand in circles over your stomach at the same time—it slows you down.

Intel microprocessors will be around for quite a while. Just to prove the point, Intel is reportedly planning to flood the market with tons of cheap Pentiums. It might be wise to wait a few more months before buying that new Pentium system...

Is My Computer Fast?

"My 386 is running at 33 megahertz," your colleague says, proudly. But, you're not sure whether this assertion is good or bad. Well, rest assured; your colleague probably doesn't know either. The speed at which a microprocessor runs, called *clock speed*, which is measured in *megahertz (MHz)*, is one of the most misunderstood measurements of a computer's capabilities.

BUZZWORDS

MEGAHERTZ

The term megahertz (MHz) refers to "one million cycles per second." This may seem like a lot, but computers have a lot of data to crunch. So, the faster, the better. With a fast computer, things happen on-screen a lot faster. Believe me, it's a pain to wait around for the screen to respond after you ask the computer to do something.

Why is clock speed misunderstood? Because these speeds aren't easily compared from one microprocessor to another. Here's why: A great, big power backhoe shoveling 20 shovel loads in 10 minutes will shovel a lot more dirt than a teeny hand shovel, even if the poor person can shovel 200 shovel loads a minute. Likewise, a 486 running at 20 megahertz is faster than a 386 running at 33 megahertz. But, most people don't know that. Most people don't care.

Clock speeds aren't a reliable guide to system performance when you're comparing two different microprocessors. But, when you're comparing two systems that use the same microprocessor, they are. The following checklist shows the relation between microprocessor and clock speed for all the popular Intel microprocessors.

Learn to talk the microprocessor lingo

- ✔ When someone says, "Oh, it's a 486DX running at 33MHz," this actually tells you a lot more than what brand the computer is, such as Compaq, IBM, Zeos, and so on. A given computer's capabilities are determined by the kind of microprocessor that's inside of it, not the company that put all the parts together.
- ✔ Advertisements often describe computers using this kind of abbreviation: 486DX-33. This means it's a 486DX running at 33MHz.
- ✔ For Windows users, 386SX PCs are going to seem really, really slow. The latest programs run like week-old mush on anything with less horsepower than a 386DX-33.

- ✔ There's one drawback to faster clock speeds—the other components have to be faster, so the faster the clock speed, the more expensive the computer. That's why your boss gave you a 386DX-33, while he has a 486DX2-66.
- ✔ If you think you might run Microsoft Windows, you need all the speed you can get.

Is my computer fast?

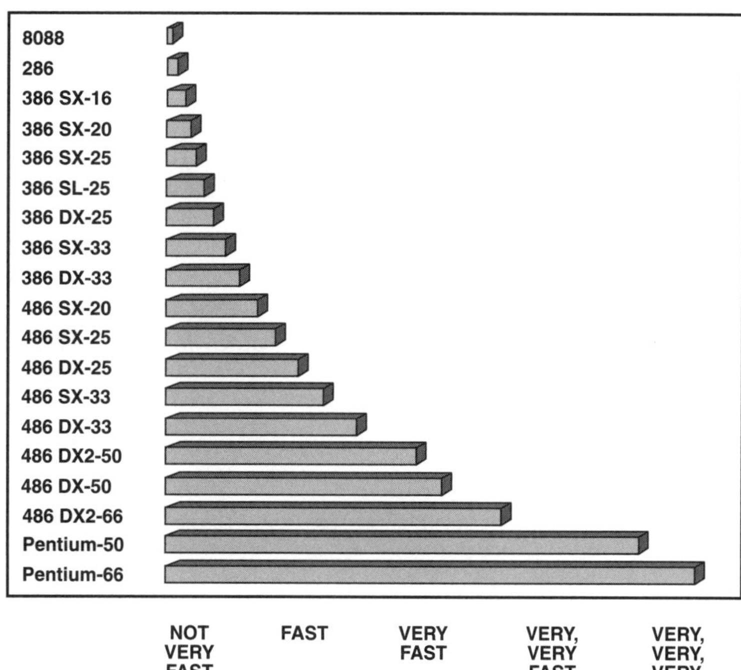

TIP

If your computer seems painfully slow, don't run out and blow 3,000 bucks on a new system. You might be able to upgrade your system much more cheaply, as the following checklist indicates. But please, get a competent computer store to do this for you—some of these upgrades are difficult to perform and you could damage your system if you don't know what you're doing.

Upgrading your microprocessor

- ✔ If you have a generic clone (i.e., not a Tandy, Epson, Leading Edge, or Packard Bell), and it has a 386SX or 386DX, you can probably upgrade to a 486 by removing the old processor and putting in a new one. This is tricky, though, and should be done only by a competent repair shop. The bright side is that it may cost as little as $300 to make a huge, noticeable improvement in your computer's performance.
- ✔ An easy processor upgrade: If you have a fairly recent 386DX or 386SX machine, you can probably upgrade it yourself with a Cyrix 386-486 Upgrade Microprocessor (about $400). This comes with instructions and a chip removal tool.
- ✔ If you have an older 386 that won't take an upgrade chip, you can replace the whole motherboard for a lot less than buying a new computer. For example, a 486 motherboard costs as little as $400, installed. You use the same old case, disk drives, keyboard, and monitor.
- ✔ If you have a system with a 486SX or 486DX processor, you can upgrade if your computer has an Intel OverDrive slot. Into this, you (or, preferably, a computer technician) can insert an Intel OverDrive processor. This gives you the same performance as a 486DX2 chip, an improvement of up to 70%.
- ✔ There will be a Pentium OverDrive chip someday (Intel promises), so you'll be able to make your zippy Pentium even zippier.

TIP

Just because your computer has a little clock ticking away inside, don't assume your computer can keep time accurately! PCs gain or lose as much as 15 seconds per day. The time you see on Microsoft Windows' little clock accessory may not be as accurate as the time you keep on your el cheapo wristwatch!

Hard Disk

(There's no such thing as enough hard disk space)

There's one more thing inside the system unit that determines your system's capabilities: the hard disk drive.

What's a disk drive, in general? (We'll get to the "hard" part in a minute.) A *disk drive* is like a cassette recorder that uses round cassettes (disks). Only rather than playing and recording music, the drive *reads* (puts information into the memory) and *writes* (stores information back on the disk).

In *floppy disk drives*—the ones you see slots for on the outside of the system unit—you insert floppy disks. Without a disk in the drive, the drive is useless—just like a cassette player without a cassette.

In a *hard disk drive*, though, the disk is built-in. It's an inflexible platter (Get it? Hard, not floppy.) It rotates much faster than a floppy disk does, which is why it can pump data in and out at much faster speeds. In order to function, the drive needs a dust-free environment. That's why the whole thingamajig is located inside the system unit—it lives in its own, permanently closed case. Hard disks have a lot more storage space, and they operate much faster than floppy drives.

Most computers have two disk drives: one hard and one floppy. Some have three drives: one hard and two floppy. A few computers even have two or more hard drives or three or more floppy disk drives, but this is going a bit far.

In general, the more capacity your hard disk has, the happier you'll be with your PC. You use your hard disk to store all the application programs, as well as the work that you do with your computer. The more space you have, the less chance that you'll run out. (Running out of space is a real pain.) When you run out of space, you have to move some programs or data files off the hard disk, which means they aren't readily accessible when you want to use them.

For more information about disks and disk drives, see Chapter 6.

BUZZWORDS

CAPACITY

The amount of data that you can *store* on a disk. This is a measurement of *storage*. Storage is different from *memory*. Storage is where you keep data when the computer's switched off. Memory is where you keep data while the computer's working with it. (This distinction confuses a lot of people—and it doesn't help that you measure capacity and memory the same way, as the following section explains.)

What Does "200MB" Mean?

To understand your drive's capacity, you need to learn a little lingo. Drive capacities are measured in *bytes*, which correspond to the amount of space needed to store a single *character* (a letter or number). I realize this is painful, but once you learn this stuff it does double duty; you use the same measurements for memory as well as storage.

BUZZWORDS

CHARACTER

Anything you can type at the keyboard, such as a letter, number, or punctuation mark.

BUZZWORDS

BYTE

The amount of space needed to store the equivalent of one character; a basic unit of measurement for computer storage.

Term & Abbreviation	Approximate Measurement
Byte	One character
Kilobyte (K or KB)	One thousand characters
Megabyte (M or MB)	One million characters
Gigabyte (G or GB)	One billion characters

TIP

There's just no such thing as enough disk space. A few years ago, it was considered a very big deal to have a 40-megabyte (MB) hard disk. But nowadays many people feel that 200MB is the practical minimum, especially if you're running Windows. Windows programs really hog the disk space—oink, oink.

EXPERTS ONLY

Technical minutia about access speed that only a toolie could love

Hard disks vary in speed, too. The faster the disk, the faster things go on-screen. The most widely quoted measurement of hard disk speed is *access speed,* which is the time it takes the disk drive mechanism to find data and start feeding it back to the computer. Really slow drives are rated in the 50 to 85 *microseconds* (millionths of a second, abbreviated *ms*) range; very fast drives are rated in the 9 to 17ms range.

Help! I'm Out of Space on My Hard Disk!

(Disk compression software to the rescue)

This cry is heard wherever computer users are found, but now there's hope: disk compression software. For a small sacrifice in performance, you can run a *disk compression program* that will squeeze the existing data onto the disk more tightly. This will free up as much as half of the disk for more programs and stuff!

Some doubt the safety of disk compression software, but the best-selling programs (such as Stacker) seem safe enough.

Memory—It Isn't Storage

Memory refers to those RAM chip things inside the system unit, where your programs are kept while the computer's running.

TIP

Be sure to remember the distinction between *memory* (RAM) and *disk space* (capacity). A shortage in one doesn't necessarily mean there's a shortage in the other! "Oh, Dad, I was trying to run Word, and it said there wasn't enough memory. So, I deleted a whole bunch of your files from the disk." If DOS says there isn't enough memory to run a program, you need more memory, not more disk capacity. See the checklist below for tips on how to get more memory.

Facts about memory (RAM)

- ✔ Technoid types, like myself, like to call memory *RAM*. You hear this term a lot—as in "How much RAM do *you* have?" (RAM, incidentally, stands for *random-access memory*.) RAM and *memory* are synonymous. Other terms for memory are *primary memory* and *internal memory*. They all mean the same thing.

- ✔ RAM has one very, very unfortunate drawback: it's *volatile*. No, this doesn't mean that it has a short-fuse personality. It means something far worse, actually. It means that you lose all of your data if there's a sudden power loss. RAM needs power to maintain the data stored in it.

- ✔ Because RAM is volatile, you need to *save your work to disk*, as computer people put it. Disks don't need power to keep the data; after you save (that is, transfer your work from RAM to a hard or floppy disk), you can turn off your computer without wiping out your work.

- ✔ Do you have enough counter space in your kitchen? Probably not. There's never enough counter space. RAM is the same way. There's no such thing as enough memory. That's particularly true if you're running Windows.

- ✔ The amount of memory you have depends on the number of memory chips installed in your computer.

- ✔ If you have a 386, 486, or Pentium computer, there's probably room on your motherboard for adding more memory. Most computers come with just enough memory to seem competitive. The inside of the computer case probably contains empty places where you can add more memory chips. Computers do impose limits on the amount of memory that you can add; this limit depends on your computer model.

- ✔ Some intrepid computer users install their own memory chips, but I don't recommend it. If you want to add more memory to your system, get your dealer to put in the memory chips. This isn't very expensive—for about $250 you can probably buy enough memory chips to double your computer's memory.

Do I Have Enough Memory?

I JUST DON'T UNDERSTAND THESE THINGS!!

Confusingly, memory (RAM) is measured the same way that storage (hard disk) is measured—in *kilobytes* (abbreviated *K* or *KB*), *megabytes* (M or MB), and *gigabytes* (G or GB). But how much is enough?

Figuring out whether you have enough memory

- ✔ This one's pretty easy: you need enough to run your programs. A program's memory requirements are usually listed right on the program box. Look for an area called "System Requirements." Microsoft Word for Windows, for example, requires 4MB of RAM. To run this program, you need at least 4MB of RAM installed in your system.
- ✔ Most DOS programs require 640KB of *conventional memory*. You should have at least this amount. If you don't have 640KB, upgrade your system to that level.
- ✔ Windows programs require humongous amounts of additional memory (called *extended* memory)—at least 3MB (to make 4MB total). However, 8MB of total memory is necessary to run some particularly piggish Windows programs.

BUZZWORDS

CONVENTIONAL MEMORY

This is the name used to refer to the part of your computer's memory, up to 640KB. This is the maximum that DOS can use. If you're running Microsoft Windows, your Windows programs can use much more memory than this.

BUZZWORDS

EXTENDED MEMORY

This is the name used to refer to the part of your computer's memory over 1MB. DOS can't use this memory, but Windows and Windows applications can. What about the memory between 640KB and 1MB? It's called *upper memory*, and it's set aside for various secret system functions that you'd be wise to ignore. There are some tricks that you can use to make use of some of this, though, as the next section discusses.

What Is "Memory Management," and Do I Have To Do It?

Whether you're using DOS or Windows, you need to clear up as much conventional memory as possible if you want get the maximum performance out of your system. This used to be a tedious task that required learning a lot of weird commands and procedures. If you're running DOS 6 or 6.2, you can take advantage of a program called MEMMAKER that does this automatically. (Whew!) For more information on MEMMAKER, see this book's companion volume, *I Hate DOS*.

This Game I Just Bought Requires "Expanded Memory"! What's That?

Basically, *expanded memory* is a technical trick that lets DOS programs use more than 640K of RAM. Expanded memory was kept on an expansion board in those old 8088s and 80286s. On a 386, 486, or Pentium computer, there's a way you can set up your computer so that the program thinks the computer's *extended* memory is really *expanded* memory. Chances are that the program includes instructions that tell you how to set up a floppy disk to pull off this trick. To play the game, you put the disk in and then boot (start) your computer. This disk sets up your computer so that the program thinks there's lots of expanded memory. After you shut it off and restart it, without the disk in the drive, things are back to normal.

Ports

(What we would call a socket)

Practically speaking, a *port* is a socket on the back of your computer's case, through which you can connect the computer to accessory devices, such as printers. (There are more electronics inside, though, that are linked to these plugs and handle the linkage to the computer.) There are several types of ports: serial, parallel, and other special ports for the keyboard and mouse.

We Wouldn't Want Things To be Too Simple, Would We?

If you look at the back of your computer, you see that the ports aren't labeled. Isn't that nice? This makes it impossible to tell which is which without getting some help. As you see in this section, you can tell the difference yourself if you're willing to inquire into the sensitive subject of whether the plug is male (has pins sticking out) or female (has holes for male cables).

Know your ports (parallel, serial, and otherwise)

- ✔ The *parallel port* is designed for printers. It has 25 holes that are ready for the male end of the printer cable.
- ✔ You can use a *serial port* for printers, modems, scanners, and neat stuff like that. The serial port plug has either 25 or 9 male pins, all ready for a female cable.
- ✔ The monitor cable goes to a plug that looks deceptively like a 9-pin serial port, except that the plug has 15 female holes for a 15-pin male cable.
- ✔ Your mouse might be plugged into a 9-pin serial port, or into a special round plug with 9 pins.
- ✔ Your keyboard is plugged into a round port with 5 pins.
- ✔ That pink lump on the back is actually a piece of bubble gum that somebody stuck there when the boss walked in suddenly.

CHAPTER 5

INSIDE THE BIG BOX

25 holes or 9 holes

Serial port

25 pins

Parallel (printer) port

15 pins

Monitor port

5 pins

Keyboard port

9 pins

Mouse port

10 pins

Bowling alley

Quick guide to the ports (sockets) on the back of your PC.

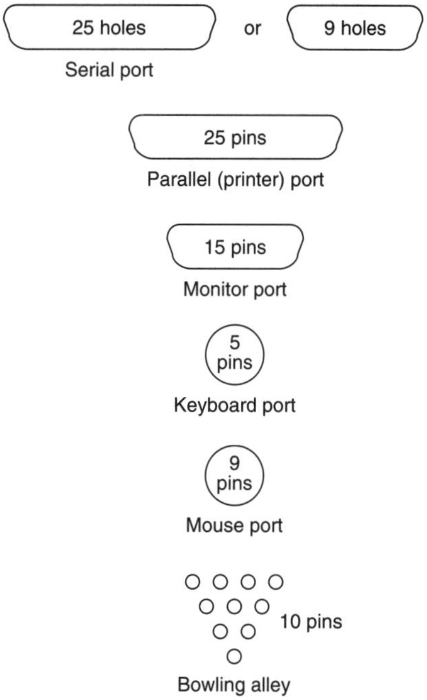

Top Ten
Uses for Dead Disks

10. Office Frisbee

9. Affix to coworker's hat to make cute Mickey Mouse ears

8. Spray with snow and glitter to make "Information Age" Christmas tree ornaments

7. Beer coasters

6. Create a mystery! Just before leaving for a trip, give someone a disk and say, "If anything happens to me, give this to Bob."

5. Lay flat on dirt, cover with mulch, to keep weeds down

4. Pile up 3.5-inch disks to level legs of sofa or ottoman

3. Fuel for space-age Databurner fireplace insert

2. Keep near computer to take out your aggressions after a computer crash or data loss

1. Target for popular Data Dart game

CHAPTER 6

Disks and Disk Drives

IN A NUTSHELL

- ▼ What disks are for
- ▼ The difference between floppy and hard disks
- ▼ How to tell which is drive A and which is drive C
- ▼ How to buy the right floppy disks for your system
- ▼ How to insert and remove floppy disks
- ▼ How to prevent the computer from changing the information on a disk
- ▼ How to format floppy disks

What are disks? Basically, they're the computer equivalent of the tape in a tape cassette. Just as a cassette recorder can play your cassette tape, the disk drive can read what's on your disk. Just as a cassette recorder can record on your cassette tape, the disk drive can write new information to the disk.

To understand why this is such a good thing, remember the point made in the last chapter about the volatility of RAM—its unfortunate tendency to forget everything when you turn the power off. Expecting RAM to remember something when you turn the power off is like expecting your teenage kid to remember to clean up his or her room.

Before you shut off the power, you save your work to a disk—normally, your hard disk (see Chapter 5 for the lowdown on hard disks). Learning how to do this is one of the most important aspects of learning how to use a program, period. If you don't save your work, you might as well not bother doing it. (Great excuse, huh?) The hard disk is big, and holds a lot of stuff. Floppy disks don't hold as much, but they're still useful, as this chapter explains. Floppy disks are the subject of this chapter, apart from occasional asides concerning worrisome things that can happen to hard disks (like getting full).

Floppy Disks vs. Hard Disks

Your system is probably equipped with one hard disk drive and one (or maybe two) floppy disk drive(s). A *disk drive* is the mechanism that makes the disk go around and access the information that's on it. The *disk* is the round thing (which, in the case of floppies, is inside a square case).

A hard disk is nonremovable; that is, you can't take it with you. You can't see the hard disk because it's inside the system unit (the big case that houses the CPU and the other stuff discussed in Chapter 5). A hard disk can store much, much more information than a floppy disk. And it's faster.

When speaking about floppy disks, computer addicts make a distinction between the disk itself and the *disk drive* (the thing that makes it go round and round). That's because floppy disks are removeable. Technically, you could make the same distinction between a hard disk and a hard disk drive, but because "hard disk drive" is longer, people just say "hard disk."

In case you're curious, the term *floppy* refers to the fact that the disk itself is flexible. (With 3.5-inch disks, you can't tell, because the disk is enclosed in a hard plastic case.) Hard disks aren't floppy; the disk consists of a rigid aluminum platter that's coated with magnetically-sensitive material.

Which drive is which?

- ✔ Floppy drives look like mail slots on the front of your computer.
- ✔ If you have only one floppy drive, it's drive A.
- ✔ If you have two floppy drives, the top one is drive A, and the bottom one is drive B. On some systems, the disk drives are side by side—hopefully, they're labelled. On a few systems that must have been set up by practical jokers, drive B is on the top and drive A is on the bottom. But, if this is the case, the drives are probably labeled.
- ✔ Your hard disk is drive C. You can't see this because it's inside the computer (it's nonremoveable, remember?). But, there's an activity light for drive C that tells you when it's doing something.

Usually, the top drive is drive A and the bottom one is drive B, while your hard disk is drive C.

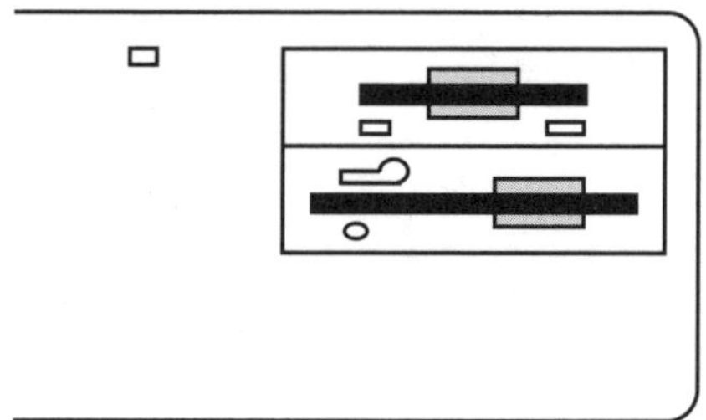

TIP

It says I have a drive F!

If you use a computer that's connected to a network, you may have an additional "drive"—a *network drive*—which acts just like another hard disk. It's probably called drive F, although the exact drive letter varies. If there are programs available on this "drive," you can run them as if they were installed on your computer. But, take my advice: Get some help from the person who set up or maintains the network. Every network has its little peculiarities, and you'll need personal assistance to learn how to navigate the network correctly.

Buying the Right Floppies for Your System

Most computers now have a hard disk as standard equipment. Still, floppy disks have lots of uses. You can use them when you want to exchange files with someone, and you can also use them to make safe, backup copies of your work.

Sooner or later, you'll find yourself at the office supply or computer store, ready to buy some disks. You learn how in this section.

What Size Drive Do You Have?

You have to decode a little technical information in order to understand the different types of floppy disks. Here are the basics.

Disks come in two sizes: 3.5 and 5.25 inches in diameter. Which size do you have? In the previous figure, drive A is a 3.5-inch drive, while drive B is a 5.25-inch drive.

5.25-inch disk

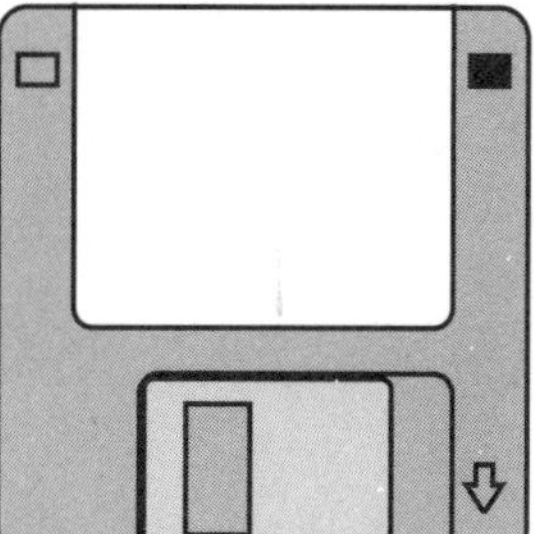

3.5-inch disk

Density and Capacity

(Fraternal twins)

Not only do disks come in different sizes, they also come in different densities.

Density refers to the recording method (how DOS crams the information on a disk). There are two densities: double density and high density.

Density is related to *capacity*—how much information can be stored on a disk. *Double-density disks (DD)* cannot store as much information as *high-density disks (HD)*. On the positive side, double-density disks are cheaper.

Capacity refers to the amount of data you can store and is measured in *kilobytes (KB)* or *megabytes (MB)*.

BUZZWORDS

BYTE, KILOBYTE, and MEGABYTE

A byte equals about one typed character. A kilobyte (abbreviated KB or K) equals around 1,000 bytes. A megabyte (abbreviated MB or M) equals around 1,000,000 bytes.

If your computer is new, chances are it has one or more high-density drives. A high-density drive can use a double-density (DD) or high-density (HD) disk. If your computer is more than three or four years old, however, you may be stuck with double-density drives. Too bad. You can't use high-density (HD) disks.

TIP

If you're using DOS 6 or 6.2, you can quickly find out which kind of disk drive(s) you have. At the DOS prompt, type **CD** followed by a space and **\DOS** (it doesn't matter whether you type uppercase or lowercase.) This switches to DOS's directory. Then type **MSD** and press Enter. This starts Microsoft System Diagnostics. Type **D** to see a dialog box explaining the facts about your disk drives. To exit, press Enter followed by F3.

360KB 5.25-inch disks

These double-density disks are obsolete—don't buy them. If you're using an old PC and really need these, almost any computer user probably has a drawer full of hundreds of useless 360KB disks that you can get for free!

You can use these disks even if you have a high-density disk drive. But, don't do this just to save money. 360,000 characters (approximately) may sound like a lot, but you'd be amazed at how fast these disks fill up. It's really frustrating to use 360KB disks.

1.2MB 5.25-inch disks

You can only use these if you have a high-density 5.25-inch drive. They hold a lot more information than 360KB disks, but they still have the drawback of that open access hole, which is just waiting for you to smear thumb grease on it.

TIP

Not sure whether you're holding a 360KB or 1.2MB disk? Take a look at the spindle access hole. If the disk has a metal reinforcing hub on the spindle ring, it's probably a 360KB disk.

If you try to put a 1.2MB disk into a double-density (360KB) drive, it will fit just fine. But, you'll get one of DOS's most horrifying error messages, `GENERAL FAILURE READING DRIVE such-and-such`. This makes you think your whole computer has blown up. Not true. You'd think the message could just say, "Can't read this disk"; but, apparently, the DOS programmers think that people can do with a few more jolts of adrenalin.

720KB 3.5-inch disks

These double-density disks are also obsolete, but not quite as obsolete as 360KB disks, because they do hold quite a bit of information. And they do have those cute little aluminum sliding doors, which keep you from ruining your disk.

You can use a 720KB disk in any 3.5-inch drive. A high-density drive has no trouble with a 720KB disk.

1.4MB 3.5-inch disks

You can tell these high-density disks from 720KB disks right away because of the letters "HD" that are usually printed on the case. If the disk is upside down, though, it look's like "CH," making you think that the noted sugar corporation has moved into computing.

These are great disks and have become the standard nowadays. Chances are your new programs will come on 1.4MB disks.

What happens if you put a 1.4MB disk into a 720KB (double-density) drive? The same `GENERAL FAILURE` message. This just means that the drive can't read the disk.

TIP

> There's a new, 2.8MB standard for special, extended-capacity disks, but you need a 2.8MB drive to use them. These are still pretty rare.

The Floppy Disk Match Up

Now that you know the different sizes and capacities, you have to match the right disk with the right drive. It's easy to figure out the size: you can't put a 5.25-inch disk in a 3.5-inch hole (unless you fold it, maybe).

It's more difficult to pick the right capacity. The trick is to determine the capacity of your drive. Remember that the drive has to be able to read the disk. The easiest way to find out the capacity of your computer's disk drives is to ask someone at the store where you bought your computer. Or, check the manuals that came with your system.

After you find out what kind of drive you have, use this table to figure out what disk you need:

If you have this drive:	Buy these disks:
3.5-inch, 720KB	3.5-inch, DS, DD
3.5-inch, 1.44MB	3.5-inch, DS, HD
5.25-inch, 360KB	5.25-inch, DS, DD
5.25-inch, 1.2MB	5.25-inch, DS, HD

Abbreviations related to disks

- ✔ KB=Kilobyte
- ✔ MB=Megabyte
- ✔ DS=Double sided (they're all double sided these days)
- ✔ DD=Double density (stores less)
- ✔ HD=High density (stores more)

Buying Disks

OK. You know what kind of disks you need. Now, here are some tips on how to purchase disks:

Tips for buying disks

- ✔ Check out one of those discount office supply stores, such as Office America, or a membership store like Sam's. You'll get great prices on disks and other computer supplies.
- ✔ Buy by the box (you get 10 per box).

continues

Tips for buying disks, continued

- ✔ Buy formatted disks. You can format disks yourself, if you must, but this process is tedious; formatting a whole box of disks might take a half hour—maybe longer. Look for disks labeled Formatted IBM. The IBM part refers to the IBM formatting standard; you can use these disks even if your computer wasn't made by IBM.
- ✔ You can save a little money by buying generic, no-name disks. Some say the disks might contain flaws. I don't really believe this, myself. All the different brands probably come from the same big factory in Taiwan.
- ✔ If you have 3.5-inch drives, you can buy disks in lots of different colors. This means you could color-code your disks. Consider getting red disks for backup purposes and yellow disks for storing old (but maybe still valuable) files.

Inserting and Removing Floppy Disks

You've probably had some experience inserting and removing floppies already, so you know there's only one way you can look like a goof doing it: inserting it the wrong way.

Inserting and removing disks

- ✔ No matter what kind of disk you're inserting, hold it with the label facing up and the access hole closest to the drive.
- ✔ If you're inserting a 5.25-inch disk, make sure that the drive door is unlatched. After you insert the disk, close the latch.
- ✔ If you're inserting a 3.5-inch disk, there's no latch. Just push the disk into the drive until it clicks into place. The drive button (which is just below the door) pops out when a disk is inserted.

- ✔ To remove a 5.25-inch disk, release the latch. The disk should pop out. If it doesn't, there's a space that lets you put two fingers in far enough to grab the disk.
- ✔ To remove a 3.5-inch disk, just press the button under the drive door. The disk pops out.

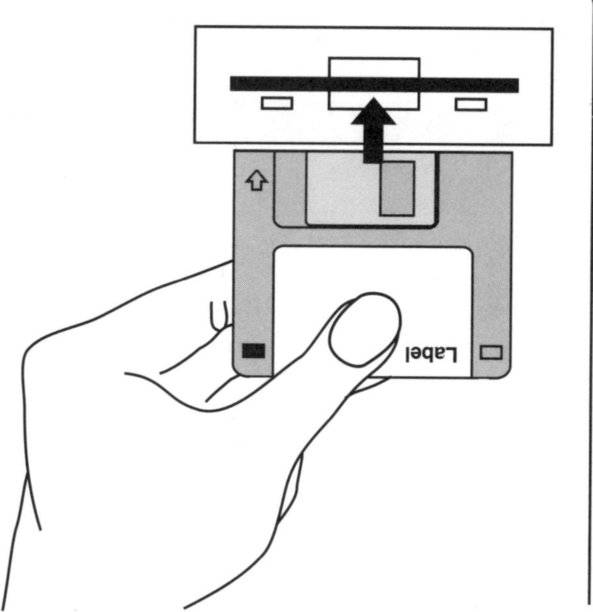

The correct way to insert a disk.

TIP

Don't force a disk into a drive. If it won't go in easily, there may be another disk in the drive, or you might be inserting the disk upside down or backward. Also, don't insert or remove disks when the little light is on. If you do, you could scramble the information on the disk.

Don't Mess with This Disk

Both kinds of floppy disks can be *write-protected*, which means you can prevent the computer from erasing what's on the disk or adding any new information to it. The computer can still read the information that's on the disk; it just can't alter the disk in any way. For this reason, you might want to write-protect a floppy disk that contains valuable data that you don't want to alter accidentally. Also, you should write-protect original program disks.

Write-protecting (and un-write-protecting) floppy disks

- ✔ To write-protect a 5.25-inch disk, you use the little adhesive labels that come with the disks. Wrap the tab over the notch so that half of the tab covers the notch on one side and half of the tab covers the notch on the other side. To unprotect the drive, remove the label. If you used all the adhesive scraps to wrap Christmas presents, you can use Scotch tape instead.
- ✔ To write-protect a 3.5-inch disk, turn the disk over and find the little write-protect slider, which is in the upper-left corner on the back of the disk. When you move it up to uncover the hole, the disk is write-protected. To unprotect the disk, move it down to cover up the hole again.
- ✔ If you've write-protected a disk and try to save data on it, DOS gives you its `Write protect error` message. Just remove the disk, unprotect the disk, and try again.

Keeping Your Disks and Disk Drives Happy

Disks are vulnerable to damage and drives can go out of alignment. But, disk drives don't need to be cleaned, really. The following sections elaborate.

Dire Warnings Concerning Things Not To Do With Disks

(Murphy's law section)

The most important thing to remember here is that if you deliberately try to ruin a disk you don't need, it will survive. However, if you have important data stored on a disk, the slightest little thing will ruin it.

Things not to do with disks containing valuable data

- ✔ Don't get them near magnets. A magnetic field can scramble the data, which is magnetically encoded. Electromagnets are just as bad as refrigerator magnets. Things that have electromagnets include boom box speakers, telephones, and "Electro-Shiatsu" back massagers.
- ✔ Keep them away from dust and dirt.
- ✔ If you're using a 5.25-inch disk, be really careful not to smear finger grease on the disk surface. And, when you write on the label, don't use a ballpoint pen.
- ✔ Don't leave them in a hot car. You'll come back to find cup-shaped things instead of plate-shaped things.

TIP

This drive works fine with *MY* disks!
(what's wrong with *YOURS?*)

If your disk drive works just fine with disks that you have formatted using this drive, but chokes when reading other disks, it's out of alignment. This requires a fairly inexpensive repair, but it needs to be done.

Does My Drive Need To Be Cleaned?

(Open wide, please)

You'll see disk drive cleaning kits in office supply stores, but opinion is divided on whether this is really necessary. These days, floppy disk drives are infrequently used—you use them just for getting new software into your system, for backing up your work, or for swapping files. Cleaning probably isn't necessary.

Formatting Floppies

(The rite of initiation)

If you buy formatted floppy disks, you don't need to read this section. Lucky you! If you didn't buy formatted floppies, read on. This section explains the why and how of formatting.

Why format? A floppy drive can't use a disk unless it's formatted. *Formatting* is a disk version of boot camp—it makes sure the disk is ready to serve you with loyalty, honor, and courage. DOS makes the disk do lots of pushups and chin-ups and run 25 or so miles. If you want to get technical, formatting creates a magnetic pattern that's needed to store the data—but you don't really need to understand everything that DOS does to the disk. You just need to know that this stuff must be done.

TIP

There's no visual difference between an unformatted and a formatted floppy disk. To help you tell which ones you've formatted, put blank labels on the formatted ones. To be really sure about which ones are formatted, write a little "f" in the upper-right corner of the label.

Formatting with DOS

You format a disk from the DOS prompt (C> or C:\>). Here's what you do:

1. Insert the unformatted disk into the drive.

2. Type the formatting command and press Enter.

   If you're using drive A, type **FORMAT A:**

   If you're using drive B, type **FORMAT B:**

If you see the message, Warning: All Data on Non-Removable Disk Drive C Will Be Lost, press N to cancel the operation! You're about to reformat your hard disk, which would cause endless grief. You should only format floppy disks, and those go in drive A or B. Don't ever, ever, ever type **FORMAT C:**. Ever.

3. You're asked to press Enter before proceeding. Make sure that you've inserted the correct disk in the drive, and that it doesn't contain any valuable data. Then press Enter. The formatting process begins!

   At the conclusion of the format, you're prompted for a *volume label* (a fancy DOS term meaning name).

4. Type a volume label of up to 11 characters. This volume label will appear when you use the DIR command. If you're crazy about names, type one. Otherwise, just press Enter to skip the volume label.

   After the format is complete, you see a message telling you how many bytes (characters) of storage are available on the disk. The message looks something like this:

```
1213952      bytes total disk space
1213952      bytes available on disk

512          bytes in each allocation unit
2371         allocation units available on disk

Volume Serial Number is 1D19-0FFD
```

5. After the message, you see a prompt informing you that you can format another disk. Press Y to format another one, or N to stop formatting and return to the DOS prompt. Then press Enter.

If you're using DOS 6 or 6.2, FORMAT checks to see whether the disk is already formatted. If so, FORMAT makes a backup copy of important information on the disk so that you can unformat the disk, should you later find that formatting the disk was a terrible mistake. (Say you happened to format a disk that contained information necessary to the known free world.)

TIP

Sooner or later, a "helpful" colleague will tell you that you can "save money" by buying double-density disks and then formatting them for high-density storage. Don't do it—the format won't be reliable.

Formatting with Windows

If you're using Microsoft Windows, you use File Manager to format your disks. File Manager is a program included with Windows that does the same stuff DOS does—in a much more user-friendly manner. This is how you format a disk using File Manager:

1. In Program Manager, choose Main from the **W**indow menu. (To do this, click on **W**indow on the menu bar, and then click on Main from the Window menu.)

2. In the Main program group, double-click on the File Manager icon.

3. Put the unformatted disk into the disk drive.

4. Pull down the **D**isk menu and choose the **F**ormat Disk option.

5. From the **D**isk In list, click the drop-down button (the down arrow). From the menu that appears, click the name of the disk drive that contains the disk you want to format.

6. If you're formatting a low-density disk, click on the drop-down arrow next to the Capacity box, and then choose the capacity of your disk (360KB for a 5.25-inch disk, or 720KB for a 3.5-inch disk).

7. Click on OK or press Enter.

8. You see an alert box warning you that formatting will erase all the data on the disk. Are you sure you want to proceed? If so, click on Yes. If you're not sure, click on No.

9. When the disk is formatted, you see an alert box asking you whether you'd like to format another disk. If so, click on Yes. If not, click on No.

10. To exit File Manager and return to Program Manager, hold down the Alt key and press F4.

Did Everything Go Smoothly?

Sometimes you run into problems while formatting disks. If you can't solve it, toss the disk into the trash—disks are cheap, but your time and data aren't.

You might see the error message `Track 0 is bad, disk unusable`. This message indicates that there's something wrong with the surface of the disk. Try again. If you still get the message, toss the disk.

Note that you might get the `Track 0 is bad` message if you try to format a low-density disk using the high-density setting. If this happens, display the Format Disk menu again, choose a low density format (360KB or 720KB for 3.5-inch disks) in the Capacity box, and click OK.

If DOS or Windows reports that the disk has any "bad sectors," discard the disk.

What's On This Disk?

Soon, you will accumulate dozens and even hundreds of disks, some of them containing valuable stuff. Trouble is, you can't tell what's on the disk unless you take a look with DOS or File Manager (Windows). Incidentally, it's a good idea to write down the names of important files on the disk label, but sometimes even experts, such as your author, forget to do this.

To see what's on a disk with DOS, follow these steps:

1. Insert the disk that has who knows what on it.
2. Activate the drive by typing **A:** (for drive A) or **B:** (for drive B); then press Enter.
3. Type **DIR /w** and press Enter. (The /w part of the command displays the file names across the screen, so you can read them easily—otherwise, the list would scroll by in a flash. By the way, it doesn't matter whether you type uppercase or lowercase letters—it's all the same to DOS.) Be sure to leave a space between the DIR and the /w.

   You'll see a list of the files on the disk.
4. Take out the disk and jot down some notes about the disk's contents on the disk label.

To see what's on a disk with Windows, follow these steps:

1. Insert the disk that has who knows what on it.
2. In Program Manager, double-click the Main program group.
3. In the Main program group, double-click File Manager.
4. In File Manager, click the little disk drive icon that corresponds to the drive that contains the disk (A or B).

You see the disk's contents in the files window.

TIP

If you'd like to be super-organized, you can print the directory and then store the file list with the disk. Begin by turning on your printer (insert and adjust the paper, if necessary). To print the directory, hold down the Ctrl key and press P; this tells DOS to route output to the printer as well as the screen. Then type **DIR** and press Enter. Your printer will then print the directory. Don't forget to press Ctrl+P again to turn off printer output!

Top Ten

Substances Found on Dirty Computer Screens

10. Dust from recent Philippines volcanic eruption

9. Orange film left from eating Cheetos too close to monitor

8. Spray globules of Pepsi from opening can too close to monitor

7. Smog fused with coworker's perfume (Warning: Possibly explosive)

6. Fingerprints from little kids pointing to where Mother Goose went

5. The type of lint you get in your dryer, only smaller fibers and more of it

4. Little white hairs from coworker's angora sweater

3. Little brown hairs from coworker's pet Chihuahua

2. Dandruff

1. Coworker's solidified tobacco smoke fused with your other co-worker's hair spray; carcinogenic mixture made radioactive by monitor emissions

CHAPTER 7

Monitors (Get the Picture?)

IN A NUTSHELL

- Why you need an adapter and a monitor to get a picture on-screen
- What all those acronyms, like VGA, mean
- Why Windows users need video accelerators
- What a "local bus" is and why it's cool to have one
- What resolution is
- What size monitor you need
- Why you should get a color monitor
- How to protect yourself from electromagnetic radiation (EMR)
- How to adjust your monitor for optimum picture quality
- How to clean the screen, and why you'd better
- How to amuse yourself (and visitors to your office) with those clever screen saver programs that show things like flying toasters

Most of the time that you work with the computer you're staring at that television thing, the monitor, except for those brief moments when you take a longing look at the Real World, which is passing you by as you work. Since you spend so much time at the monitor, the monitor had better be good. It would be nice, too, if it didn't zap you with insidious rays that Science Thinks Might Be Dangerous, even though the "experimental" evidence (so far) is contradictory. Funny, that's what they said about tobacco once, too.

In this chapter, you learn what it takes to display a high-quality image on your monitor, and how to tell whether what you're seeing is the latest and greatest.

The Monitor and the Adapter

(It takes two)

Your computer requires two components to come up with a screen display: a *monitor* (the television-type thing) and a *video adapter* (an electrical thing housed inside the computer where you can't see it).

BUZZWORDS

VIDEO ADAPTER

Electronic stuff inside the computer that generates the screen display. There are lots of different video adapters, and they vary in quality. It's called an adapter because, in most computers, its circuitry is on one of those plug-in expansion boards that fits into one of the expansion slots in your system unit. (Some people call these adapter boards, just to confuse others.) In other computers, though, the video stuff is built into the motherboard.

Basic video adapter facts

- ✔ More than the monitor, the video adapter determines the quality of the text and graphics you see. Like your television, your monitor is just a receiver; something else has to be a transmitter. That's where the adapter steps in; it creates the signal that the monitor displays.
- ✔ If you want a better display, you probably need to upgrade your adapter, as well as your monitor.
- ✔ Adapters fall into two general categories: color and monochrome (black and white).
- ✔ *Black and white* is a misnomer for early monochrome systems, which display green or amber characters on a black background. More recent monochrome systems display black text on a white background.
- ✔ There are lots of different kinds of video adapters, but the best for most folks are VGA adapters.

The Acronym-Collector's Guide to Computer Monitors

Your computer's video adapter creates the signal that's then conveyed, via cable, to your monitor. The older ones don't do such a hot job of this. The newer ones do better: they show sharper text, handle graphics better, and offer hundreds of colors or gray shades. Among the computer community, all this knowledge is summed up in terse acronyms, like CGA and VGA, which you're just expected to know. If you don't, you can read on, or you can just take my advice: Super VGA is good. You want Super VGA.

Fake your way to video adapter knowledge.

Adapter type	Acronym	Faker's guide
Color Graphics Adapter	CGA	The oldest color adapter, and pretty obsolete unless you only occasionally use the computer. Generates fuzzy text and just a few, garish colors. Not usually included with today's systems.
Monochrome Display Adapter	MDA	The oldest monochrome adapter. Great text quality, but one huge disadvantage: it can't display graphics. If you try to display a graph, for example, you just see a blank screen. Like the CGA, this adapter isn't often included with today's systems.
Hercules Graphics Adapter	HGA	Also called a monographics adapter, this adapter solved the MDA's no-graphics problem. Great text, good graphics. Often included in "budget" systems, and fine if you just want to use your computer for basic word processing and number crunching.
Enhanced Graphics Adapter	EGA	A much better color adapter than the CGA, this adapter produces great-looking text and graphics with lots of cool colors. But the VGA came soon afterward and offers even better performance for just a bit more money. You don't find too many systems with EGA adapters these days.
Video Graphics Array	VGA	The current "standard" adapter, which you find in almost all the budget systems being sold in places

Adapter type	Acronym	Faker's guide
		like Sears and K-Mart. Great text, lots of colors, and beautiful graphics. Good for both DOS and Microsoft Windows.
"Gray Scale"	VGA	This adapter is also monochrome, but it produces lots of intermediate gray shades that make pictures and drawings look really cool. You find this on notebook computers.
Super Video Graphics Array	SVGA	The sharpest and latest color VGA adapter, with even more colors. Awesome. The better computers sold today usually include an SVGA adapter.

Do I Need a Video Accelerator?

If you're using Windows, there's a quick answer to this question: Yes, unless you just love sitting around to watch the screen get updated (reflect the changes you've made or requested). Windows screens use lots of pictures made up of little tiny dots. This takes a lot of processing horsepower to update.

Getting a video accelerator card is a very good way to improve the performance of a system that's having trouble with Windows.

BUZZWORDS

VIDEO ACCELERATOR

This is a plug-in expansion board that replaces your computer's video adapter. It contains its own processing chip, which takes the load off your computer's poor microprocessor. The result is an amazing improvement in screen updating times, sometimes as much as 200 to 300%.

TIP

Video adapters and accelerators come with memory—usually, 1MB or 2MB. Unless you plan to display color photographs at your adapter's highest resolution, 1MB is enough. If you later find that you need more, you can usually add more memory to the adapter.

What's a "Local Bus"?

We're not talking about Bus 18A, which makes the loop once an hour between the hospital and the Kroger supermarket. This is the hottest new technology for video circuitry.

BUZZWORDS

LOCAL BUS

As far as you're concerned, this is a special expansion slot inside the computer, into which you can plug an adapter that's designed to work with it. Computers that have a local bus video system give you very fast video performance. You can get video accelerators that fit into the local bus slot.

TIP

Local bus designs vary. It isn't good to get stuck with a computer that has a "proprietary local bus." This means that the manufacturer wants to force you into buying their video board—probably at a stiff price. If you're thinking of getting a new computer and running Windows on it, by all means find one that has a "VESA-compatible local bus." (VESA is short for Video Electronics Standards Association.) There are lots of great video adapters for a VESA local bus slot (also called a VL-Bus).

EXPERTS ONLY

More about busses than most people really need to know
What is a "bus"? Chapter 5 briefly and delicately broached the subject of the bus inside your computer. This is basically a kind of electronic highway that different parts of the computer are plugged into. This includes your video adapter.

Chances are pretty good that your computer has an ISA (Industry Standard Architecture) bus. This is the bus design that first popped up with the IBM Personal Computer AT in 1984. When IBM brought out its PS/2 computers in the late 1980s, a new bus was introduced, called MCA (Micro Channel Architecture).

Now that people are using Windows, the ISA and MCA busses turn out to be too slow for the video adapter. Some computer companies came up with an EISA (Extended Industry Standard Architecture) bus, but this didn't really solve the problem.

That's why the newest computers employ a *local bus*. These computers also have an ISA bus; the local bus is provided mostly so you can use a local-bus video adapter.

The local bus is a lot faster because it's directly connected to the computer's microprocessor, so it runs at much higher speeds.

There are several different local bus designs. The VESA local bus design, also called VL-Bus, is a good standard, and there are lots of video adapters available that fit into VESA local bus slots. Intel has offered what it calls the Peripheral Component Interconnect (PCI) bus, and lots of video adapters are also available for this design.

Just beware of the "proprietary" designs, which, to put it bluntly, are offered by certain computer manufacturers in an attempt to make sure that you buy *their* video adapter. Avoid these like the plague. The VESA local bus (VL-Bus) is the best way to go.

And What Adapter Do You Have?

Which video adapter is "under the hood" of the computer you're using? If you're using DOS 6 or 6.2, the MSD (Microsoft Diagnostics) program can tell you pronto. If you don't have DOS 6 or 6.2, find out which adapter you have by asking the person who sold you the system or set it up for you.

To find out which video adapter your system is using, type **MSD** and press Enter. You see a screen with a lot of big buttons. Just look next to the button labeled Video. You see the acronym of your adapter (like VGA or SVGA), followed by the manufacturer's name. If you really want to know more, press V or use your mouse to click on the Video button. You see a screen full of information, some of which is useful—such as whether your system is capable of color.

Press Enter to exit the Video dialog box, and then press F3 to quit MSD.

Monitors Are Pretty Simple

(Compared to that awful adapter stuff)

The type of adapter you have generally determines what type of monitor you're using.

What kind of monitor do *you* have?

- ✔ If you have a CGA adapter, you have a CGA monitor—also called an *RGB monitor*. RGB stands for "red, green, blue," which are the colors that make up the color display.
- ✔ If you have an MDA adapter, you have a monochrome monitor. The text looks great, but you don't get graphics. This is a pain when you're using a program, such as Lotus 1-2-3, that allows you to see graphs that are automatically generated from the numbers you're crunching. But read on for a quick, cheap fix!

- ✔ MDA users, you can replace your MDA adapter with a *Hercules graphics adapter* (HGA) at a very low cost. Then you can see graphics on-screen without having to purchase a new monitor.
- ✔ If you have an HGA adapter, you have a "monographics" monitor. This is just fine if you're planning to run nothing but DOS programs, like WordPerfect. But it isn't the best choice for Windows.
- ✔ If you have a VGA adapter, guess what? You have a VGA monitor. And it's probably color.
- ✔ If you have a Super VGA adapter, you probably have a monitor designed to work with Super VGA adapters. But, you might have what's called a *multisynch* or *multiscanning monitor*, which automatically senses the type of signal your adapter is putting out and adjusts itself accordingly.

Screen Sizes

Monitor screen sizes are measured diagonally. The standard size is 14 inches, but you can get bigger monitors. They used to be expensive, but these days you can get a 17-inch monitor for less than $700.

What's the point of having a large screen? If you have a Super VGA adapter with high resolution (1,024 x 768), you can display more data on a single screen. That's a real benefit for applications such as electronic spreadsheets, desktop publishing, and word processing.

TIP

> If you're a writer, it's nice to see a whole page of text at one time. That way, you can tell where you're going (and where you've been) as you write. Thanks to Portrait Display Labs, you can display a whole page with the *Portrait monitor*. Basically, this is a 15-inch monitor that's oriented vertically
>
> *continues*

instead of horizontally. (No, you can't do this just by standing your VGA monitor on its side—special software and circuitry is required.) The full-page view only works in Windows, though. If you need to use DOS (perish the thought), you can swivel this monitor so that it's oriented to the horizontal. (That's the only way DOS can display things.)

What's the Difference Between an Analog and a Digital Monitor?

You've probably heard that "analog is out, digital is in." An *analog* device uses continuously varied signals to simulate a sound or picture, while a *digital* device uses nothing but numbers. LP (vinyl) records are analog devices, while audio CDs are digital.

But it isn't necessarily the case that digital is better than analog. In fact, for computer displays, exactly the opposite is true. All the video adapters, up to the EGA, produce digital output, which limits the number of colors you can display. VGA adapters of all kinds (including Super VGA) produce analog output, which can make more colors. Some Super VGA adapters and monitors can produce several million distinct colors.

What Is Interlacing and Dot Pitch?

Two characteristics of VGA and SVGA monitors affect their quality: whether or not interlacing is used, and the monitor's dot pitch specification.

Interlacing is a method of faking a high-quality display by "painting" half the screen in one cycle, and then doing the other half in the second cycle. This produces a faintly detectable screen flicker that can be fatiguing to the eyes. The best monitors are non-interlacing monitors; they don't use this trick. But they cost more. Just remember, they're your eyes.

The *dot pitch measurement* tells you how detailed an image a monitor can display. The smaller the measurement, the better. For example, .28mm (millimeters) is very good; .43mm isn't so hot.

What Is This Resolution Number All About?

When I said earlier that adapters have been getting "sharper" as time goes by, I was talking about *resolution*. And just what is resolution?

BUZZWORDS

RESOLUTION

Resolution is a measurement of the amount of detail your monitor can show. It's measured by the number of dots (called *pixels*) that can be displayed on each line, as well as the number of lines that can be displayed on each screen. (Why use an unfamiliar word such as pixels? Because the word dots doesn't sound nearly so impressive.)

Basic stuff about resolution

- ✔ You'll see figures like 680 x 480 in advertisements and manuals. This figure means "680 dots per line and 480 lines per screen." 680 x 480 is the standard resolution for a VGA monitor, which is pretty basic. Generic systems, the kind that are sold for less than $1,000 in the K-Marts of the world, tend to have basic VGA adapters.
- ✔ Super VGA resolutions are higher, such as 800 x 600 or 1,024 x 768. With a higher resolution, your computer system can display more detail in the same amount of screen space.
- ✔ If you have a Super VGA adapter, you can switch display resolutions. You can display your work using the VGA standard

continues

Basic stuff about resolution, continued

680 x 480 or higher resolutions. With the higher resolutions you can see more on the screen (with a word processing program, you can see half or two-thirds of a page, instead of just one-third).

- ✔ High resolution adapters (1,024 x 768) are at their best with big monitors (more than 15 inches measured diagonally); on a standard size monitor, the highest resolution makes for pretty teensy characters.
- ✔ Your video adapter determines your monitor's display resolution. You can't improve the screen resolution just by getting a better monitor; you have to get a better adapter that offers higher resolution.

Monochrome or Color?

PC displays fall into two broad categories: monochrome (such as white on black) and color. Which is better? The short answer: color, although monochrome still has its advocates.

Why a color monitor?

- ✔ Color is worth having even if you're planning to do nothing but word processing (text only). Most programs use color to highlight menu options and display messages. A message displayed in a bright, garish yellow is a lot easier to see than one that blends with the text.
- ✔ Most programs designed today assume that you're using a color system. Of course, you can still run a lot of programs on a monochrome system, but they don't look as nice.
- ✔ If you think you'll ever run Windows, color is desirable. Windows makes great use of color.

- ✔ Take a break and play a computer game. If you really want to distinguish the friendly space ships from the enemy space ships, though, you'll need a color monitor to tell the difference.

What Are Those Funny Knobs?

Monitors usually have two knobs in addition to the On/Off switch. In keeping with the spirit of the PC, these knobs are usually carefully hidden. One knob controls brightness, the other controls contrast. Very few monitors actually label these knobs Brightness and Contrast. Most use incomprehensible symbols. A little experimentation, however, will reveal which is which.

Cleaning the Screen

Computer monitors attract an unbelievable amount of dust, thanks to the static charge that accumulates on the glass surface. Keep some glass cleaner and paper towels handy—you'll need them frequently. But don't spray the glass cleaner directly on the glass; some of the liquid might seep into the monitor's innards. Instead, spray the glass cleaner on the paper towel, and then clean the glass.

The Joy of Screen Savers

A screen saver program blanks your screen, or uses moving pictures, so that there isn't one set image on-screen if you don't type anything or move the mouse for, say, 5 or 10 minutes. Screen savers can even include sound to enhance the image. The current rage among Trekkies is a program called Star Trek, a screen saver that shows pictures of the Enterprise, Mr. Spock, and Captain Kirk.

Why use a screen saver? On older monitors, this was necessary to prevent *phospher burn-in*, the recording of a permanent image on-screen.

But that's not true with today's VGA and Super VGA monitors, despite allegations to the contrary by screen saver publishers. But what the heck. It's cool to see the Enterprise on your screen.

TIP

If you plan to run Windows, you don't need to go out and buy a screen saver program—one is built in. Unfortunately, it doesn't run with DOS or DOS programs. To turn on the Windows screen saver, double-click the Control Panel icon in the Main program group. Then double-click the Desktop option. In the Screen Saver area, choose a screen saver option from the list box, and then click OK.

TIP

If your screen goes blank, some "helpful" colleague has probably installed a screen blanking program on your computer. Just press a key or move the mouse to see your screen again.

Are These Things Safe?

(Will I glow in the dark after using my monitor?)

Don't worry about X-rays, gamma rays, and all the rest of the really nasty stuff you may have heard about; today's computer monitors don't emit them in any measurable quantities. What may prove to be more dangerous to your health is a type of radiation that's emitted by just about every electrical device in homes and offices.

Many household devices, such as electric shavers, electric blankets, and computer monitors, emit *extremely low-frequency (ELF) electromagnetic radiation (EMR)*. After years of denying that this radiation is dangerous, the scientific community is now coming up with some studies that suggest that prolonged exposure to such devices leads to elevated rates of leukemia.

What about monitors? Most of the EMR emitted by computer monitors goes out the sides and the back of the monitor. And no matter which direction it goes, it falls off to undetectable (and presumably safe) levels, at a distance of about 28 inches from the monitor.

To be ultra-safe, here are some tips:

- ✔ Work at least 28 inches from your monitor.
- ✔ Don't sit at a desk where you're close to the back or sides of someone else's computer.
- ✔ Those ever-cautious Scandinavians have worked out standards for EMR radiation. If you're really concerned about EMR, get yourself a low EMR radiation monitor that conforms to the Swedish MPR II standards.
- ✔ Notebook computer screens emit no EMR radiation.
- ✔ Be sure to turn off computer devices you're not using, such as monitors or laser printers.

It Says It's an "Energy Star Monitor"!

That's good. An Energy Star monitor conforms to the Environmental Protection Agency's specifications for energy conservation.

One of the most energy-efficient monitors available at this writing is Nanao's FlexScan monitor, with the PowerManager system. You can use these monitors with any PC, even if the PC itself isn't so efficient. When your screen saver cuts out the screen, PowerManager follows suit, reducing power consumption by up to 92%. If your computer tends to be on all day, this monitor can save you $50 or more per year. And that means significantly less smoke pumped into our fragile atmosphere.

Top Ten

Reasons to Use a Typewriter Instead of a Computer

10. A lot cheaper
9. No nasty on-screen error messages
8. Real writers do not use computers
7. Electricity optional
6. Combines keyboard, CPU, and printer in one compact, space-saving case
5. No agonizing decisions over which text typeface (font) to use
4. No software needed—load 8 1/2-by-11-inch paper for word processing, index cards for database management, and so on
3. Less clutter: no disks, no manuals, no nerds
2. You only have to learn a couple of terms, like *platen* and *carriage*
1. Tap-tap-tap clatter drives coworkers nuts

CHAPTER 8

Keyboards, Mice, and More

IN A NUTSHELL

- Why the computer keyboard has more keys than a typewriter
- The purpose of all those keys with weird names
- What to do if you hear a beep while typing fast
- Rules of the keyboard
- How to avoid repetitive strain injuries (RSI), such as Carpal Tunnel Syndrome, while using the computer
- Mouse mysteries revealed
- How to keep your mouse happy
- Why some people think trackballs are better than mice
- The heartbreak of pen computing
- Why you can't talk to your computer yet

The computer is a genuine Space Age thing—sleek, incomprehensible, and electronic. So, why does it have a nineteenth-century keyboard? Because nobody has figured out any better way to get text into the computer—at least, not yet. (They're working on it, but more about that later.)

Oh, sure, some computers are equipped to recognize a few dozen spoken words, but you'll have a lot more luck typing a letter into the keyboard than trying to dictate it to the computer. For now, computers have one trait in common with people: they talk better than they listen. So, you're stuck with the keyboard for text input.

Next to the keyboard, you'll probably find a mouse, which has lots of uses in Windows. Some DOS programs use the mouse, too. My cat certainly knows what to do with one.

The Computer Keyboard

(I don't think this is a typewriter anymore, Toto)

Computer keyboards look somewhat like a typewriter's keyboard, but they pack a few nasty surprises.

Keyboard basics

- ✔ Keep that keyboard plugged in. Your computer probably won't start—and might crash—if the cord's disconnected. With most computers, you'll see an on-screen message right after you start your system if your computer can't detect the keyboard. Your keyboard usually plugs into the back panel of the computer, in a round plug that has five little holes.

- ✔ The standard, 101-key, extended keyboard has lots of keys that you won't find on a typewriter. Why is it called extended? Because it has more keys than the old, 88-key, nonextended keyboard, which hardly anyone uses anymore. The *extended keyboard* has four major regions: typewriter keys, function keys, cursor-movement keys, and the numeric keypad.

- ✔ The "old" typewriter part of the keyboard is laid out just like a standard typewriter keyboard. You press Shift to create capital letters, symbols on the number keys (such as a dollar sign), or certain punctuation marks (such as a question mark). If a key shows two things, you press Shift to get the one on top.

- ✔ The *function keys* (F1, F2, F3, and so on) appear along the top of the typewriter keys. (On older keyboards, you find them to the left of the typewriter keys.) They do different things, depending on which program you're running. In most programs, for example, F1 is the Help key.

- ✔ The *cursor-movement keys* let you move the on-screen cursor. (The cursor is the little blinking underline, or vertical bar, that shows you where your text will appear when you start typing.)

- ✔ *Numeric Keypad*. If you know how to do the fingering for super-fast number entry, like they do at the bank, you can use the numeric keypad.

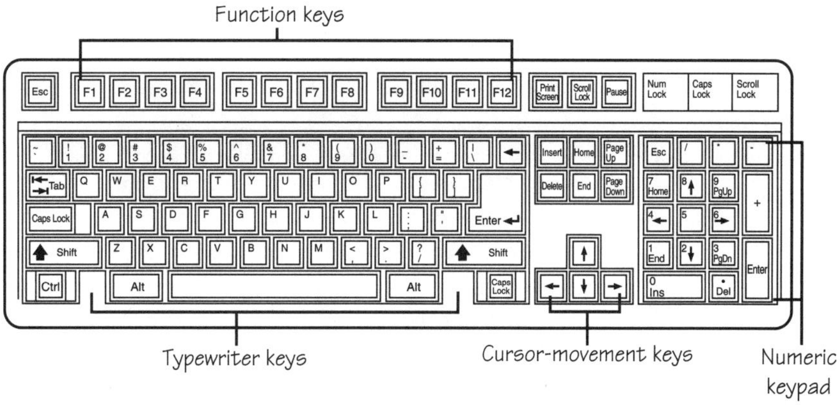

Function keys

Typewriter keys

Cursor-movement keys

Numeric keypad

Areas of the computer keyboard.

Those Highly Irritating Toggle Keys

The word toggle is highly familiar to anyone who spent his or her childhood building model railroads, ham radios, or those Lego structures. For the rest of us, toggle doesn't mean a whole lot—there's only the suggestive fact that it rhymes with boggle. Here's a tip: the word basically means switch. When you *toggle* something, you switch it back and forth between two modes or states (this is usually on and off).

The first time you press a toggle key, you turn on whatever it does. On most keyboards, a helpful little light comes on to let you know that you've engaged the key. The second time you press it, you turn it off. And right in synch, the light goes off.

Your keyboard has three toggle switches: Caps Lock, Num Lock, and Scroll Lock. Note them and beware. If you accidentally press them, the keyboard may do unexpected, funny things, such as entering uppercase letters when you weren't expecting them.

If your computer starts doing funny things, check the keyboard to see whether you've accidentally pressed one of the toggle keys.

Avoiding problems with toggle keys

- ✔ When you press Caps Lock, you get uppercase letters, just as you do on a typewriter. That's not so weird. What's weird is what happens when Caps Lock is on and you use the Shift key while you are typing. You get lowercase letters! lIKE tHIS. vERY iRRITATING. Of course, you only notice this after typing half a page of text.

- ✔ Almost as irritating is the Num Lock key, which controls the way the numeric keypad operates. When Num Lock is on, you get numbers when you press the number keys. When Num Lock is off, you can use the numeric keypad to move the cursor. So what's so bad about that? Unlike the other toggle keys, Num Lock is set up on most computers so that it's on when the computer starts. I like to use the numeric keypad to move the cursor, but I get 44288666 instead. Irritating, isn't it?

- ✔ In contrast to its two pesky counterparts, Scroll Lock isn't a troublemaker. In fact, it doesn't do much of anything these days. The key actually does something interesting when you're running a spreadsheet program, but otherwise it doesn't do much more than turn the Scroll Lock light on or off.

TIP

Using Caps Lock while typing gives you the same result as using the Shift key while typing: uppercase letters. However, remember learning that when a key contains two characters, you need to use the Shift key to get the one on top? Well, this still holds true when Caps Lock is on.

Decoding All Those Keys with Arrows on Them

Some keyboards helpfully put the words Tab and Enter on the so-named keys, along with arrows. Some keyboards have only the arrows. Here's how to decode what the keys mean:

Arrow	Name of key	The scoop
←	Backspace	You press this key to rub out the character to the left of the cursor. It's a pretty neat key because it lets you correct mistakes right after you make them.
↵	Enter	In DOS, you press Enter to send a command to the computer. In Windows, this performs an action on whatever is selected. It does different things in different programs.
|← →|	Tab	This key doesn't do much in DOS, but it works a lot like its typewriter counterpart in word processing programs.
→	Right arrow	This cursor-movement key moves the cursor right one character.

continues

Arrow	Name of key	The scoop
←	Left arrow	This key moves the cursor left one character.
↓	Down arrow	This key moves the cursor down one line.
↑	Up arrow	This key moves the cursor up one line.

TIP

You'll also see arrows on some of the numeric keypad keys. With some programs, these keys work like the cursor keys—but only when Num Lock is switched off.

The Cursor Won't Move!

Don't bother trying to move the cursor if you're working with DOS (you can tell you're working with DOS if you see the C:\> prompt). You can't use the arrow keys to move the cursor with DOS. You can use the arrow keyswith most programs, though. If you're using a *program* and the cursor won't move, it's probably bad news: your computer may have crashed. See Chapter 20 for help.

TIP

Keep your keyboard clean. Occasionally, when your computer is turned off, turn the keyboard over and shake it—you'd be amazed how much junk falls out. Also, use a paper towel moistened with Windex occasionally to clean the finger grease off the keys.

Weird Keys That Typewriters Never Had

In addition to the arrow keys, you'll notice some other unfamiliar keys on the keyboard. Nope, you're definitely not using a typewriter anymore.

Key	The scoop
Esc or Escape	This Escape key generally cancels the current operation, or takes you back to what you were doing previously.
Del or Delete	When you press this key, in most programs, it erases the character that the cursor is on or the character to the right of the cursor.
Ctrl or Control	Some programs use this key with another key to select a command. For instance, you might press Ctrl and B (written as Ctrl+B or Ctrl-B) to select the Bold command.
Alt or Alternate	You use this key, like the Ctrl key, for commands. It works the same way the Ctrl key does; you hold it down and press another key.
Ins or Insert	For the most part, this key turns on a program's Insert mode, which lets you insert characters within text you've already typed, instead of typing over the text (this is called the *typeover* or *overtype mode*). In a lot of DOS programs, the cursor changes from a thin little underline to a big fat block after you switch to the Insert mode. Windows programs signal this mode in different ways.
Home	Programs usually use this key to move the cursor to the beginning of a line or the beginning of a document. Sometimes, however, this moves the cursor to the first on-screen character.
End	Programs usually use this key to move the cursor to the end of a line or the end of a document. Sometimes, however, this key moves the cursor to the last on-screen character.
PgUp or Page Up	Programs usually use this key to scroll the screen up toward the beginning of your file.

continues

Key	The scoop
PgDn or Page Down	Programs usually use this key to scroll the screen down toward the end of your file.
Prt Scr or Print Screen	In DOS (but not Windows), you can this key to get a quick printout of what's on-screen. Don't expect great quality, though. Use your program's Print command to print your work.
Pause/Break	You can press this key to stop a DOS command, such as DIR, from scrolling. When used in combination with the Ctrl key, this key cancels a DOS command. This doesn't work in Windows; in Windows you use the Cancel button to accomplish the same thing.
\	This is the backslash key. It's used a lot in DOS to indicate subdirectories.
/	This is the forward slash key. It's used in spreadsheet programs, such as Lotus 1-2-3, to display the Command menu. In mathematical expressions that you sometimes type, it means divide. For example, 4/2 means, "4 divided by 2."

It Tells Me to Type Ctrl+A, but I Can't Get It To Work!

Computer manuals use expressions like "Ctrl+A" to indicate a key combination. Key combinations work like this: you hold down the first key (Ctrl in this case), and then press the second key (A in this case—either uppercase or lowercase). You don't actually type the plus sign. If you see an expression like "F10, M," it means, "Press F10 and release the key. Then press M." (Note: Sometimes, key combinations are indicated with a hyphen rather than a plus sign, like this: Ctrl-A. The hyphen means the same thing as the plus sign. For example, Ctrl-A is the same thing as Ctrl+A.)

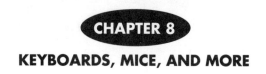

What to Do If You Hear a Beep While Typing Really Fast

The quick, easy answer: slow down and let the computer catch up.

There is, of course, a boring technical explanation. Sometimes, programs have to stop accepting keyboard input because they're busy doing something else, like saving your data to disk. You can keep typing for a little while, thanks to something called the *type-ahead buffer*. That's a temporary storage area that can store keystrokes while your computer is busy. But, as soon as the type-ahead buffer is full, you hear a beep that warns you that the characters you're typing at the moment will be lost. Wait until the program finishes doing what it's doing, and then resume typing.

Most programs can handle keyboard input as fast as you can dish it out.

TIP

Do you have to type the same character twice? Just hold down the key; most keys on the keyboard—even the cursor-movement keys—repeat when you hold them down. Try it. There's a delay, and then the repeat kicks in at a pretty fast rate.

I Spilled My Pepsi On It!

Rule #1 of computing is don't drink coffee or anything while you're working with the computer. Right. And by the way, the speed limit is 55.

The best thing to do is flip the keyboard over immediately and spank the liquid out. Then wipe off the excess. Chances are pretty good that there won't be any damage.

Keyboard Styles of the Rich and Famous

The computer elite follow a set of handy, try-this-first rules, which, naturally, are never explicitly given to beginners.

Things they ought to tell you about the keyboard

- ✔ Never indent by pressing the space bar. The text might not look aligned when printed, even if it looks right on-screen. Always use the Tab key to indent text.
- ✔ When typing text, only press Enter when you want to start a new paragraph. Most programs use a thing called word wrapping, which makes it unnecessary for you to press Enter when you reach the right margin. In *word wrapping*, the program automatically detects when a word would go over the margin, and wraps (moves) it down to the beginning of the next line. If you make changes in the paragraph, the program automatically adjusts the line wrapping for you.
- ✔ In many DOS programs, and in all Windows applications, pressing Alt or F10 activates the *menu bar*, the bar across the top of the screen that lists menu names. After activating the bar, you can use the left and right arrow keys to highlight different menus, then use the up and down arrow keys to scroll through the selected menu. A faster alternative is to activate the menu bar, press the highlighted or underlined letter to "pull down" a menu, then press the highlighted or underlined letter of the command you want to select.
- ✔ Esc is the universal get-me-out-of-this command. You can use Esc to cancel a menu or on-screen dialog box, if you've decided against choosing an option.
- ✔ In Windows and most DOS applications, pressing F1 gets you on-screen help.
- ✔ In DOS, use Ctrl+C or Ctrl+Pause to cancel a command that's not working out right. If you've just used DIR to display a directory and it's scrolling by too fast, press Pause to stop the scrolling. Then press any key to continue.

- ✔ Don't try to attack key combinations by crashing down on them at the same time. Hold down the Alt or Ctrl key, and then press the second key in the combination.
- ✔ Some programs make extensive use of key combinations that might involve three or more keys—kind of a computerized version of Twister. For example, you may be told to press Shift+Ctrl+Q. This means, "Hold down the Shift and Ctrl keys, and while both of them are being held down, press Q."
- ✔ A lot of programs come with a thing called a *keyboard template*. This is an adhesive "cheat sheet" that fits on your keyboard. You can use the template to remember frequently used keyboard commands that you keep forgetting. If you use one program most of the time, stick its template to your keyboard.

TIP

With many Windows programs, you don't really need a keyboard template because of the easily accessible buttons that enable you to perform commands with one simple click of the mouse. Windows also lists the shortcut key combinations next to the commands in the menu drop-down list, so that you see it every time you use it. The more you use a command, the easier it'll be to remember it.

TIP

Ctrl+Alt+Del reboots your computer, but it's dangerous—it wipes out everything in the computer's memory (RAM). If some of that stuff includes unsaved work, it's G-O-N-E, forever, period. Press Ctrl+Alt+Del only if you're sure your computer has crashed. A pretty good way to tell: nothing is happening on-screen, and when you try to type, you just hear beeps—even after 5 or 10 minutes.

What's That Funny Numb Feeling

(And that shooting pain)?

As rhythm guitarists have known for a long time, repeating the same hand action over and over and over can lead to a health problem that doctors call *repetitive strain injury* (RSI). This condition can cause a really painful nerve disorder when scar tissue builds up in narrow nerve channels within the hand and wrist. RSI can be serious and debilitating. A symptom of the injury is numbness in your fingers.

You can reduce your chances of contracting a repetitive strain injury by using the keyboard correctly.

Ways to avoid repetitive strain injuries

- ✔ Don't use a keyboard that's way up on the top of the desk. It should be positioned so that you can type with your elbows forming a right angle, or going slightly downwards. That usually means lowering the keyboard. If necessary, get a keyboard shelf that fits under your desk and slides out as needed. The key point: your hands should not angle up from your wrist while typing.

- ✔ Be sure to use an adjustable chair. Raise or lower the seat until your elbows are at the correct angle. If you're experiencing back pain, you might try angling the seat so that it slopes downward slightly.

- ✔ To make sure your hands aren't angled up while typing, rest your palms on a wrist pad. Check out an office supply store such as Office America; you'll find wrist pads that will fit your keyboard and mouse pad.

- ✔ Take regular breaks—at least once an hour. Stretch and massage your fingers, wrists, and arms to make sure there's plenty of blood flowing through them.

- ✔ If you feel numbness or shooting pains in your wrist or forearm, stop typing immediately. Take a break and stretch. If the pain continues, see a physician immediately. Repetitive strain injuries can be extremely painful and may require surgery to correct.

Mice Are Nice

(Especially with Windows)

Most computers now come equipped with a *mouse,* that little soap-sized thing that sits on the table next to the keyboard. Inside the mouse is a ball that spins when you move the mouse around on the table top. As you move the mouse, a pointer (it usually looks like an arrow) moves around on-screen. There are (usually) two buttons on the mouse; most of the time, you use the left one.

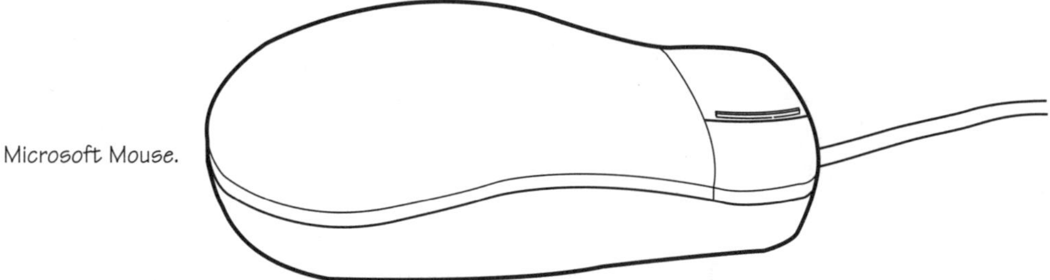

Microsoft Mouse.

The basic mouse actions (first mentioned in Chapter 4) are *pointing* (moving the pointer to something), *clicking* (clicking the left button with the pointer on something), *double-clicking* (clicking the left button twice in rapid succession), and *dragging* (holding down the button and moving the mouse so that you move something on-screen). A few programs make use of the right button, but most of the time it just sits there. If your mouse has three buttons, it's a safe bet that the middle one's about as useful as a hood ornament on a '56 Chevy.

What's a mouse good for? With DOS, nothing, although some DOS programs make use of a mouse, if you have one. But, it's in Windows that the mouse really comes in handy.

Things you can do with a mouse

- ✔ In most programs, you can use a mouse to move the cursor really fast—just point to where you want the cursor to be, and click the button. No fussing with those arrow keys.
- ✔ When you choose commands by using the mouse, you cut down on keyboard fussing. If your application has a menu bar—a bar across the screen with names of commands—you can just point to a command and click to display the command menu. To choose an option from the menu drop-down list, such as Print or Save, just click the option name.
- ✔ You can use Windows without a mouse, but lots of cool Windows features are designed with the mouse in mind.
- ✔ A mouse is very handy if you intend to use graphics programs, such as a presentation graphics program for making color slides or overhead transparencies. This isn't so much for drawing. Instead, the mouse comes in handy for positioning and sizing things on-screen, such as clip art pictures, lines, and little boxes with text in them.
- ✔ A mouse is also really handy for *selecting* text for editing and formatting. To do this, you hold down the button and drag over the text you want to select. This text appears in *reverse video* (white letters on black background). The next formatting command you give affects only this text.
- ✔ If you're left-handed, most mouse programs give you a way to swap the functions of the left and right buttons. This way, your index finger will be on the right button, which you can then use for most mouse functions. If you use Windows, you can do this with the Control Panel. Double-click the Control Panel icon in the Main program group, and then double-click Mouse. In the Mouse dialog box, click the Swap Left/Right Buttons check box so that an "X" appears in it, and then click OK.

Who doesn't like the mouse? Some people who are expert typists dislike having to take their fingers away from the keyboard. If you agree, you can ignore the mouse; most programs, including Windows programs, include keyboard equivalents for most mouse procedures. Even so, you'll probably still find a mouse useful for some things, like selecting and editing text.

Mouse pointers

- ✔ Don't let the cord get tangled up in stuff. You won't be able to move the mouse freely, which is pretty frustrating.
- ✔ Keep an area clear for the mouse's use. You need about one square foot.
- ✔ If you run out of room to complete a mouse maneuver, you can pick up the mouse (while holding down the button), reposition it on the desktop, and complete the maneuver.
- ✔ Some programs, including Windows, let you adjust mouse characteristics, such as how fast the mouse pointer moves as you move the mouse. To adjust the mouse with Windows, double-click on Control Panel in the Main program group, and then double-click on Mouse. You see lots of things you can change. Make your changes, and then click on OK to confirm your changes.
- ✔ If your desk has a smooth top and the mouse ball doesn't seem to find its footing, get a mouse pad. This provides just the right "feel" for the ball.
- ✔ About once every two weeks (longer if you don't use your computer much), remove the mouse ball and clean it. Use Windex and a paper towel.
- ✔ Windex is also pretty good for getting potato chip grease off the mouse case.

EXPERTS ONLY

Mouse Technology

The cheapest type of mouse is the *mechanical* mouse, which has a little rubber ball inside. The ironic thing is, this is probably also the best.

At one time (about 1988), *optical mice* were all the rage. These didn't use a ball at all. But, you had to keep the mouse on a little metal pad with little lines on it. If you ran off the pad, the mouse lost its bearings. You don't see these much anymore.

You can also get *cordless mice*. The cheaper ones use an infrared thingie like your TV set remote control. But, if something gets between the mouse and the little receiver eyeball that you put near the computer, it won't work. The more expensive kind uses a radio transmitter and receiver. Both of these are probably overkill unless, like me, you have a very messy desk and are constantly fighting to free the cord from 2-liter Pepsi bottles, stacks of computer magazines, and three-week-old coffee cups.

How Do I Hook This Thing Up?

Mice come in three varieties: PS/2, serial, and bus (in case you are curious). A PS/2 mouse is designed to plug into a round, 9-pin socket that IBM introduced with its PS/2 computers. Nowadays, almost all clones and notebooks have a PS/2 mouse port.

If your computer doesn't have a PS/2 mouse port, you can hook it up to one of the serial ports. If there isn't a serial port, you can get a bus mouse that plugs into an expansion board, which you have to install inside the computer.

If you already have the mouse and it's working fine, you probably don't need to fret over what kind you have. If you want to add a mouse, keep in mind that a serial mouse is a lot easier to hook up, and it's the one to choose if your computer has a special mouse port. If your computer lacks such a port, and your serial ports are all taken up with other things, you can get a bus mouse. Get your local computer wizard to install it for you.

It Says I'm Not Using the Right Mouse Software!

To use your mouse, you or someone else must install the mouse software on your hard disk. Programs sometimes require you to use the latest version of this software. If you're using a Microsoft mouse, you automatically get the latest mouse software when you upgrade to the latest version of DOS. (DOS itself doesn't use the mouse, but some DOS applications do.) If you're using a non-Microsoft mouse, write to the company that makes the mouse and ask for the latest version of the mouse software. Hopefully, they're still in business!

There's No Pointer!

Don't worry, your computer isn't broken. There's no pointer because DOS doesn't use the mouse. Look for the pointer again after starting Windows (or a DOS application that uses the mouse). If you still don't see it, get someone who's knowledgeable about computers to install the mouse software for you.

Heavy mouse users sometimes experience problems with *tennis elbow*—a painful form of tendinitis caused by lifting your arm up to reach the mouse. Make sure the mouse is at the same level as your keyboard. If you're right-handed, try using the mouse with your left hand—this takes some getting used to, but it's possible. You might also consider a trackball designed to minimize arm movements, such as Kensington's Expert Mouse.

Trackballs

Some computers are equipped with a *trackball*, which is like an upside-down mouse. Instead of moving the mouse (which rotates the ball), you move the ball itself, usually with your thumb. This takes some getting used to. You use trackballs to accomplish the same things you accomplish with a mouse, but they have one advantage over mice: you don't need a desktop to operate a trackball. Some keyboards include trackballs. One available trackball even fits onto the side of notebook computers, which are discussed in Chapter 12. In fact, lots of notebook computers come with trackballs built in.

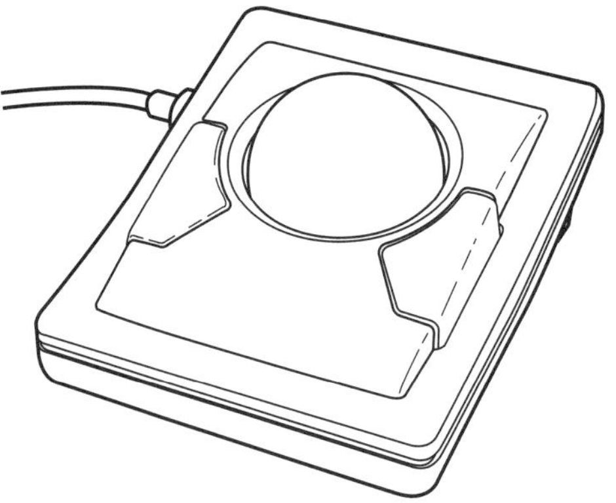

Trackball (an upside-down mouse, sort of).

The latest innovation in the mouse-equivalence game is IBM's *Stick Shift*, a pointing control device that's included with its Think Pad notebook computers. This is a little red rod positioned right between the G and H keys on the keyboard, where it won't get run over by flying fingers. You put your index finger on the end of this thing and, as you move it, the pointer flies around on-screen. You use your thumb to click buttons on the Stick Shift.

Handwriting Recognition

(Jot this down)

It sounded like such a great idea. You just write on the screen with what looks like a pen. The computer captures what you've written, and converts it to ASCII text.

That's the idea behind several new products, including Apple's Newton (a Personal Digital Assistant, discussed in detail in Chapter 12) and Microsoft Windows for Pen Computing. The only trouble is, it doesn't work very well. The system tries to guess what you've written, and sometimes the guesses are wildly inaccurate.

But they're working on it, folks. After all, the first PCs weren't really anything to write home about, either. In the near future, look for better handwriting recognition systems, which you'll be able to plug into your PC. A pioneering product is Handwriter for Windows (Communication Intelligence Corp.), which gives you a handwriting recognition tablet, a pen, and plenty of software. You teach Handwriter your writing style, and once it learns your peculiarities, the recognition is much better than the first-generation Newton's. A great feature: An ostensibly hacker-proof system security program, which won't allow access to the computer until it recognizes your signature.

Speech Recognition

(Why won't you listen?)

It's ten years from now. You're sitting in front of your computer. You say, "Open Word. New document. Insert date. Get address 'Dave.' Insert text: 'Dear Dave, [new paragraph] Remember that $500 I loaned you last year?..."

Actually, this technology exists right now, but it's expensive ($2000 to $8000) and primitive. One system, for instance, recognizes up to 20,000 words with an accuracy of 95%, but you have to speak each word slowly, one word at a time—you know, the way you have to talk to your teenager. Worse, these systems eat up humongous amounts of computing

power. There are only a few of them installed, mostly for people with disabilities.

But there *is* something you can do with speech synthesis today: tell your computer what to do. (Unfortunately, this does *not* include telling it where to *go.*) Equipped with the right hardware and software (see Chapter 10), your computer will let you boss Microsoft Windows around.

With many popular sound boards (see Chapter 10), you get speech synthesis software that "reads" a text file to you. This is pretty cool if you want to hear how a story or letter "flows" when read aloud—as long as you don't mind putting up with what sounds like a thick Eastern European accent.

SHOE®
BY JEFF MACNELLY
THIS BEEPING PILE OF PLASTIC JUST AIN'T A TYPEWRITER.

WHERE'S THE DING?

IN THE GOOD OLD DAYS OF NEWSPAPERING YOUR TRUSTY TYPEWRITER WOULD HELP YOU EXPRESS YOURSELF...
EDITOR

YOU COULD POUND THE KEYS HARDER WHEN YOU WERE MAD...
@★!#

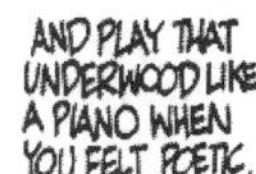
AND PLAY THAT UNDERWOOD LIKE A PIANO WHEN YOU FELT POETIC.

MOST IMPORTANT, THOUGH, WAS THE WAY YOU COULD BLOW OFF STEAM WHEN YOU MADE A MISTAKE...
TAPPA... TAPPA... TAPPA... PATTA....

YOU COULD RIP OUT THE PAPER, CRUMPLE IT UP AND HEAVE IT ACROSS THE NEWSROOM.
ZIP!

SOMEHOW IT MADE YOU FEEL A LOT BETTER WHEN YOU DID THAT...

BUT TODAY, WITH THESE WORD PROCESSORS AND COMPUTERS,... WELL, IT JUST AIN'T THE SAME...
10/9

BUT IT'S STILL PRETTY SATISFYING.
EDITOR
MACNELLY

Top Ten
Rejected Font Names

10. IRS Tax Form Gothic
9. Twinkie Sparkle (little stars over the "i")
8. USDA "Choice" Block Letter Bold
7. Graffiti Dingbats
6. FinePrint Rip-Off Narrow (small font sizes only)
5. Gang Territory SprayPaint Italic (outdoor use only; large-caliber automatic weapon strongly suggested)
4. Olde Obituary
3. Publisher's Clearinghouse FormLetter Ultra (large font sizes only)
2. Tantrum Bold Frantic
1. Terror Threat Calligraphic (requires hostage)

CHAPTER 9

Nobody Loves Printers, But We Do Need Them

IN A NUTSHELL

- What kind of printers are available, and how they differ
- The best kind of printer for you
- What fonts are, and how you can get more of them
- How to hook up a printer to your computer
- How to deal with common printing problems

A few years ago, geniuses at a major West Coast think tank predicted that the use of paper would soon disappear completely. We'd be working in "paperless offices," reading everything on computer screens. The atmosphere in the board rooms of paper companies was very gloomy. Hunched over, with their heads in their hands, the directors said things like, "We're doomed."

But it wasn't to be. Instead of giving up on paper, computer users have led the biggest paper-gobbling boom in history. Much to their surprise, paper company people watched profits and stock prices zoom upward. Today, the "paperless office" idea is dismissed as a joke.

Part of the reason is that just about every computer application program is designed to help you print stuff on paper. Word processing programs, for example, take the place of typewriters, while spreadsheet programs take the place of those vertically lined sheets that accountants and bookkeepers use. Maybe we'll use computers differently in the future, but for now, getting it down on paper is what completes the job.

The weak link in the whole chain is the printer, which all too often is an unwilling accomplice. It won't respond, the paper gets jammed, it runs out of paper—there's a whole string of annoyances that these devices are all too ready to spring on the unsuspecting user. This chapter surveys the world of printers, and tells you what to do when one of these annoyances comes up.

Types of Printers

(Laser and inkjet are best)

Only four kinds of printers are in widespread use today:

The Printer	The Scoop
Dot-Matrix Printers	The cheapest printers, these work by hammering a pattern (or *matrix*) of little wires against a ribbon, making an impression on paper. These printers tend to be noisy, and sometimes the dots don't connect very well. The best ones produce OK output, but they're slow

The Printer	The Scoop
	because they have to go back over the printed text two or three times to connect all the little dots.
Inkjet Printers	These printers are more expensive than dot-matrix printers, but less expensive than laser printers. They work by spraying the paper with ink. The output looks something like the print created by a laser printer. Inkjet printers are slower than most laser printers.
Laser and LED Printers	These printers use parts from and work like copying machines, except that the image comes directly from the computer. Print quality is very good, and they print quickly (the best ones can print eight or more pages of double-spaced, plain text per minute). LED printers use a different technology to make the image, but they work just like laser printers.
PostScript Laser Printers	These printers are much more expensive than any other type of printer because they have their own built-in computer. The computer is needed to interpret printing instructions given in the printer's language (called PostScript). PostScript is needed only if you're doing professional desktop publishing.

TIP

Do you have to print lots of labels, such as press-apply mailing labels? This can be done if you have a Ph.D. in word processing layout—believe me, it's tough—and you're willing to mess up dozens of "test" label sheets in your printer. The easy way: take a look at a label printer, a little printer that specializes in printing labels only. These printers use rolls of

continues

press-apply labels (they come in a variety of colors, shapes, and sizes). Accompanying software handles the details on the computer end.

What About Color?

This used to be a no-brainer—you could just forget it. If you think that color printers are still expensive luxuries, though, you're in for a shock. There are very good ink-jet printers that sell on the street for $300. The quality is much, much better than that produced by color dot-matrix printers, which, in retrospect, can only be considered to have been a not-so-funny prank. Because today's color printers are much better, they're well worth investigating.

On the down side, though, the output produced by today's color ink-jet printers isn't as good as the print output of monochrome printers using the same technology. Actually, it is, but it's just that the inherent limitation of ink jet printers—their tendency to splatter a little extra ink where it's not supposed to go—shows up more when you're using four colors instead of one. Another limitation: color printers are slower than their monochrome counterparts.

So, What's the Best?

Laser (or LED), hands down, followed by inkjet printers. Both are quiet, fast, and produce very nice-looking output. Avoid dot-matrix printers like the plague that they are. The only justification for dot-matrix printers (besides their low price) is the need to print multipart (carbon) forms.

Inkjet printers claim to produce "laser quality" output, which is almost true. (You can tell the difference, though, if you look closely.)

TIP

If you're using an inkjet printer, get high-quality 20-pound bond paper with a smooth finish—you'll get much better results.

NOBODY LOVES PRINTERS, BUT WE DO NEED THEM

Laser printer basics

✔ You can get laser printers for less than $700 these days—a sore point for me, since I paid $2,500 five years ago for a *used* Apple LaserWriter.

✔ One drawback to laser printers is the cost—those toner cartridges cost money (up to about 5 cents per printed page). You can save money, though, by sending your cartridges off to be refilled. Look in the back advertising section of computer magazines, or your local Yellow Pages, for addresses of firms that refill toner cartridges. Be forewarned, though—sometimes the refilled cartridges leave streaks on your printouts or leak like crazy. If this happens, change suppliers.

✔ Use your laser printer in a well-ventilated room—they throw out a lot of ozone, which is an air pollutant.

✔ The quality of a laser printer is measured by the number of dots per inch (*dpi*) it can print. Most laser printers can print 300 dpi, but the latest thing in printers is a new generation of 600 dpi printers—and amazingly enough, they're not much more expensive. 300 dpi is good for text, but you'll need 600 dpi if you want to print really professional-looking graphics. For some extra bucks you can get 1200 and even 2400 dpi printers, which let you print good-looking halftones (photographs).

✔ The speed of a laser printer is measured in pages per minute (*ppm*); the slower printers manage only four per minute, the faster ones eight. But, this is measured by printing text pages only, so this is a fairly meaningless measurement. Pages with graphics take a lot longer to print.

✔ Most laser printers come with built-in fonts, which is a good thing, even if you're using Windows (which has its own fonts). The reason is that the fonts built into the printer work much faster than the fonts on your computer.

Will It Work with My Programs?

Good question. The problem with printers is that each of them has its own pet language for talking to the computer. Unless your program knows how to "talk" to your printer, you may not be able to use it.

Can your program talk to your printer? If you're using DOS, there's only one way to tell—read your program's manual to find out whether your printer is *supported*. And what does "supported" mean? It means that the program comes with a *printer driver* that's designed to work with your printer. Check your printer's manual, too, since many printers come with printer drivers designed to work with specific programs (including Windows).

BUZZWORDS

PRINTER DRIVER

A file that contains the information a program needs to work with your printer. Without a printer driver, your printer may not work, or you may not be able to take advantage of all of its features.

If you're using Windows, there's less to worry about. One of the best things about Windows is that the printer drivers are handled at the Windows level—the individual programs don't have to worry about it. They just say to Windows, "Hey, Windows, here's what to print," and Windows takes it from there. Windows includes printer drivers for hundreds of printers.

TIP

One way to make sure that your printer is compatible ("supported") is to go with the herd: use a printer that just about everyone else is using. That means sticking with name brands, such as Hewlett-Packard or Epson. Hewlett-Packard is abbreviated HP. Incidentally, a lot of printers are capable of emulating popular printers, such as HP printers. If your printer is said to have "HP emulation" or "Epson emulation," it'll probably work with just about any program.

What Is a "Page Description Language?"

There are few standards in the printer business; that's why you need a printer driver to support the printer you're working with. The printer driver is always necessary to deal with peculiarities, such as switching fonts or using a different paper tray.

When it comes to printing graphics and other fancy stuff, though, there are some standards—and woe to you if you're stuck with a printer that doesn't follow them. These standards are called *page description languages*. They do pretty much what you'd expect—they tell the printer how to print a page.

Why is this important? If you want to print graphics, you're smart to stick with printers that use popular page description languages, such as Hewlett-Packard's Graphic Language (the latest version is called PCL 5). HP is one of the biggest printer manufacturers. They make great printers.

Does this mean that you have to get an HP printer? Not necessarily. Almost all laser printers can *emulate* (work the same way as) HP printers and recognize HP's page description language.

BUZZWORDS

EMULATE

To work the same way as a popular computer device made by another, well-known company. Bogus Banana Printers, Inc. produces printers that *emulate* a certain well-known California firm's products.

Another popular page description language is PostScript. PostScript is also widely recognized and supported. But, PostScript comes with a hefty price tag. It's actually a programming language. (You don't have to write the program—that's all automatic.) But, the printer needs its own mi-croprocessor (and lots of memory) so that it can interpret all those programming instructions and make sense out of them. And that adds considerably to the price of a printer. The additional expense of Post-Script is only necessary if you're doing professional desktop publishing.

What Are Those Funny Buttons?

Most printers have two basic buttons that you'll come to know (but probably not love): *On Line* (also called *Select*) and *Form Feed* (or *Page Eject*). The On Line button is the most important one. When this is turned on, your printer is connected to the computer and ready to receive instructions. When it's turned off, the printer isn't connected to the computer.

Why would you turn the On Line button off? Mostly by accident. However, sometimes there's a good reason—for example, suppose your computer crashed while the printer was in the middle of a page, and you need to press the Form Feed button to get the page out of the printer. You need to turn off the On Line button before you can press Form Feed.

TIP

> If your printer isn't working, check to see whether the On Line button is turned on. There's usually a little indicator light next to the button. If it's off, press the button, and try printing again.

The Joy and Confusion of Printer Fonts

Fonts: distinctive, cool typeface designs, with impressive-sounding names like Garamond, Avant Garde, and Bodoni. They're all the rage. Your coworkers are using them. And, they impress the boss. You want to get on the bandwagon. But how?

NOBODY LOVES PRINTERS, BUT WE DO NEED THEM

There's an unfortunate distinction to learn here, the distinction between *printer fonts* and *screen fonts*. The tragedy is, what you see on the screen ain't necessarily what you get on the printer.

BUZZWORDS

SCREEN FONTS

The fonts your program uses to display your text on-screen.

BUZZWORDS

PRINTER FONTS

Fonts that are built into the printer or available in a plug-in cartridge. Most printers these days come with at least a few fonts; some come with as many as 80.

Font Basics

- ✔ Fonts that are used for the text of your document are called *text fonts* or *body type fonts*. These are designed for readability.
- ✔ Fonts that are used for headings and titles are called *display fonts*. These are designed to catch your attention.
- ✔ Fonts that include nothing but symbols, such as hands pointing in various directions, are called *dingbat fonts*. These symbols are great for special purposes, such as adding eye-catching bullets next to items in a list.
- ✔ Windows comes with several fonts built-in, such as Arial and Times New Roman. These are good for everyday use, but they are kind of boring.
- ✔ Don't use more than two fonts in a document—one for display and one for text—unless you have a Master of Arts degree and you're *sure* you know what you're doing.

Some commonly used Text and Symbol Fonts.

FONTS

3 Commonly used Text Fonts
Courier
Helvetica
Times New Roman

2 Commonly used Symbol Fonts
Symbol: αβχδεφγηιϕκλμνοπθρστυϖωξψζ
Wingdings: ♋♌♍♎♏♐♑♒♓🙰🙵●❍■ □□❑❒⬧⧫◆❖⬥⌧⍓⌘

Fonts with DOS

(You'll just have to imagine what they look like)

If you're using DOS, chances are pretty good that your program will show clunky-looking typewriter-like text on the screen. And, no matter what font size you choose, all the characters will seem like they're the same size on-screen. But, you'll be able to choose one or more of your printer's fonts. The document will print with the printer's fonts. (With some programs, you can see a preview of your document's fonts on-screen, but this requires a special preview mode.)

What Is TrueType and Why Do Font Lovers Prefer Windows?

Windows users have a much easier time with fonts. Windows 3.1 comes with some TrueType fonts, and you can get others. The amazing and wonderful thing about *TrueType fonts* is simply this: what you see on the screen (font choice *and* font size) is what you get on the printed page. This is true even if your printer doesn't have a printer font corresponding to the font or fonts you've chosen. Neat, huh?

TIP

TrueType is the way to go for Windows users. Still, you may wish to switch to your printer's fonts if you're in a hurry—they print faster. If you have a Hewlett-Packard laser printer, a very wise move is to purchase the Microsoft Hewlett-Packard Font Set, which gives you Windows TrueType fonts that exactly correspond to the fonts built into your printer. This way, you get the best of both worlds—nice fonts on-screen and fast printing, too.

I Paid *Thousands* for This System. How Come I Get Courier on the Printouts?

Courier is probably the least-loved font in computerdom. It's meant to look like the output of an office typewriter. That's like buying a Ferrari and then putting a Pinto body on it.

For reasons only known to themselves, the people who make computer programs and printers think that Courier is by far the best choice as the *default font*.

BUZZWORDS

DEFAULT FONT

The ugly, cheerless font that your program automatically uses, unless you specifically instruct it to use something a little nicer.

Check your program's manual for ways to override the default font. You may be able to change this setting permanently, so that all your works come out in something with a little more class than Courier.

It Says, "24 Points." Huh?

Font sizes are measured in printer's points (72 per inch). The standard size is 12 points, which equals six lines per inch—the same as an office typewriter. For titles, 18 or 24 points looks good. Don't use fonts smaller than 10 points, unless you want your readers to squint.

What Are "Soft Fonts?"

If your printer has a lot of memory, it might be able to use soft fonts. *Soft fonts* are stored on your computer's hard disk until needed, at which time they are sent (the term is *downloaded*) to your printer. Good word processing programs, such as WordPerfect, handle soft fonts automatically.

Hah hah! She Has to Install Her Printer

(Smirk)!

This *should* be easy. And, it is, pretty much, if you have a printer that's designed to connect with your computer's *parallel* (printer) port (that's the socket with 25 holes). If you're trying to connect a printer to the *serial* port, however, take my advice—stop right now and get someone to help you. Because it's such a hassle to connect printers through the serial port, most of today's printers are parallel printers. (For more information on ports, see Chapter 5.)

If you're using a system that's already set up and is working fine, don't worry about which port the printer is connected to. Someone has made the system modifications that are necessary to get the darned thing to work. Lucky you.

What Does "LPT1" Mean?

(Besides "#$%&!")

Your computer is designed so that it can be hooked up to three or four printers. Because you're probably just hooking up one printer, the whole process should be uncomplicated, no? Well, of course not. After all, DOS is involved.

To give you the ability to use more than one printer, DOS has a set of printer names, such as LPT1:, LPT2:, COM1:, COM2:, and so on. (The colons are part of the name; they make the names easy to misspell.) The LPT ports are parallel ports, while the COM ports are serial ports. If you're a lucky person, your computer has just one parallel port, and if so, it's LPT1:.

DOS, as well as your programs, assumes, by default, that you're using LPT1: to connect your printer. Moral of the story: your life will be much easier if you connect your printer to LPT1:. You won't be able to use a printer connected in the other ports unless you make modifications to your programs or to DOS.

TIP

You've got more than one parallel port, huh? Oh, too bad. Beg, cajole, threaten—whatever it takes—but get the dealer who sold you your computer to show you which parallel (printer) port is LPT1. Occasionally, this is actually indicated on the back of your computer with a helpful label, but don't count on it.

Making the Physical Connection

To connect your printer, you need a printer cable. Finding the right printer cable should be a snap, but it isn't—thanks to a lack of printer cable standards. There are a lot of different kinds of connectors, and to top it off, you have to know the sex of the connectors (male or female). Obviously, this is a very distasteful and embarrassing subject, one that is best left to the salespeople at the store where you bought the computer. Just say, "I want a cable to connect my printer," and take the one that is given to you. Be sure to ask where you need to plug in the cable because some computers have two connectors that look exactly the same. And if the cable doesn't work, take it back, make a bit of a fuss, and force the salesperson to give you the right cable.

Test Your Printer

(And your ability to withstand stress)

To test whether your printer works, make sure that the power's on and the printer is loaded with paper.

To print, your printer must be on line or selected (ready to receive stuff from the computer). This is usually the case, but check to make sure. Look for a button called On Line or Select. This button probably has an indicator light. When it's on, the printer is ready to go. (If it's off, press the button to turn on the light.)

Testing, Testing, 1, 2, 3...

When your printer is on and selected, type **DIR > PRN** at the DOS prompt and press Enter. This command tells DOS to send the command's output to the printer. This command prints the current directory.

If you're using Windows, you have to double-click the MS-DOS Prompt icon in the Main program group to display the DOS prompt. Then you can use this command. When you're finished using DOS, type **EXIT** and press Enter to return to Windows.

It Won't Respond!

Is the printer on? Is the printer selected (on line)? Is there a cable between the printer and the computer? Did you type the command correctly? Is there paper in the printer? Is there a user at the keyboard? Is the user reading a Harlequin romance again, instead of typing these wonderfully cool DOS commands?

If you've checked all the obvious stuff and your printer still doesn't work, don't torture yourself. Find someone who knows this system, and get help. That's especially true if you're using a printer that's on a network. Almost always, you have to do something unusual to get network printers to respond.

Setting Up Your Printer with Windows

Once you've gotten your printer to work with DOS, you're almost home. But, you still need to tell Windows which printer you're using.

To install your printer with Windows:

1. Open the Main program group and double-click the Control Panel icon.

2. In the Control Panel, double-click the Printers icon. You'll see the Printers dialog box.

3. Look for your printer's name in the Installed Printers list. Click the down arrow next to the list to see more options.

   If your printer is on the list, click it so that it's selected (highlighted), and click the Set as Default Printer button.

   If your printer isn't on the list, click the Add button. You'll see another, longer List of printers. Look for your printer's name on this list. If you see it, click it so that it's selected, and click the Install button. Windows will tell you to put in one of the Windows disks. When the name of your printer has been added to the Installed Printers list, click the Set as Default Printer button.

   Some printers come with a disk containing a custom printer driver that's especially designed for the printer you have. If so, choose the Install Unlisted or Updated Printer option. You'll find this option at the top of the List of Printers. You'll see a dialog box prompting you to insert the disk containing the driver. When the name of your printer has been added to the Installed Printers list, click the Set as Default Printer button.

The Pain and Heartbreak of Printing Problems

When you're printing, lots of things can go wrong. However, most of them aren't too serious.

Dealing with printing problems

- ✔ The printer might not respond. Check to see whether the On Line or Select light is on. If it's not, push the On Line or Select button.
- ✔ The paper can jam. If you're using a laser printer, you may have to open the cabinet and extricate the jammed pages from various rollers, clamps, and other sadistic devices. But, be careful! One of those rollers is really hot.
- ✔ Your printer can run out of paper. If so, your program will probably display a message informing you of this development. Load some more.
- ✔ If you have a laser printer, loading paper is easy. Just refill the tray. Loading paper is a feat unto itself with a dot-matrix printer. Sometimes you have to weave and bob and weave and clamp the paper through the printer. Ask someone to help you.
- ✔ If there aren't any page numbers, don't be surprised. With most word processing programs, you have to add page numbers—they're usually not added automatically.
- ✔ You might see funny-looking garbage on your printout. If you're trying to print with a program, something's wrong. Maybe the program isn't set up for the printer you're using. Get someone who knows the program to help you.

WHAT'S THE SCORE?
WORD PROCESSOR–17,930 ...PERFESSER–ZIP.
MACNELLY

Top Ten
Least Popular CD-ROM Discs

10. Scenic Metropolitan New Jersey
9. Gunshot Wounds: An Illustrated Emergency Room Guide
8. Ten Easy Steps to an Uncontrolled Nuclear Reaction
7. The Accordion from A to Z
6. The Sayings of Chairman Mao (On-Line Edition)
5. Charles Manson's Prison Notebooks (Full Text Edition)
4. Recognizing Intestinal Parasites: The Multimedia Experience
3. Get Rich Quick By Raising Chinchillas
2. Know Your Vice Presidents
1. Save Big By Making Your Own Casket

CHAPTER 10

Sound! Action! Multimedia! (Sound Boards and CD-ROM)

IN A NUTSHELL

- What multimedia is
- Why multimedia equipment is worth the additional cost
- What equipment you'll need
- How to pick the right sound board
- How to pick the right CD-ROM drive
- Why you should spend some time finding good speakers
- Other stuff to spend lots of money on

THAT'S THE GREATEST THING ABOUT ALL THIS HIGH-TECH EQUIPMENT:
HIGH-TECH EXCUSES.

It's the latest computer fad, and supposedly the greatest thing to hit learning since—well, the human teacher. On the computer screen, you don't just see text. You also hear sounds and see animations, pictures, even full-motion video clips from movies and TV. Click on the tiger—you hear the roar and see the leap. It's super. It's expensive. It's... Multimedia!

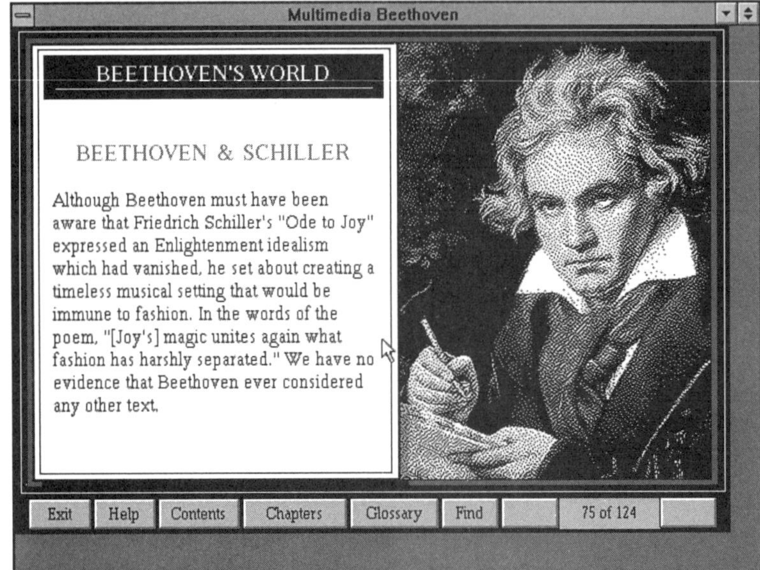

A multimedia application.

A segment of a full-motion video image in a multimedia application.

CHAPTER 10

SOUND! ACTION! MULTIMEDIA!

BUZZWORDS

MULTIMEDIA

In a computer program, the use of more than one medium to convey facts or ideas. A multimedia presentation may include sounds, pictures, full-motion video images, and animations, in addition to text. The best multimedia programs are *interactive*, which means you can choose your own pathway through the material. You can review it, skip it, or even group it as you please.

Why Bother?

Good question. But here's a clue. This is supposed to be the Information Age, right? Humble folks like you and me were supposed to be able to get our hands on humongous amounts of information, which we would then use to empower and enrich our lives.

If you listen to the people talking about the Information Superhighway, the thing that's supposed to bring you 500 channels of junk TV, you'll think that the best route to getting this information is through a sort of group marriage between your TV, telephone, and cable TV converter. Maybe that's really going to happen 10 or 15 years down the road. For now, though, there's a simpler, cheaper, easier way: it's called *CD-ROM*.

BUZZWORDS

CD-ROM

A compact disc that's stuffed with huge amounts of computer-readable information, which can include sounds, animations, and graphics, as well as text. To use a CD-ROM disc with your computer, you need a CD-ROM drive. Because multimedia presentations eat up huge amounts of storage space, most of them are distributed on CD-ROM discs rather than floppies.

CD-ROM provides a great way to get tons of information into your computer. A single CD-ROM disc can hold up to 600MB of data—the equivalent of an entire encyclopedia. And, the computer can search through all this stuff lickety-split. If you're having trouble with Japanese Beetles attacking your rhododendrons, just slip in your gardening reference disc, type "Japanese Beetle AND rhododendron," and Bam! Seconds later, you see three articles describing exactly what to do.

TIP

If you have kids in the house, the question of getting a CD-ROM drive is a no-brainer. You can equip your computer with a good CD-ROM drive, a sound card, and the Microsoft Encarta encyclopedia for less than it would cost to get a set of World Book or Britannica encyclopedias.

But aren't CD-ROM titles in short supply? That used to be true. But the cost of manufacturing CD-ROM discs is dropping rapidly, and supply is expanding very rapidly. It only takes about $8000 now to buy the equipment needed to manufacture CD-ROM discs that people can use in their computers. As a result, street prices of CD-ROM discs are dropping—you can get them for as little as $25. Computer magazines have recently learned that it's actually cheaper to put a CD-ROM disc in the magazine (as a freebie for introducing their readers to free or sample programs) than it is to include a floppy disk! There are a lot of organizations out there that have tons of valuable information, and they're putting it on CD-ROM discs that will soon sell for less than the audio CDs that you see in record stores.

CD-ROM discs that you shouldn't miss

- ✔ *Microsoft Encarta Multimedia Encyclopedia for Windows*. This shows what it's supposed to be like. The well-written articles—more than 21,000 of them—include photographs, seven hours of sound, brief animations, and full-motion video.

- ✔ *Microsoft Cinemania Interactive Movie Guide for Windows*. Over 19,000 capsule reviews of films—plus stills and audio clips—with an emphasis on the classics. Check out what's on tonight!

- ✔ *Monarch Notes on CD-ROM*. Remember Monarch Notes—just what you needed to help you with tomorrow's test on F. Scott Fitzgerald's novels? Monarch Notes give you a quick, readable rundown on important areas of knowledge. This CD contains the *entire Monarch Notes collection*, in every conceivable field of knowledge.

- ✔ *Mayo Clinic Family Health Book*. A multimedia version of the best-selling home health reference, this disc includes animations, photographs, voice, and video.

- ✔ *Global Explorer*. Imagine having so many maps that, when they are spread out edge-to-edge, they occupy more area than an entire football stadium. Global Explorer contains a computer version of the Earth that lets you zoom in wherever you like, by clicking one of the 20,000 icons found on the maps. You see textual information on the feature you've selected (such as museums, waterfalls, parks, and volcanoes).

- ✔ *Berlitz Learn to Speak Spanish*. It's the third most widely-spoken language in the world—and it's becoming increasingly popular as a second language in North America. A lot of employers are looking for people who can speak Spanish, as well as English, and this is a great way to start learning it. It's like having a textbook, a patient instructor, and an audio language lab all rolled into one!

But Isn't All This Just Hype?

Maybe so. A lot of CD-ROM discs end up in their cases, just gathering dust on the shelf. There are lots of CD-ROM discs available, but very few of them are produced with the high standards found in a disc such as Microsoft's *Encarta*, which was meant as a multimedia showpiece.

The truth is, lots of people buy a few of these information discs to justify buying all that expensive CD-ROM and sound equipment (see the next section), but then they set out to do what they really wanted to do in the first place: play games. The new generation of CD-ROM games, with full digital stereo sound, is really pretty awesome. With all that storage space, these games offer far more options, much better graphics, and more complex plots. Why do you think some sound boards (see the next section) come with a joystick port?

What Do I Need for Multimedia?

The trouble is, most of the computers that have been sold aren't equipped for multimedia. (This is changing, though.) If you want to get into multimedia, you'll probably have to upgrade your system. That's a torturous process. But, here you'll find the help you need. Let's take it one step at a time, with an overview of the equipment you need for multimedia. The following sections go into the details.

The equipment you need for Multimedia

- ✔ **A pretty darned good PC system.** The newest Multimedia PC (MPC) standards call for the following *minimum* system: a 486SX-25 with 4MB of RAM, a Super VGA display, a 160MB hard drive, and the rest of the stuff on this list. If you're really thinking about getting into multimedia, I'd get as much computing horsepower as you can afford—minimally, a 486DX2 running at 50 or 66 MHz and a 400MB hard drive. (If "486SX-25" doesn't mean anything to you, see Chapter 5 for a quick, relatively painless explanation.)

- ✔ **Sound Board**. This is an expansion board that fits into one of the slots inside your computer. Beware of the inexpensive ones (less than $100)— they sound tinny.

- ✔ **CD-ROM Drive**. This is like a floppy disk drive, except that it's designed to "play" CD-ROM discs.

- ✔ **Computer Speakers**. You can't just use that extra pair of hi-fi speakers that you're not using—unless you're willing to put up with an irritating hum, caused by the computer's radio frequency interference. Computer speakers shield out the computer's bad vibes, and keep the speaker's radio interference from disturbing the computer.

✔ **A nice, big monitor**. Do you really want to look at these cool multimedia presentations on that little 14" screen? Even a 15" monitor seems bigger (it actually has 10% more screen area), and a 17" monitor starts to get you into the minimum of what you'd tolerate in a TV. For more information on monitors, see Chapter 7.

There's also some optional stuff that you don't need, but might want, such as interfaces (ports) for hooking your computer up to a synthesizer keyboard, a full-motion video adapter with VCR camera input, and an electronic camera. But, this stuff gets expensive—bank account, look out!

Sound Boards

(Beyond the beep)

That little, squeaky 3" speaker inside your PC dates back to the ancient days of personal computing, when large lizards roamed the earth. Meanwhile, the Macintosh came along with digital sound built in. Macintosh users got to listen to great game sounds and, with a little clever fiddling, could get the Mac to say "Yes, my master" in Darth Vader's voice whenever they clicked an icon to open a file.

Your PC probably doesn't have digital sound capability—you have to add it, in the form of a *sound board*. (The "board" part refers to the fact that this is an expansion circuit board that fits into one of the expansion slots inside your PC.) A lot of people are adding sound to their systems—shipments of sound boards tripled last year. Increasingly, the newer systems are coming with sound boards already added.

I JUST DON'T UNDERSTAND THESE THINGS!!

Which sound board is right for you? The following checklist tells you what to look for.

What to look for in a sound board

- ✔ **16-bit data sampling.** This refers to the number of pieces of audio data that the board can process in one gulp. The more bits, the better the sound. 8-bit boards are cheap, but the sound isn't very good.

- ✔ **Software Compatibility.** Simple one, here: No matter who makes your sound board, it should have SoundBlaster compatibility. With this, you can get stereo digital sound from hundreds of SoundBlaster-compatible applications, including cool games, such as X-Wing. Also, look for MPC 2 compatibility—which means the board can both record and play in full 16-bit sound.

- ✔ **Synthesis Method.** Two choices here: *FM synthesis* uses built-in, fake sounds to "emulate" orchestral instruments, but it's cheap; the best synthesis method, by far, is *wave-table synthesis*. This uses sounds of actual recorded instruments that are kept on a ROM chip. But, it's expensive. You can compromise by getting an FM sound board that allows you to add a wave-table "daughter board" upgrade later, if you just can't live without it. (A *daughter board* is a small circuit board that plugs into another circuit board.)

- ✔ **Digital Signal Processor (DSP).** This is very nice to have because it takes over a lot of the processing work that your poor computer would otherwise have to do. That makes the sound board work faster and gives your computer the freedom to do other things. But, it's an expensive option. Again, look for a board that allows you to add this later, if you decide you need it.

- ✔ **CD-ROM Drive Compatibility.** Check this out carefully. If you want to hear the sound in multimedia CD-ROM discs, the sound board you have must be compatible with your CD-ROM player.

TIP

Plan your sound board and CD-ROM purchases together so that you can make sure the two devices will work with each other. For example, the Sound Blaster 16 Basic Edition board only works with Creative Labs and Panasonic drives. The Sound Blaster 16 Multi CD works with Sony, Panasonic, and Mitsumi drives, while the SoundBlaster 16 SCSI-2 will work with any SCSI-2 compatible drive (more about SCSI in the next section). To make sure you get a CD-ROM drive and sound board that are compatible with each other, you might want to consider buying a multimedia upgrade package (which typically includes speakers as well).

My Notebook Doesn't Have Any Expansion Slots! Can I Get Sound?

Yes, you can. One option is PORT-ABLE Sound Plus (DSP Solutions). A 16-bit external sound board with SoundBlaster compatibility and two speakers, it plugs into your notebook's parallel port. Want to keep printing? No problem; there's a parallel port pass-through. Another solution, if your notebook computer has a PCMCIA slot: Turtle Beach System's Audio Advantage, a sound board that's the size of a credit card. You'll need speakers or headphones to hear it, though. (For more information on PCMCIA, see Chapter 12.)

I Can't Hear Anything!

Duh! That's because you don't have speakers. Or headphones. Or a microphone, for that matter. Sound boards don't come with these things. We'll get to speakers later in this chapter—we'd better look at CD-ROM drives first.

What Is MIDI?

(It isn't a skirt length)

If you really want to get into musical composition, you can get yourself a MIDI-compatible keyboard or synthesizer and a sound board that includes a *MIDI (Musical Instrument Digital Interface)*. With the addition of some software, you can turn your PC into a recording studio, laying down multi-track recordings and playing them back in crystal clear, digital sound.

This might sound great, but the truth is that most of the sound boards for PCs have very limited MIDI capabilities, if any. If you really want to get into this you'd be wise to consider a sound board that's especially designed for MIDI purposes, such as one of the MIDI boards made by Roland (one of the top makers of synthesizer keyboards).

CD-ROM Drives

(Let's try to put the right spin on this)

Let's start with the most important fact about CD-ROM drives up front—CD-ROM drives, even the best of them, are *a lot slower* than your hard disk. If you've been working with your PC for a while, you'll surely agree that it's frustrating to have paid all this money for a fancy computer and then have to wait a minute while it loads a program. Well, CD-ROM is worse—much worse. You'll be very wise to invest in the fastest CD-ROM drive you can get.

But, there's more. The following checklist sums up the stuff you need to look for in a CD-ROM drive.

What to look for in a CD-ROM drive

✔ **Double Speed (at least).** These drives rotate that little disc twice as fast, producing much better performance. You can get triple speed and even quadruple speed drives, but they're expensive. A single-speed drive transfers data at a decidedly clunky 150KB per second; double-speed drives do 300KB per second.

✔ **Average Access Time.** This is a measurement of how long it takes the drive to find the information you've requested. This is measured in microseconds (abbreviated ms). Hard disks can access data in 15ms or less—and even then, you see a little delay on the screen. The best CD-ROM drives can manage 200ms average access times. Drives with access times of 400ms or more are slowpokes; you should avoid them like the plague that they are.

- ✔ **Compatibility with Standards**. The bottom line is MPC 2 (Multimedia Personal Computer) compatibility—and, if you're wise, you'll also look for a drive that's compatible with the next generation CD-ROM standard, called XA. But, while you're at it, look for "Multisession Photo CD" compatibility too. Here's why: you may not realize it just yet, but your old chemistry-based Nikon may be on the endangered species list. Computer cameras are here already. The Kodak Photo CD system records your snaps on a CD, which lets you display, process, and print your pictures on your computer—*if* your drive is compatible. These days, all the top-rated drives are MPC 2, XA, and Multisession Photo CD compatible (but check to make sure).

- ✔ **Compatibility with Your Sound Board.** You may not get any sound if you ignore this! The best way to go is to pick a drive *and* a sound board with SCSI-2 compatibility. For example, the SoundBlaster 16 SCSI-2 includes the SCSI-2 port, to which you can connect an SCSI-2 compatible drive.

- ✔ **Internal Mount.** There's no reason to get an external drive (one that has its own case) if you have a spare expansion slot inside your computer. You'll just be paying for something you don't need (the case and power supply).

This Drive Is Only $99!

Skip it, unless the only use you foresee for your CD-ROM drive is to read discs crammed with text. Probably, it's a single-speed drive that they're frantically trying to get rid of. You can bet it isn't MPC 2-compatible, and that means you can forget using the newest and best multimedia applications.

Can I Play My Audio CDs?

Why not listen to Corelli—or Mariah Carey—while you're working? Well, you can. Almost all CD-ROM drives can play audio CDs. You'll need software that can play the discs; usually, this comes with the drive. Or, you can just use Windows' Media Player accessory. For committed music freaks, get a copy of CD Player 3.0 (Graphical Bytes), which puts a familiar CD-player control panel on your Windows' screen.

It Says It Comes with a Caddy!

(This is Golf?)

There are two ways you can get the CD into your CD-ROM drive—via a motorized tray, like the ones in audio CD players, or a *caddy*, a little plastic holder. To use the caddy, you have to put the disc in the caddy and then push the caddy into the drive.

TIP

Using a caddy sounds like a hassle, but remember, there's no motorized tray to break down. With electro-mechanical devices, the simpler, the better (i.e., fewer repair bills). And if your drive is mounted vertically, you need a drive that uses a caddy.

Do I Need a Drive That Can Play More Than One Disc?

If you really get into CD-ROM, it may become something of a pain to be stuck with just one CD-based resource at a time. So, you'll see a lot of ads for CD-ROM readers that can handle six, eight, or more discs at a time. Remember, though, that these are changers—they still can only access one disc at a time. If you request information that's on another disc, there'll be a lengthy delay while the system loads this disc. And, the complicated mechanism may do a very good job of making local service technicians rich.

Speakers

(What's that awful buzz in the background?)

It happens every day. People spend hundreds on CD-ROM drives and sound boards, and then buy cheesy, little speakers that make 1950 transistor radios sound good in comparison. Here's what to look for in computer speakers:

Computer speaker basics

- ✔ **Shielding.** Your computer pumps out a lot of radio frequency interference. That's one reason why computer speakers have protective shielding. Without this, you'll hear an awful buzz in the background.

- ✔ **Self-Power.** Sound boards don't pump out enough juice to power speakers to reasonable volume levels. Unless you want to mess with adding a stereo amplifier to your system, look for self-powered speakers.

- ✔ **Headphone jack.** Most sound boards have only one stereo output, making it a chore to switch from speakers to headphones. Speakers with headphone jacks let you plug in headphones conveniently.

- ✔ **Good frequency response.** You wouldn't settle for limited frequency response in your stereo speakers—and you won't like it in computer speakers, either. With their small speakers and cases, most computer speakers aren't going to win any audio magazine prizes for bass response, but they should be able to handle the high end well. To get good bass response, look for a speaker system that includes a subwoofer (not really recommended if you live in an apartment or work in a crowded office!).

Digital Photography

(The end of chemicals?)

Photography. Remember that course you took? Lots of smelly chemicals. But chemical processing might be an endangered species. If it becomes a thing of the past, you can also say good-bye to high film costs and pollution from processing chemicals. Not such a bad prospect, is it?

If you buy a Kodak Photo CD-compatible CD-ROM drive, you can get involved in the new world of digital photography. You don't even need a digital camera. There's still a chemical step—you get your film processed normally. You then send your negatives to a processing station, which scans your pix and gives you a CD-ROM disc back. With Kodak's software, you can then view and edit your pictures on-screen. You can even make custom slide shows.

Can you eliminate the chemical step completely? Already, you can buy pure digital cameras, which record the image directly on computer-readable discs, but they're costly. And frankly, the quality isn't as sharp as going the chemical route—a high-resolution color photograph may contain up to two million bits (units) of information, compared to the 200,000 or so that the less expensive digital cameras can capture. The fun comes in once you have the image in your PC. With a program such as Adobe Photoshop, you can crop the picture, correct the color, retouch blemishes, and add zillions of special effects. With a reasonably good color printer, you can produce nice-looking prints, even if they're clearly not magazine quality.

If you're resolved to get your pictures into your PC, and you already have a good VCR camera, then you might consider adding a *frame grabber* to your system. This is another one of those expansion board things that fit inside the system unit. This one lets you "grab" (capture and record) a still frame, as well as motion video clips of short duration, from a VCR camera—or, for that matter, from a VCR player or a TV.

Right now, you'd have to pay about $10,000 to get a digital camera that could tempt you to put the Nikon away. But, just wait. Nikon itself is reportedly developing a digital camera that will sell for less than $1,000 and produce a resolution of 1.1 million bits—enough to satisfy all but professional photographers.

Top Ten

Least Popular Public Forums on CompuServe

10. Tips for the Socially Clueless
9. Ingrown Toenail Experiences—Shared!
8. I'm Happy! (And Barney Loves You)
7. Bambi's Mommy: Support for Guilty Hunters
6. Psychotic Loners On-Line Chat Group
5. What We've Learned about Our Neighbors by Exploring Their Garbage
4. Let's Share Our Poems from Summer Camp
3. Dates that Ended in Embarrassment
2. Whitewater Investment Club On-Line
1. Processed Cheese Product Hotline

CHAPTER 11

You've Got Your Modem (or Fax Board) Working!

IN A NUTSHELL

- What a modem is
- Why you should buy a fax/modem
- Why you should buy a *fast* fax/modem
- What people do with modems
- What people *shouldn't* do with modems
- The best on-line services
- What the Internet is
- How you can send and receive faxes from your computer
- What a local area network (LAN) is and what it does

Most people don't realize that computers are used as much for communication as they are for crunching numbers and printing reports. If you'd like the latest stock quotes and weather, if you need to exchange documents with coworkers in distant regional offices, or if you just like getting involved in a computer equivalent of a late night talk show, your computer can assist you. That is, it can help you when it's suitably equipped. Yes, pull out your Visa card, because we're talking about more irresistible accessories here: modems, fax boards, and networks.

What is a Modem—and, for That Matter, a Fax/Modem?

A *modem* is a computer accessory that allows your computer to send and receive computer signals via the telephone system. If there's a computer on the other end that's also equipped with a modem, the two computers can "talk" to each other and share files. If there's a human on the other end, he's going to hear nothing but annoying honks, beeps, and moans, and you won't even be able to say, "Sorry, wrong number."

A *fax/modem* includes a modem, but it can also send and receive faxes. These days, most modems are fax/modems; it doesn't cost much more to get the fax part thrown in.

Why Are Modems Needed?

The world's telephone system is one of humanity's most astonishing creations. Virtually anywhere on the globe, you can pick up the phone, direct-dial, and talk to someone who's on one of billions of other telephones.

There's a significant word in the above paragraph, though, and that word is "talk." The phone system is designed to carry the human voice, not computer data. That's why the modem is necessary. It takes the computer's signals and changes them into the warbling tones that the phone lines can carry. That's where the term *modem* comes from, incidentally—it's short for *modulator-demodulator*, which really means "warbler-dewarbler" (if you prefer bird talk over computer talk).

9600 Baud? Huh? v.32 bis! What?

Oh-oh, it's jargon time. 2400 baud, or is it bits per second (bps)? Do I need a 14.4 bps modem, or will 9600 do? What is v.32 bis? Rather than dragging you through all the technical details, I'll just tell you what your best options are.

What to look for in a fax/modem

- ✔ **Get a fax/modem**. Even if you're not sure you want to get into computer faxing, get a fax/modem anyway. It probably comes with fax software which will let you send and receive faxes from your computer, and I'll bet you anything that this will come in handy someday.

- ✔ **Go for 14,400 bps**. 2400 bps modems are passé, zilch, finished. They're still for sale for up to $50, but if you buy one, you've been snookered. You can get a much faster 9600 bps modem for a little more. At this book's writing, the best price/performance point is found in 14,400 bps modems that can manage up to 57,600 bps with compression (you can get one of these for $150 or less). These are also known as *v.32 bis* (this is a standard that applies to the 14,400 bps speed), with v.42 bis data compression (compressing the data is as good as getting a faster modem, since there's less data to send). Why go for speed? Sending a 1MB file from LA to the East Coast would cost $17.48 with a 2400 bps modem—but, sending the same file with a 14,400 bps modem will cost you just 73 cents.

- ✔ **Internal modems are cheaper**. An internal modem doesn't require a separate power supply and case. Why pay for stuff you don't need? The internal modem plugs into one of those expansion slots inside your system unit. An external modem is needed only if all your expansion slots are taken up.

continues

What to look for in a fax/modem, continued

- ✔ **Look for Hayes compatibility**. This refers to the command set that your software uses to tell the modem what to do. This command set was originally designed by Hayes (a company that makes modems). Almost all modems are Hayes-compatible, but a few aren't, and they may not work with your programs.
- ✔ **Insist on full send/receive fax capabilities.** Beware of "bargain-basement" deals on fax/modem boards—you could get stuck with a receive-only fax, which can't send out faxes. You can get a send and receive fax/modem board for just a little more money.

TIP

Got cable TV? In the next few years, more and more cable TV systems will be offering services such as Internet, CompuServe, and Prodigy via their cable systems, which can transmit data at much faster speeds than the telephone lines can handle. To connect with these services, you'll need a cable modem, which can send and receive data about ten times faster than the fastest telephone-line modem. Don't look for these at your corner computer store yet, though, since cable modems (and cable data services) are still in the experimental stage.

Hooking Up Your Modem

Installing an internal modem should be easy—just follow the instructions. Hopefully everything will work out. If not, it's because of a horrible thing called a *port conflict*. This happens when two accessories are trying to access the same port. This is going to be difficult to resolve and you'll definitely need help. Get a computer wizard to help you, call technical support, or read the manual—but *do* get help.

Most modems have two phone jacks, one for the phone line and the other for an extension phone. You can plug your phone into the extension phone jack so that you don't have to give up having a phone in your office. But bear in mind that you can't use this phone when your modem is in action. If you spend a lot of time on-line, the only solution is to get an extra phone line.

You'll Need Communication Software

Like everything else in computer-land, you need software to get all that hardware to work. Specifically, you need two programs to work with your fax modem: a communications program and a fax program.

The communications program handles everything that's needed to help you communicate, via your modem, with distant computers. It helps you determine the communication settings, stores the phone numbers of computers you dial frequently, and handles the details of giving orders to your modem. Once the connection with the distant computer is made, that computer takes over your computer's screen, and you work with the distant computer's commands. But, your communications program is waiting in the wings. With it, you can *upload* (send) or *download* (receive) files to and from the distant computer. You can also *capture* your session (record everything you type, as well as everything your computer receives, in a file).

Fax software lets you send and receive faxes with your fax/modem. These programs have features that are actually a real improvement on fax machines: they can store frequently-accessed fax numbers, keep trying at intervals if the other fax is busy, and receive faxes in the background while you're working on other things.

TIP

If you think you're going to get into computer faxing in a big way, be sure to get a modem that can distinguish between incoming fax and incoming voice calls (Intel's Satisfaxion 400 can do this). Fax/modems with this capability will ignore voice calls, passing them on to the telephone, but will intercept and receive incoming fax calls automatically. If your fax/modem can't do this, you can get inexpensive accessory devices that will do the job.

Things to Do with Your Modem

With your computer linked to the world's telephone system, there's no end to what you can do. Most modem activities, though, boil down to the following five.

Sharing Data with a Friend or Coworker

Any two computers equipped with modems can communicate, although this requires a lot of coordination. You have to call, and say, "Hey, Ralph, turn on your modem, and set it to auto-answer; I'm ready to upload that file." People use this a lot to send files back to the office (or home) when they're off traveling with one of those neat little notebook computers (see Chapter 12).

Electronic Mail

Electronic mail (abbreviated *e-mail*) works like this: you use your modem to upload a letter to Fred; it's stored on the electronic mail service's gigantic computer. Later, when Fred contacts the e-mail service, the computer says, "Fred, you have mail." Fred then reads your letter, and can respond, if he likes. The problem is, what if Fred never contacts the service? He won't get the mail. E-mail is only useful when all the parties who are trying to keep in touch agree to log on (contact the service) at a set interval, like once a day or once a week.

Calling On-Line Services

An *on-line service* is a giant computer that's stuffed with resources for people calling in with their modems. These computers can receive hundreds, or even thousands, of calls at once. You see a menu with lots of options, such as Weather, Stock Quotes, and Soap Opera Twists.

Popular information services include Prodigy, America Online, CompuServe, and Dow Jones News/Retrieval Service. All of these offer electronic mail. In addition, most services offer thousands of files to download, topically organized forums for discussing subjects of specific interest (ranging from computer subjects to social topics), vendor software libraries (very good for getting updated drivers for things like monitors and printers), encyclopedias, full-text magazines, newspapers, news wires, sports results, local weather, aviation forecasts, stock market quotes, mutual fund rates, movie reviews, interactive games, air travel reservations, and on-line shopping.

A big drawback to commercial on-line services, such as CompuServe or Prodigy, is the subscription price. There's usually a flat monthly fee, and you'll incur extra charges for premium services, such as plane reservations and bibliographic searches. It isn't difficult to run up bills of $50 to $100 per month.

Popular information services

- ✔ **America Online.** This service gives you software that you install on your machine, and this makes AOL very easy to use. It's best for chatting with other users and sending electronic mail. There are lots of files to download, and good vendor forums, but not much in the information resources department.

- ✔ **CompuServe Information Service.** This is the best all-around service, with excellent information, thousands of great files to download, wonderful entertainment resources, and the best selection of financial and research information. Beyond the flat monthly fee, though, the things you'll want to do turn out to cost more money. The default (standard) CompuServe interface is very difficult to use, but you can get a GUI-based program called CompuServe Information Manager for a reasonable fee.

- ✔ **Delphi.** This is the smallest of the on-line services. It's cheap, but there are few resources available beyond an on-line encyclopedia and forums for special interest groups.

- ✔ **Dow-Jones News/Retrieval Service.** This is an expensive service designed for corporate and professional services. It offers up-to-the-minute financial news and business information, including on-line versions of *The Wall Street Journal* and *Barron's*.

continues

Popular information services, continued

- ✔ **GEnie.** This service is much smaller than CompuServe, but it's cheaper, and it's trying to provide a wide range of research and financial information resources. The trouble is, accessing these additional resources can be expensive.

- ✔ **Prodigy.** The most popular service, Prodigy, is geared to homes and families rather than computer nuts. You'll find travel information, home shopping services, lots of financial service resources, and great resources for kids (including on-line editions of *National Geographic* and *Where in the World is Carmen Sandiego*). But, you can't download files and e-mail resources are limited.

Having Fun with Local Bulletin Boards

A *bulletin board* is a do-it-yourself information service that local computer hobbyists set up. All it takes is an unused PC, a modem, an available phone line, and bulletin board software. Most bulletin boards keep huge storehouses of shareware and public domain software, which you can download and use on your computer.

BUZZWORDS

SHAREWARE

A computer program that you can copy and distribute freely, on the understanding that you will pay a registration fee to the program's author if you like the program and decide to use it.

Also available are discussion groups, mail, and *GIFs*—graphics files that you can download and view on your computer in full, living color. When my computer starts, Windows displays a gorgeous picture of Mt. Rainer and a mountain lake—which lets me dream about my favorite recreation activity, backpacking. Many bulletin boards address specific themes or topics, like Hatha Yoga Central or the Matchbook Collector's Hotline.

Contacting a local BBS is a great way to get started with your modem. Chances are that it's free, or very cheap. This is great while you're learning; you won't have to worry about running up huge on-line charges that produce nothing but frustration.

TIP

To find out whether or not there are any computer bulletin board systems operating in your local calling area, check out *Boardwatch* magazine or the BBS section of *Computer Shopper*.

Using the Internet

The *Internet* is probably the most talked-about development in computing these days. It's also hard to describe. First, it's not an on-line service, like CompuServe. Rather, it's a collection of linked networks that are set up so that messages can travel freely from one network to another. Connected to this network are more than *two million* computer systems, with an estimated 20 million users.

The backbone of the Internet is a U.S.-funded high speed data pathway called NSFNet, which links colleges and universities. In fact, Internet has been something of a collegiate plaything for years, since Internet access is free for most college students and professors. But more and more corporate and commercial services are getting linked to the Internet. You can also access the Internet through subscription on-line services such as Delphi and CompuServe.

What is the Internet for?

By far the most frequently-used Internet application is electronic mail, the sending and receiving of mail messages through the computer medium. The Internet is the world's largest electronic mail system.

There are several other Internet applications that you may find valuable, including Gopher (a way of exploring files and resources on other computer systems) and the World-Wide Web (a futuristic project to make gigabytes of information available in documents that let you "jump" to another document when you see a boldfaced word).

Of all the Internet applications (apart from electronic mail), by far the most popular is *Usenet* (composed of thousands of discussion groups on every conceivable subject). In these discussion groups, you'll find messages from people all over the world, expressing their opinions and joining in dialogue on subjects such as politics, the environment, hobbies and sports of all kinds, human sexuality, and—naturally—computers.

How Do You Get Connected to the Internet?

There are different ways to get connected to the Internet.

Many on-line services offer Internet access, but this access may be limited to just electronic mail. Check with your on-line service to find out what's available.

Many universities, companies, and private firms offer dial-up (modem) access to the Internet, but this has its drawbacks—you'll probably find yourself using an Internet computer that's running UNIX, an operating system that only a computer scientist could love. You can still use all the cool Internet capabilities, but you'll have a tough time learning to use the UNIX programs and commands.

The best way to connect to the Internet is through a *local area network* (LAN) that's connected to your personal computer. (LANs are discussed later in this chapter.) If your computer is hooked up to such a network, and this network in turn has Internet access, you can run user-friendly, GUI-based programs for electronic mail (Eudora) and other Internet applications (Mosaic).

TIP

Many people have access to the Internet without realizing it. If you work for a large corporation or a university, chances are you can get an account on a computer that is linked to the Internet. If you're connected to a local area network, you may already have the best kind of access you can get.

Fax It to the Max!

Fax machines are popping up everywhere, but they aren't cheap—you have to shell out about $300-$600 to get a decent machine. You've probably seen them work: you feed sheets of paper into the machine, which takes a picture of the page line-by-line, transforms the picture into data that can be transmitted over a phone line, and contacts a fax machine at the other end, which then spits out copies of the pages on yucky thermal paper.

Fax machines are expensive. But, you can equip your computer with an excellent fax/modem board for about $100-$150, as mentioned earlier in this chapter.

However, computer faxing has one gigantic drawback. You can receive any fax, but you can only *send* documents that you've created with your computer and saved on disk. If you want to be able to send *anything* as a fax, including the menu from the Chinese take-out down the road, you need to equip your system with an expensive accessory, called a *scanner*. This brings the total cost of computer faxing up to, and probably beyond, the cost of a good fax machine.

A lot of people have fax machines at the office, and a computer fax at home. This way, they can at least receive a fax at home, and they can still send anything that they create within their computers. If they need to send a copy of a Chinese take-out menu to somebody, they can do this at the office (if their boss doesn't mind).

Computer fax facts

- ✔ Computer faxes have one big advantage over fax machines—incoming faxes are confidential. They're captured inside your computer and you don't print them unless you want to.
- ✔ When you print your incoming faxes, you print on plain paper, not that crinkly thermal stuff that most ordinary fax machines use.

continues

Computer fax facts, continued

- ✔ To send a computer fax, you use one of your programs (such as a word processing program) to prepare the document. Then you "print" the document to a special file, which the fax software then "reads" and sends via the fax/modem.
- ✔ When you receive an incoming fax, you see a dialog box informing you of this. You can view the fax on-screen, if you wish, or print it. With most fax programs, a utility program can even translate the incoming fax message to computer-usable text that you can access, modify, and print with a word-processing program.
- ✔ You can schedule a fax to be sent automatically in the dead of the night, when rates are low.
- ✔ If you receive a lot of faxes with your computer, you'll need to leave it on all the time. But, that would also be true if you had a fax machine. Some people leave their computers on all the time, anyway, out of concern that switching them on and off actually shortens their life.

If I Had a Scanner

If you want to go the computer faxing route whole hog, you'll need a *flatbed scanner*—and thanks to big, recent price drops, you can get a good one for about $650. A flatbed scanner looks like a personal photocopying machine—it has a flat glass plate and a lid—but it doesn't make copies. It scans a piece of paper, and converts the information into a form the computer can use.

So, why not just get a fax machine if you're going to spend so much money? The computer route probably isn't worth the money, unless you can use the scanner for something else besides faxing. For example, an antique merchant could scan photographs of collectible pieces, and create a newsletter featuring the pictures.

This Hand-Held Scanner Is Cheap!

Yes, but is it wide enough to capture the stuff you want to scan? Hand-held scanners are best for capturing snapshot-sized photographs, columns of text, corporate logos, business cards, and other small-scale stuff.

Local Area Networks (LANs)

(Hello, Central?)

From the beginning, the basic idea of personal computing was to give each individual his or her own computer, and also the freedom to decide how to use it. A great idea. But, it did create some problems. Does everybody have to have an expensive printer? How do we share stuff?

These questions stumped the computer geniuses, but they went to work. Their solution? The *local area network* (abbreviated *LAN*, which rhymes with Dan). In brief, a local area network is a bunch of cables and connectors that let two or more PCs share printers and files. All the computers on the network have to be physically connected through special, high-speed cables—the phone line is just too slow.

BUZZWORDS

LOCAL AREA NETWORK (LAN)

A set of computers (from three or four to several hundred) that are directly linked by means of high-speed data exchange cables. These computers can share files and exchange electronic mail.

Why a Network?

One of the most common reasons for creating a network is to share an expensive printer. A network means that all of your coworkers can print gorgeous documents from the same laser printer—thus saving the company thousands of dollars.

Another common reason for creating a network is to share information. In a real estate office, for example, every realtor wants to see the list of currently available properties. It makes sense to keep just one copy of this information and let everyone access it. Also, networks allow you to use electronic mail. You write a letter to someone else on the network, and when that person logs on, he is alerted that mail is waiting for him. You can also send messages to groups of people, or to everyone on the network.

Yet another reason for creating networks is to let people use network versions of software. A *network version* of a program, like Lotus 1-2-3, is a version that is—you guessed it—designed to work on a network. What this means is that just one copy of the program can be accessed by two or more people at once. (This is all perfectly legal as long as the software in question is a "network version" of the program.)

Basic network facts

- ✔ Typically, local area networks link anywhere from a few (two or three) to several dozen computers. The largest LANs link several hundred computers.
- ✔ If you're using a PC in a large, up-to-date corporation bent on effective international competitiveness, you're probably hooked up to a network already. Don't be embarrassed if you didn't know; networks are so slick that they let you use your PC as if the network didn't exist.
- ✔ If you're connected to a network, you probably have a *network adapter card* in one of your computer's expansion slots. There's also probably a cable coming out of the back of your computer.
- ✔ Most networks have *file servers*, computers that are completely given over to handling network tasks. Here's where you find the files and programs that everyone shares, and also the programs that help the network run.
- ✔ You have to use special commands and procedures to access the network resources, such as printers and programs. Because these

commands and procedures vary depending on the type of network, you need to get the details from the person in charge of the network. This person is probably called the *network administrator*. If no one is in charge of the network, look out—it's not going to be very reliable!

- ✔ Possibly, you'll need to *log on* to the network. This means typing your *user name* (a moniker that lets electronic mail find you) and *password* (a secret code that keeps other people from posing as you and doing nefarious things, such as writing nasty letters to the boss).

It Says I Have a Drive Called "F!"

In a lot of networks, the network's presence is felt by the appearance of what looks like an extra hard disk—often named drive F—on the system. This drive, which is actually on the file server, is called a *network drive*. The network drive works just like an ordinary hard disk, with all those maddening directories and such. This drive contains the network versions of software you can run. You start these programs just like you would start any program on your hard disk.

Questions To Ask Your Network Administrator

If you have a network, ask the network administrator the following questions:

1. How do I get onto the network? Exactly what do I have to type?
2. What is my user name? Do I have to type a password?
3. Is there a network drive? Which drive is it?
4. How do I access the network printer to print my documents?
5. Are there any programs available on the network? How do I use them?

6. How do I send a file to someone else on the network?

7. Are there any shared files on the network that I should be using?

8. Is there a way I can send a fax through the network?

9. Is this network set up for electronic mail? How do I use it?

10. Wouldn't it be nice if this network were easier to use?

#?!!
LOST AGAIN!!
BEEP
BEEP
©Jefferson Communications, Inc. 1983
Distributed by Tribune Company Syndicate, Inc.

Top Ten

Rejected Notebook Computer Names

10. Peewee Pixel Hound
9. DataDwarf Deluxe
8. The Dashing Diminutive
7. Peerless Processing Pygmy
6. Byte Bantam
5. SuperShrunk II
4. IBM InfiniTesimal (IT)
3. Le Petite Portable Peckboard
2. TinyTyper
1. Wee Workstation

CHAPTER 12

Take It With You... And Work All the Time!

(Notebooks and Personal Digital Assistants)

IN A NUTSHELL

- Find out what notebook computers are—and why they're cool
- Get a charge out of examining notebook batteries
- Explore the limitations of notebook keyboards
- Find out what determines a quality display in a notebook computer
- Examine the pointing devices used with notebook computers
- Look at ways to connect a notebook to your desktop system
- What personal digital assistants (PDAs) are and why people make fun of them

It's amazing. My 7.7-pound notebook computer, which fits into my slimline briefcase, has all the power of that behemoth system that's taking up two-thirds of my desk back home. And it's portable. I'm writing this right now at 30,000 feet, somewhere over Rapid City, South Dakota. The only problem is, the nosy guy next to me just can't keep his eyes off my screen. I don't mean to be unfriendly, but could you move over one seat so I can use my mouse? Thanks.

If you're thinking about buying a portable computer instead of (or in addition to) a desktop mammoth, or if you're just curious about portables, this chapter should prove interesting; it surveys this intriguing, miniature world. And, as you'll discover, some very tiny machines are actually good enough to give your desktop machine serious competition.

From Luggable to Palmtop

My very first computer, way back in 1982, was ostensibly a "portable"—a Kaypro II. In one system unit, you got the computer, the disk drives, and monitor (but the keyboard wasn't built in). The tough, metal case was actually developed for use in the M-1 tank, and it was built on the assumption, apparently, that the enemy would be shooting at it. All this meant weight. Lots of it. The Kaypro weighed in at a hefty 28 pounds. These and similar "portables" earned the derisive epithet "luggable." Mine stayed put, right on my desk. Since that time, the only computers that legitimately earn the epithet "portable" are those that weigh under 12 pounds—and the keyboard must be built in. There are lots of different kinds, as the following checklist attests.

Types of portable computers

- ✔ *Laptop computers* weigh 12 pounds or less (down to about 7) and are pretty much obsolete. They're too big to fit in a notebook or to fit comfortably on an airplane's seat tray, and they're a real pain to lug around.

- ✔ *Notebook computers* weigh in at about 7 pounds, on average, but their key characteristic is their ability to fit inside a briefcase. They're about the size of a college textbook (8 by 11 by 2 inches). Notebooks can give desktop computers serious competition. They offer big, fast hard disks; a single 3.5-inch floppy disk drive; decent screens; and reasonably good keyboards. You can get good accessories, too, such as modems and fax boards. Notebooks are the most popular type of portable computer, but a good notebook costs two to three times what a comparable desktop system costs.

- *Subnotebook computers* average about 4 pounds, and are half the thickness of notebook computers. You have to use an external floppy disk drive, and the keyboards are cramped. Some of these machines could replace a desktop computer, but they tend to use older, outmoded microprocessors, like the 386SX. This could pose problems if you expect to run Windows at anything other than a glacial pace. These machines can't really replace a desktop computer, unless you only use the computer to write an occasional short letter or memo.

- *Palmtops* (such as Sharp's Wizard) weigh in at 1 pound or less. They have little, cramped keyboards, often with keys the size of Chiclet gum. Mostly, they're used for appointment scheduling and expense tracking for busy people "on the go." They're also dearly loved by gadget freaks. Some can run DOS and DOS applications, though, so they make sense if you need to use something like Lotus 1-2-3 while you're on a plane or calling on customers in their homes or offices.

- *Personal Digital Assistants (PDAs)* look like a palmtop, but they don't have a keyboard. You work it by "writing" on the screen; the computer decodes your writing—sort of (but therein hangs a tale—more about that at the end of this chapter). With such devices, you can do things like keep appointments, send faxes via cellular phone connections, and jot down notes just like you're using a notebook.

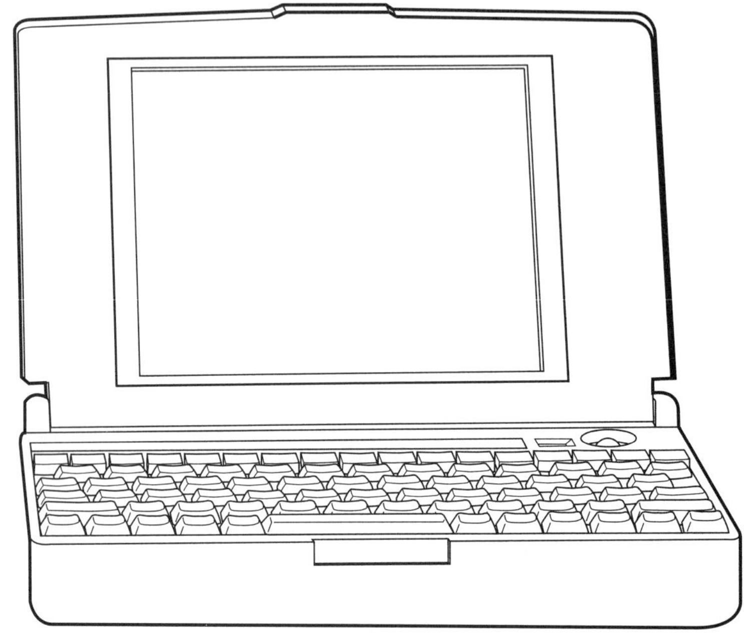

Zeos subnotebook.

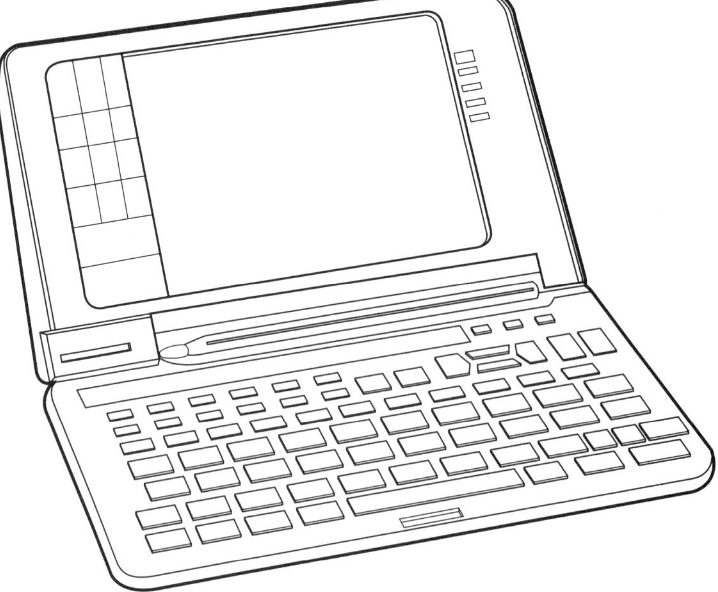

The Sharp Wizard palmtop.

TIP

Notebook computers are your best bet right now. You can get lightweight notebooks that pack as much computing power as a desktop computer, and display your work in a beautiful, big color display. (I'll let you in on a little secret: I'm writing these lines right now on a cute little Compaq notebook computer, sitting at a window watching the ducks swim by on the River Fyris.)

There Are Notebooks, and Then There Are Notebooks...

What to look for in a notebook computer

- ✔ **486SX-33 or 486DX-33.** You don't like a slow desktop computer, do you? Well, believe me, you won't like a slow notebook, either. You should be able to get a notebook with at least this much horsepower.

- ✔ **Under 9 pounds *with* the AC adapter/charger unit.** A weight that doesn't include the adapter and charger unit, as well as the power cord, is pretty meaningless; you'll have to lug all this stuff around as well as the notebook computer, unless you have oodles of spare batteries—but they're heavy too.

- ✔ **Go for color.** The most expensive, and best, color technology for portables is called *active matrix*. If you can afford this, great. I can't. The least expensive, and worst, is *passive matrix*. A very good compromise is called *dual-scan passive matrix*, which is more expensive than run-of-the-mill passive matrix, but which gives you very good color. If you don't want to go the color route, get a notebook with a gray-scale display (preferably, it should be able to display 64 shades of gray so that your graphics look nice).

continues

What to look for in a notebook computer, continued

- ✔ **PCMCIA slot.** This is a credit-card sized slot that lets you plug in a huge and growing variety of things, such as modems, fax boards, scanners, additional memory, you name it. This is a fast-growing segment of the *peripherals* (accessories) industry, and you shouldn't buy a notebook without it.

- ✔ **NiMH batteries.** Most notebooks use nickel-cadmium (NiCad) batteries. They're rechargeable, but they have some drawbacks. For one thing, cadmium is incredibly toxic, and poses a hazard to children and to the environment. The latest battery technology is the nickel hydride (NiMH) battery, which is more expensive, but is non-toxic. Plus, NiMH batteries give better performance. Additionally, you should be able to swap out an exhausted battery and slip in a fresh one without the computer crashing.

- ✔ **Advanced Power Management.** Portables that conform to the *Advanced Power Management (APM)* specification use about 25 percent less power. If you're shopping for a notebook, look for a machine that has this feature—it doesn't cost anything extra and it's a sign of good design.

Other nice things to look for in notebooks include a removeable hard drive (this lets you swap additional drives in and out), lots of ports (parallel, printer, keyboard, external SuperVGA monitor), and cursor keys in the upside-down "T" pattern. This is the same, standard pattern for cursor keys that you'll find on your desktop computer's keyboard. Although you may not realize it, you're probably used to this pattern, and you'll feel confused and frustrated using a non-standard cursor key layout (which, unfortunately, some notebook computers have).

TIP

Never buy a notebook computer without trying it out first! You may not like the keyboard, the pointing device, or the screen. It would be very wise to comparison shop for some time, until you find the machine you like.

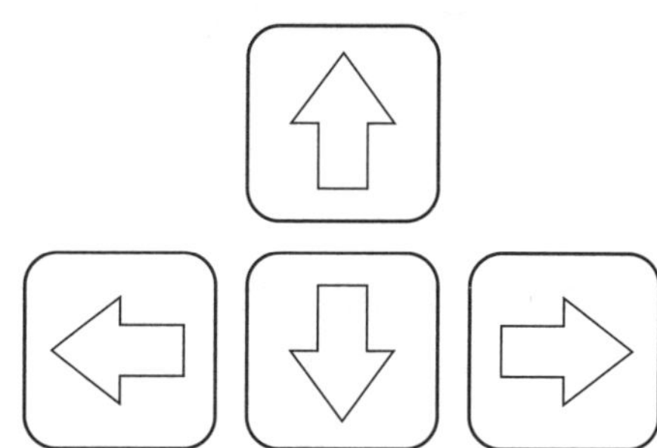

Look for a notebook that has cursor keys like this.

What Does "PCMCIA" Stand For?

I thought you'd never ask. According to one wag, it's "People Can't Remember Computer Industry Acronyms." But actually, it's Personal Computer Memory Card International Association. The Association's President, John Reimer, told a magazine writer that he regretted the association's name because the acronym is unpronounceable.

What's worse is that it's misleading, because there are a lot more things than memory cards that you can stick into a PCMCIA slot on your notebook computer. These include fax/modems, RAM memory cards, network adapter cards, ROM cards containing programs, and—get this—even hard disks.

There's more than one PCMCIA standard, just to confuse things: Type I, Type II, and Type III. You can't put a Type III device into a Type II slot, and vice versa. Aren't computers fun?

Generally, the higher the Type number, the more the slot can do. Type II PCMCIA slots can handle disk drives and modems as well as memory add-ons; Type III slots, still under development at this writing, will be able to do even more. For now, a Type II slot is a good bet.

Can I Take It to the Beach?

Thinking of using your notebook outside? It sounds great, doesn't it? But remember, dust, dirt, sand, and temperature extremes are murder on computers. If it's mild enough for you to be comfortable, it's mild enough for your computer. Otherwise, leave the computer at home. Also, don't leave your notebook computer in the car on a sunny day.

My Battery's Dead!

It sounds great, doesn't it? Instead of being stuck at your desk, you could be sitting in that big rocking chair, watching the boats go by on the Rappahannock and working with that trendy new notebook computer. Unless you have a really long extension cord, though, you're dependent on the computer's batteries. And they run down pretty fast. With today's feature-packed systems, expect a battery life of only four to five hours maximum for monochrome systems. With color screens, the figure drops to only two to three hours, maximum.

When the battery gets low, the computer's automatic detection circuitry flashes a warning on your screen—something like, `Low battery! Save your work now or lose everything`! Fun, huh?

Ways to conserve battery power

- ✔ Turn down the backlighting intensity to the lowest setting that's still comfortable for your eyes. The lower it is, the less power your screen uses.
- ✔ Don't use the floppy drive unless it's absolutely necessary. Floppy drives require a lot of power.
- ✔ Get lots of additional memory, and ask the technician to help you set up a "RAM disk" and a "disk cache." These are ways of keeping information in your computer's memory so the disk doesn't have to go into action so often.
- ✔ If your computer has advanced power management, be sure it's turned on and set for maximum power conservation.
- ✔ Use simple applications that don't need to go to the disk all the time. If you're writing, use the MS Edit utility (supplied with DOS)

to create the text; later, when you're plugged into the AC main current, start Windows and do the fancy formatting with WordPerfect or Word.

- ✔ If you pause for a few minutes, be sure to engage the computer's sleep or standby mode. Some notebooks "go to sleep" after a set period of inactivity, while others require you to press a Standby button.

No, It Isn't a Bomb! It's a Computer!

(Oh, yeah? Prove it!)

If you plan to travel with your laptop, get ready for several gigantic hassles. The first begins at the security gate of the airport. Your innocent little notebook computer is under suspicion of being a murderous device filled with plastic explosives, so you'll be asked to turn it on (proving, thereby, that it's really a computer, and not a bomb). When you're on the plane, you may find that some airlines aren't happy about the use of electronic devices, which might interfere with the plane's radio. (That wouldn't be good for you or the computer, would it?) Generally, the smaller the plane, the more likely that they'll be antsy about this. Bear in mind that you may be asked to shut down your system.

TIP

Most airlines now forbid the use of any computer device (including notebook computers and PDAs) during takeoff and landing. If you're not sure, ask.

Please, Give Me My Mouse Back!

A big area of deficiency in most laptops: pointing devices. Most come with a mouse port, which lets you plug in the same type of mouse you use with your desktop computer. But, where are you going to roll it?

If you're on a plane, you'll have to use the meal tray of the person sitting next to you, which might not be appreciated.

To solve this problem, notebooks offer a variety of solutions, none of which are particularly satisfactory. Some systems come with tiny, built-in *trackballs* that don't offer enough control to be usable. Another solution: Microsoft's BallPoint, a trackball that clamps onto the side of your notebook's keyboard. This fix is better than a built-in trackball, but not by much. The latest gizmo is IBM's TrackPoint II, a little red stick shift offered with the company's Think Pad computers. The TrackPoint juts out between the G and H keys. You move the pointer by controlling this stick with your index finger, but it takes some getting used to.

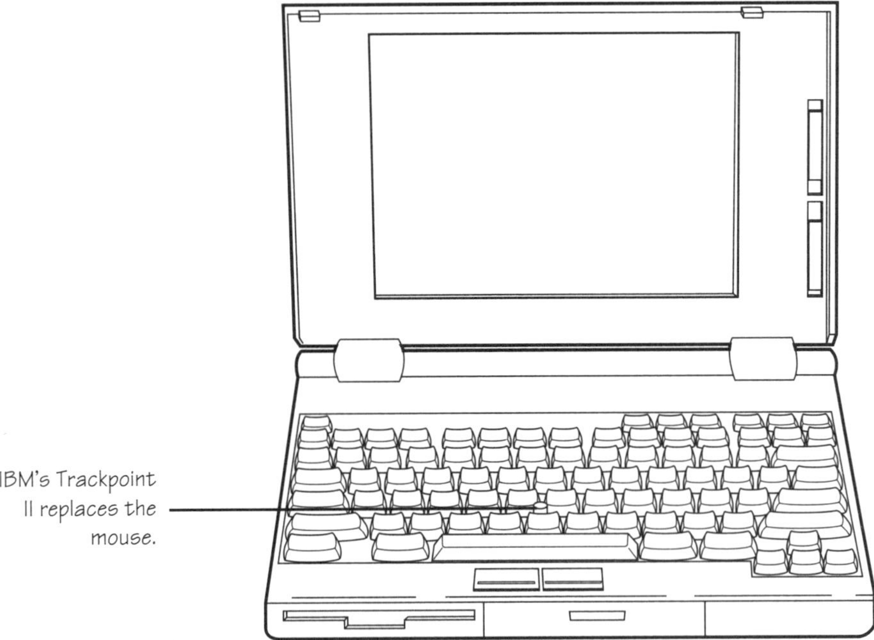
IBM's Trackpoint II replaces the mouse.

Making Connections

Notebook computers are great for making connections—use one at any airport, and every nerd within hailing distance will come over and say, "Gee, that's a great display. What's your hard disk's access time?" until you finally give up working and pull out *People* magazine. Actually, what I had in mind for this section was external connections—connecting to items like external monitors.

Connecting your notebook computer

- ✔ Do you think you'll get tired of working with that tiny little screen? Look for a system with an external VGA connector (one of those 9-pin sockets discussed in Chapter 5). This allows you to hook your notebook up to an external Super VGA monitor, like the one your desktop computer users.

- ✔ You can get a built-in modem or fax/modem for most notebooks. (Chapter 11 tells you a bit more about modems and fax/modems.) Many notebooks come with fax/modems built in. You can also get fax/modems that fit into PCMCIA slots.

- ✔ I don't recommend computing and driving at the same time, but you can get an adapter cord that lets you hook up your notebook to your car's cigarette lighter. This would be great for private eyes on stakeouts.

- ✔ Most notebook computers have a standard printer port. (Flip to Chapter 5 for information about ports.) You can even get portable printers, but they're a hassle to use and they double the weight of the junk you're carrying around. Your best bet is to print at home, or to bring a cable to hook up with friendly printers that you happen to meet along the way.

- ✔ The ultimate in connectability is the docking system. No, this isn't something from Deep Space 9. A *docking system* looks like a desktop computer—it has a monitor, disk drives, a decent keyboard, and connections for printers and the like—except that you can slide your notebook computer right into it. Instantly and automatically, your notebook is hooked up to the monitor, printer, disk drives, and keyboard. The docking station will set you back about $300, more or less depending on the accessories you want installed.

continues

Connecting your notebook computer, continued

- ✔ If you don't have a docking system, you can get utility software that lets you connect your notebook to your desktop system via a connector cord. Once the connection is established, the software lets you access the desktop computer's hard disk as if it were part of the notebook computer itself.

No Keyboard? It's a PDA!

You see them on *Star Trek*. Everyone's walking around with these little flat things. They're *personal digital assistants*—abbreviated *PDAs*. And, you don't have to wait until the 24th century to get one, thanks to Apple Computer and Sharp Electronics, makers of the Newton and the Zoomer.

These aren't computers, really. A computer is a general-purpose device that can run a lot of different programs. PDAs are designed to provide built-in applications for personal assistance, including an address book, a date book, a notebook, a pocket version of the popular Quicken checkbook program. PDAs start at about $600 for a stripped-down model that lacks a modem.

But how can you use this if it doesn't have a keyboard? The Newton and Zoomer come with pens, and the systems include handwriting recognition software. You're supposed to be able to write on the screen, and the PDA translates what you've written into text that appears on-screen. There's only one problem. The handwriting recognition doesn't work very well. In one test, an attempt to write the name Halfhill produced the following on-screen guesses: *florists*, *teachers*, *forecasts*, *four their*, and—this is truly a stroke of genius—*Clarence*. If you add troublesome words such as this one to the dictionary, though, the system doesn't choke on them again.

Apple hoped that PDAs in general (and Newton in particular) would take the world by storm, but they're selling slowly. Word has gotten around that handwriting recognition still has a ways to go before it will satisfy most users.

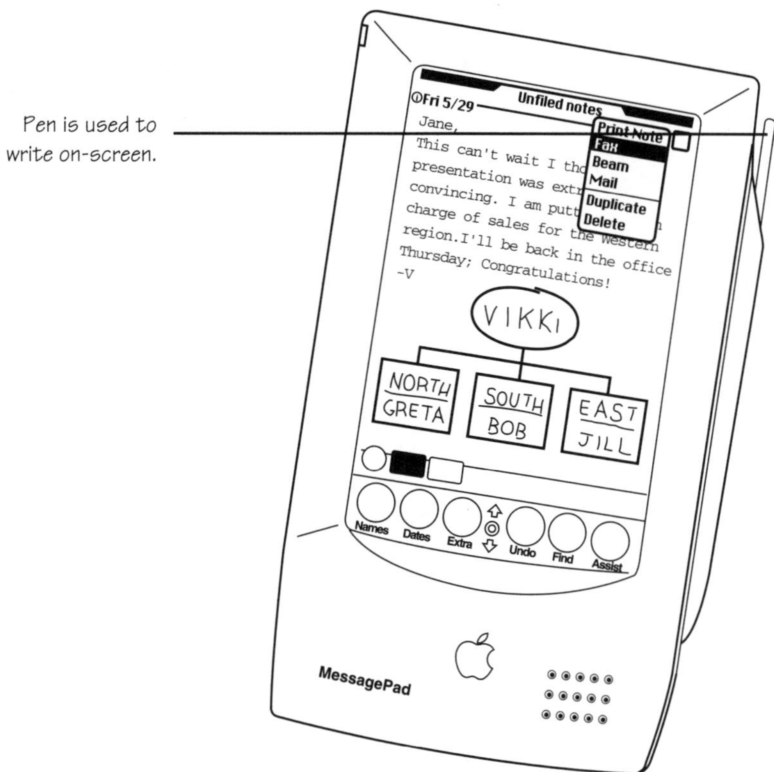

Despite all the drawbacks, there's clearly a future for PDAs. People aren't going to use PDAs for mass data entry; they'll keep using PCs for that. We're talking about jotting down a few notes or an appointment. Handwriting recognition software should be able to handle that once they get the bugs worked out. Plus, the pen comes in very handy for choosing things from menus. With wireless mobile communication already a reality, look for PDAs to come that will keep you linked up with electronic mail, satellite positioning systems, and paging systems. Imagine sitting in your car somewhere along a country road in Nebraska, and being able to access the latest world news, read the local weather forecast, check your electronic mail, and figure out exactly where in the heck you are.

Top Ten

Recent Discoveries of Computer Science

10. Computer actually invented by ancient Egyptians, who gave up the idea "because it was obviously so stupid"

9. Fans inside PC system units can be used to power model aircraft

8. Keystrokes on computer keyboards can be picked up, and recorded by neighbors who have made a simple modification to their portable telephones

7. Annual loss of 8% of U.S. Gross National Product attributed to trying to figure out the difference between 486SX, 486DX, and Pentium

6. First personal computers actually invented by Vietnam-era student radicals who hoped to "bring capitalism to its knees"

5. Large, flat area of computer system unit cabinet handy for stacking magazines and newspapers

4. DOS originally created to control remote bulldozer at hazardous waste site near Seattle, WA

3. Increase in computer orders is followed by corresponding increase in sales of aspirin and Tylenol

2. People aren't really interested in how computers work

1. Large, cumbersome computer manuals perfect for propping up short table leg

CHAPTER 13

Them Ol' System Software Blues

IN A NUTSHELL

- ▼ What an operating system is and why your computer needs it
- ▼ What system utilities are
- ▼ The most popular system utilities and what they do
- ▼ How to equip your system with the utilities you need
- ▼ The alternatives to MS-DOS—and why you should probably stick with MS-DOS for now

I JUST DON'T UNDERSTAND THESE THINGS!!

Computers are just junk without software. To some, they're still junk *with* the software. But the point is, you need software to get them to run and do things, like write letters, send faxes, and design brochures.

It's the "to get them running" part that gives people fits. We're talking here about *system software*, all the programs (collectively) that are needed so that your computer can run efficiently. This includes programs that do incomprehensible things, like handling electron collisions deep in the heart of the computer's complex data pathways. But, it also includes programs that help you do necessary maintenance tasks, such as deleting unneeded files, searching for computer viruses, and making backup copies of your work.

Beyond a doubt, the subject of system software is the least popular aspect of computing. Still, it's worth looking at. This is especially true today, now that you have some real options concerning which *operating system* you'll run on your PC.

What's An Operating System?

(What is this, the emergency room?)

Every computer needs an *operating system* (OS), a program that makes all the computer's components work together in a harmonious, gentlemanly way (they say, "After you, my fine fellow," and "Please, feel free to partake of this file"). The operating system also provides an *interface* with the user.

BUZZWORDS

USER INTERFACE

The part of a program that lets the user choose options and give commands (and explains what's happening if the option can't be chosen or the command can't be carried out). In DOS, each program has its own user interface, which is confusing because they differ. Windows provides the same user interface for every program.

THEM OL' SYSTEM SOFTWARE BLUES

Basic operating system facts

- ✔ A computer can't run without an operating system. It's the glue that holds everything together.

- ✔ Because operating systems talk directly to the physical parts of the system, they have to be designed around the requirements of specific hardware. MS-DOS, for example, is designed to be used with Intel microprocessors, while the Macintosh's System 7 is designed to be used with the Motorola microprocessors that power Macintoshes.

- ✔ Software can only run with the operating system for which it was designed. DOS programs require DOS, while Macintosh programs require System 7. (There's a way you can get DOS programs to run on the Macintosh using something called *emulation*, but it doesn't work very well—believe me.)

- ✔ The operating system used in most of the world's PCs is Microsoft's MS-DOS, which helps to explain why Microsoft CEO Bill Gates is one of the world's richest people, in the same league as the Sultan of Brunei.

- ✔ DOS is also an antique of sorts. It's actually a "clone" of an early operating system (CP/M) that was widely used for very early personal computers, way back in the Paleolithic Era (1977-1983). Back then, having 64KB of RAM was a very big deal, so operating systems had to be lean and mean.

- ✔ Windows isn't an operating system, really. It's actually a kind of fancy DOS program. Windows requires DOS. While it's running, it "hides" DOS. But, DOS is still under there, causing trouble every once in a while.

- ✔ DOS stands for Disk Operating System, which pretty much describes how DOS comes across to the user. You use DOS, mainly, to do stuff with your computer's disk drives. And the stuff you do is called system maintenance.

continues

Basic operating system facts, continued

✔ System maintenance is a necessary evil of using the computer. It mainly involves working with files—primarily your files, the ones that contain your work. (These are called *data files*.) You can look at them, copy them, and delete them. You can move them, and yes, you can lose them. With any luck, you can find them again.

What Are System Utilities?

(Keeping things hummin')

Think about the equipment it takes to keep your house looking nice. As long as you have the rock-bottom necessities—a good broom, a couple gallons of vinegar, a boar bristle brush, and can of Drano—you can solve any problem. In the same way, you need a few system utility programs to keep your computer system humming. These are extra programs that may or may not come with your computer. This section discusses the basic system utilities, and tells you why they're needed.

BUZZWORDS

UTILITY PROGRAMS

Programs that help you maintain your computer, keep it running efficiently, maximize computer resources, and solve disk-related problems. Lots of utilities come with DOS, but most computer users find that they need to buy some additional utilities.

Back It Up (Or Else...)

Fact 1: Very few people back up their work by copying it onto floppy disks or special backup tapes. Fact 2: All hard disks eventually die—and in many cases, you can't recover the files unless you have a backup. Fact 3: Many people fervently wish they would have backed up when a nasty hard disk crash wipes out several months of work. Cheerful prospect, isn't it?

BUZZWORDS

BACKUP

To copy the data on your hard disk to a different place (a set of floppies, another hard drive, or a backup tape—a storage device designed just for backups). If your hard disk fails, not to worry—you have a backup copy.

A *backup utility* is a program that copies files from your hard disk to floppy disks or other backup media, such as backup tapes. You begin by backing up all the files on your whole disk. This is a tedious job and can involve as many as 50 or 100 floppy disks. After that, it's easier. The utility "knows" which files have been backed up, and which ones haven't, so subsequent backups involve only the files you have created or changed since the first backup. And if your disk fails, you need only reverse the backup process—in an operation called a *restore*—and presto! Your disk is restored, just the way it was at the time you last backed up.

TIP

If you use your computer for professional work or business, by all means equip your system with a tape backup unit. This fits into one of your computer's empty drive bays and lets you backup your entire hard disk quickly and easily. You can get good tape drives for as little as $200.

A good backup utility (in both DOS and Windows versions) comes with DOS 6.0 and 6.2. Called MS Backup, this is good enough for most users. You'll only need a special backup program, such as FastBack Plus, if the MS Backup doesn't work with your tape drive. For information on running MS Backup, see this book's companion volume, *I Hate DOS*.

Doubling Your Disk Space

(Squeeze those files!)

It's inevitable that your hard disk will soon be crammed with programs, files, more programs, and more files. Files seem to multiply at a furious pace. Sooner or later (probably sooner), you're going to run out of space on your hard disk. That's when a disk compression program comes in handy.

A *disk compression program* works by getting your disk into a full nelson and squeezing until the disk agrees to store your data more tightly than it normally would. Don't worry; it's safe.

There are several disk compression programs available, but the most popular is Stacker (Stac Electronics). The latest version can actually more than double the storage space on your disk.

Restoring Your Hard Disk's Peak Performance

You won't like what you're about to read, but it's true: DOS is likely to store your precious data here and there all over the hard disk, rather than putting it all in one nice, continuous unit. This phenomenon is called *file fragmentation*, and it makes your hard drive run more slowly. When you tell DOS you want a file, it has to run around the hard disk, frantically collecting all the pieces. This process can take some time.

The cure for file fragmentation is running a *defragmentation utility*, a program that rewrites all the data on your disk so that all the file parts are put back together. This takes anywhere from a few minutes to about an hour. You should perform this occasionally (every couple of weeks, or every couple of months if you use your computer infrequently).

If you've got MS-DOS 6.0 or 6.2, there's no need to run out and buy a defragmentation utility—you already have one.

The Great Virus Hunt

What's a virus? Basically, a *virus* is a prank program designed to do something unexpected to your computer. Sometimes, the unexpected is something silly such as displaying a prank message on-screen on a certain day at a certain time. More often, the result is an annoyance—one virus makes your screen "melt" so that you can't see what you're doing. Sometimes, the surprise is vicious; some viruses wipe out files on your hard disk, beyond recovery. One virus even set up a video pattern that was capable of setting fire to certain computer monitors.

Viruses often propagate by traveling unseen on floppy disks. If you insert an infected disk into your system and start an infected program, the virus immediately infects as many of your files as it can. After infecting your system, many viruses operate for a long time without your being aware of their presence. During this time, you might give disks to others, who in turn infect their systems.

Your best defense against viruses is to run an anti-virus checker on any floppy disk you insert in your computer, even if you've taken the disk from a fresh, shrink-wrapped package. There are cases where software publishers have unknowingly distributed disks containing viruses! This is pretty rare, though.

Virus-checking programs, such as the one that comes with DOS 6.0 and 6.2, can detect thousands of current viruses, using a pattern-matching technique. While this is effective for known viruses, these programs can't protect you from the new ones. That's why virus checking utilities usually come with a coupon that lets you get update disks. Alternatively, you can download recent patterns from the vendor's forum on CompuServe or other on-line services.

Managing Memory

(Getting the most out of your RAM)

It isn't easy to get the maximum memory performance out of your computer. Ideally, you've cleared up as much of your computer's 640KB of *conventional memory* (see Chapter 5) as you can. This is done by moving DOS and other parts of the operating system into unused memory areas. But, this requires a lot of skill and even some programming knowledge. It's better to get a utility to do this for you. That's what *memory management utilities* are for. Whether you're planning to run DOS or Windows, it's a good idea to run a memory management utility on your system.

Many PC users believe that QEMM 7.0 (Quarterdeck Systems) is the best memory management utility available, but there's one that comes free with DOS 6.0 and 6.2. For more information on this utility (called MEMMAKER), see this book's companion volume, *I Hate DOS*.

Undelete

(Please! Give it back!)

Sooner or later, you'll delete a very, very important file, one that will require you to do hours, days, or even weeks of work to replace. So, it's nice to know that you can get an *undelete utility* which can restore the file. In fact, it would be nothing short of madness to use the computer without an undelete utility. An undelete utility comes with DOS 6.0 and 6.2, both in DOS and Windows versions (for more information, take a look at *I Hate DOS*).

Cache Software

(It's pronounced "cash")

No, we're not talking about counterfeiting twenty dollar bills. This is a utility program that sets aside part of your computer's memory to store frequently-accessed data. (The term *cache* refers to the memory hiding place where this data is kept.) Without the cache utility, your programs would have to go hunting for this frequently-accessed information on the hard disk—and that would really slow down your computer's performance. A good cache utility is practically indispensable when you're using Windows, unless you just love sitting in front of your computer waiting for the screen to update.

A cache utility called SMARTDRIVE comes with DOS 6.0 and 6.2. It's automatically installed when you or somebody else installs Microsoft Windows on your system.

Disk Repair Utilities

It isn't fun to think about. But, things *will* go wrong with your hard disk. Sometimes, when you delete files, the pieces sort of get scattered all over the place. These are called *lost chains*. They slow down your disk and take up room needlessly. And, worse things can happen. Sometimes, a little area of your disk goes bad (this is called a *bad sector*). If your operating system doesn't detect this and lock it out of future data storage operations, you could suffer data loss.

A *disk repair utility* is just the ticket for these two problems. It will find and delete lost chains. Plus, it will detect and lock out any bad sectors that it finds. You should run a disk scanning utility occasionally to make sure your disk is in top shape.

An excellent disk repair utility called SCANDISK comes with DOS 6.2. A huge improvement over the old, clunky CHKDSK program, packaged with earlier versions of DOS, SCANDISK automatically detects and fixes a variety of disk-related problems.

So, Where Do I Get All These Cool Utilities?

For years, people have been saying, "These utilities really ought to be included with the operating system." And finally, they are. As mentioned in the preceding sections, MS-DOS 6.0 and 6.2 include most of the utilities mentioned here.

Whether the DOS utilities are all of sufficient quality, however, is another matter. There's still a healthy market for *utility packages* such as PC Tools and The Norton Utilities (these are available in versions for Windows as well as DOS). These packages give you additional utilities that some people swear by, such as one that can fix certain files after they've become so corrupt that DOS can't access them. This could mean the difference between saving at least some of your work and having to do it all over again.

TIP

To get started with utilities, learn to use the ones packaged with your operating system. If these aren't good enough, consider adding a utility package to your software library.

Popular utility packages

The Program	The Scoop
After Dark (Berkeley Systems)	The famous Windows screen saver that displays flying toasters (and lots of other fun things) when you're not using your computer. How can you pass *that* up?
Close-Up (Norton Lambert)	This is a bit weird, but just imagine: it's 8:00 PM, and you're sitting at your home computer—but, you're working with the computer at your office, just as if you were sitting there. All you need is this program and a modem!
Dashboard (Hewlett-Packard)	A push-button utility panel for Microsoft Windows—a big improvement over Windows' Task Manager. This lets you open applications and switch among them with the click of a mouse button.
Microsoft Scenes (Microsoft)	Screen savers for Windows with beautiful images. Choose from Impressionist art, Sierra Club photographs, and incredible outer space views.
Norton Desktop for Windows (Symantec)	More than just a utility package, this program replaces the Program and File Managers and shows you what Windows 3.1 should have looked like in the first place. One of the best programs available in any category.
PC Tools for Windows (Central Point Software)	Offers more than a dozen system utilities that let you get into the nitty-gritty of your computer's file system. Also available for diehard DOS users.
Qemm 7 Quarterdeck Systems)	Squeeze the last bit of available memory out of your system—it's a lot better than the MEMMAKER utility that used to be packaged with MS-DOS.
Stacker (Stac Electronics)	The best-selling disk compression program.

Popular utility packages

The Program	The Scoop
Star Trek: Screen Saver (Berkeley Systems)	When you're not using your computer, Captain James T. Kirk saves your Windows screen from Klingon attacks.
Systems Uninstaller (MicroHelp)	A program to uninstall Microsoft Windows applications shouldn't be necessary, but unfortunately, it is. When you install a Windows application, it leaves stuff hither and thither on your disk—but, if you later decide you don't want to use the program and try to delete it, much of this junk is left behind (and some of it can make your computer behave oddly).

Do I Have To Use MS-DOS?

Actually, no. There *are* alternatives. But, look before you leap.

What's PC-DOS?

Not so long ago, when IBM and Microsoft were good buddies and did *everything* together, like going bowling and planning the future of the Information Age, *PC-DOS* was just the version of MS-DOS that IBM packaged with its computers. But, PC-DOS has gone its own way, and IBM has done its own work on PC-DOS. Now you can buy PC-DOS separately, if you like, and run PC-DOS on a clone.

PC-DOS looks just like MS-DOS on-screen. In fact, there's very little difference between the two in most respects. The difference lies in the system utilities packaged with the two operating systems.

PC-DOS has the edge in the utilities department. It has better anti-virus, backup, and undelete utilities than MS-DOS. In addition, PC-DOS comes with Addstor's SuperStor/DS disk compression utility.

What's Novell DOS 7?

This is another alternative to MS-DOS, created by a company that's a leader in the networking field. It's comparable to MS-DOS or PC-DOS—in fact, you'd be hard-pressed to tell the difference on-screen—but, it has one gigantic plus: it includes the software that's needed for your PC to communicate with a network. If you're trying to set up a network of a few computers in an office or small business, this is a great deal because you won't have to buy additional networking software for each PC.

What's OS/2?

You probably don't realize it, but there's a lot more horsepower under the hood of your 386 or 486 than your programs can use. These are 32-bit processors, which means that they can gobble up four 8-bit chunks of data at a time. (This is like eating four potato chips at a time—you get through the bag a lot faster.) But, DOS and Windows treat these processors as if they can only process two 8-bit chunks of data at a time. It's like having a V8, and getting four-banger performance.

But, there is a true 32-bit operating system: *IBM's OS/2*. And what's more, it runs Windows, Windows applications, and DOS programs, as well as applications specifically written for OS/2.

Is OS/2 a real alternative to DOS and Windows? OS/2 runs OS/2 applications—programs that have been specially written to run in the OS/2 environment—nice and fast. But, OS/2 doesn't give you much of an advantage when it comes to running Windows applications, some of which can actually run slower under OS/2 than they do under Windows. That's because OS/2 has to do some translation in the background so that the Windows programs can function in the OS/2 environment. Plus, OS/2 isn't strong on providing driver support for all those sound boards, video accelerators, and other nifty system goodies out there.

What's UNIX?

UNIX is an operating system that was originally developed by AT&T's Bell Laboratories. Thanks to an antitrust court decision that kept AT&T out of the computer business for many years, AT&T allowed colleges and universities to use and adapt UNIX. It's the operating system that today's computer scientists grew up with, and as a result, they retain an unreasonable affection for it. They keep saying that UNIX's day on PCs is coming, but it never quite happens. UNIX isn't really an alternative to DOS or Windows, and it can't run DOS or Windows software.

There's one place where you might run into UNIX—the Internet. When you contact a distant computer using your modem, your computer becomes a remote terminal for the host system (the one you've contacted). If that system uses UNIX (and most Internet-accessible systems do), you may need to learn a little UNIX so that you can get around. (For more information, check out the book *I Hate Unix*.)

PART III

Software

Includes:

14: Grunt-Level Operating System Facts: Files and Directories

15: All You Really Need To Know about DOS (You Learned at the C:\> Prompt)

16: Picture Yourself in a World Full of Icons (Managing Files with File Manager)

17: Finally, Programs That Actually Do Things for You (Application Software)

18: Buying, Installing, and Starting Programs

19: You Too Can Become a Global Village Idiot: Electronic Mail and Internet

Shoe
By Jeff MacNelly

Once upon...

a timeframe,

WHAT'RE YOU DOING?
WORKING.

LOOKS LIKE YOU'RE SITTING.
I'M TRYING TO WRITE, IF YOU REALLY MUST KNOW.

WHAT'RE YOU WRITING?
NOTHING, SO FAR.

BUT THE COMPUTER MAKES WRITING A LOT EASIER, I'LL SAY THAT.

WITH JUST A FLICK OF THE FINGER...

I CAN WRITE REAMS OF NOTHING.
WHIRRRRR

I CALL IT "STREAM OF UNCONSCIOUSNESS."
7-21

Top Ten

Problems if the Starship Enterprise's Computer Ran DOS

10. Away team beamed to wrong planet due to typing error
9. Can't find file containing recipe for Romulan ale
8. `Load torpedo and press any key when ready` message takes thrill out of space battles
7. Captain's personal log accidentally rerouted to public-address system
6. McCoy often heard exclaiming, "Dammit, Jim—I'm a doctor, not a computer scientist!"
5. Spock spends too much time writing batch files, never develops his human side
4. Computer can talk only by means of honks and beeps from tinny, 3-inch speaker
3. `Insufficient memory` message appears when trying to run ShieldsUp application and PHASER.EXE at same time
2. `File not found` message is only explanation when away team fails to materialize on transporter pad
1. Accidentally reformatted disk that contained navigation data

CHAPTER 14

Grunt-Level Operating System Facts: (Files and Directories)

IN A NUTSHELL

- What files are and how to name them
- How to make sense of directory concepts
- What the current directory is and why it matters a lot
- How to decode path names (and when to use them)
- What wild cards are and how they're used
- What system files are and when they need to be modified

Whether you run DOS or Windows, you're stuck with some of the basic, ugly facts about the way DOS organizes your computer. This isn't a fun subject—especially if you're using Windows because you thought that you could escape all this horrible DOS stuff. Windows makes DOS pretty; but, underneath, Windows is still DOS. All of the restrictions and peculiarities of DOS can be seen beneath all the colorful on-screen Windows action.

This chapter discusses files, file names, and directories—necessary subjects for any DOS or Windows user. The better you understand files—and how they're named and where they're stored—the less chance you'll get so frustrated that you "caress your system with a baseball bat," as we politely put it.

So, this chapter is valuable for any PC user, whether you're using DOS, Windows, or whatever. Chapter 15, "All You Really Need To Know About DOS (You Learned at the C:\> Prompt)," is for DOS users, while Chapter 16, "Picture Yourself in a World Full of Icons (Managing Files with File Manager)," is for Windows users.

Files

(And those dratted file names)

Everything on your computer—hard disk or floppy disk—is stored in a *file*. And every file has a name. Some of the files, such as program files, are already on the disk. Some files are created when you use a program. When you type and save a memo, it's stored as a file.

BUZZWORDS

FILE

A unit of related stuff that is stored on disk. There are two types of files: *program files,* which contain instructions the computer can follow; and *data files,* which contain your work. Every file has its own unique name.

CHAPTER 14

GRUNT-LEVEL OPERATING SYSTEM FACTS

Basic facts about computer files

- ✔ File names consist of two parts: a "first" name and a "last" name. You use a period to separate the two names.
- ✔ The file must have a first name, but it doesn't need a last name. Hey, we're on a first-name basis here inside the computer!
- ✔ The first name can have up to 8 characters, but it doesn't have to use this many. The last name can have up to 3 characters, but it doesn't have to use all three.
- ✔ You can use the last name, called an *extension*, to show how files are related (just like your last name connects you to your family members). You might have .DOC files for document files and .WKS files for worksheet files.
- ✔ Programs always have an .EXE, .COM, or .BAT extension.
- ✔ Stick to using letters and numbers in your file names. Except for a period between the first and last name, avoid punctuation.
- ✔ You can't use spaces in a DOS file name, but some users like to fake it by typing an underscore instead of a space (for example, SHUT_UP.DOS).
- ✔ Users who are in the know let their applications assign extensions automatically. Some applications are bossy and prefer that you let them assign the extension. Don't fight it; it's a losing battle, and you'll need to conserve your energy for more important DOS operations—like shaking your fist at the screen.
- ✔ A commonly used extension for text files is .TXT. A text file contains nothing but the standard DOS keyboard characters, without any of the weird-looking characters (such as happy faces and Greek letters) that most programs add to your files to handle things like formatting.

EXPERTS ONLY

Do you *really* want to know which characters you can't use in a DOS file name?

You can't use spaces, commas, backslashes, or periods within the file name. (You must use a period, though, to separate the file name from the extension.) You can use any of these characters:

_ ^ $ ~ ! # % & - { } @ ‘ ( )

Why Directories, Anyway?

In brief, a *directory* is a section of your hard disk that has been set aside for storing files of a certain type, like all the letters you've written to your boss over the years asking for a raise. Chances are that you're working with a hard disk big enough to hold tens of thousands of files—and somehow, they've all got to be organized.

BUZZWORDS

DIRECTORY

A section of your hard disk that has been set apart for storing files of a certain type (such as recipes or WordPerfect program files).

Why Can't I Put Everything In One Big Directory?

Suppose that you have one giant folder that holds all 6,000 of the letters you've typed in the last three years. Even if the letters are alphabetized, it would still be difficult to find a letter when you need it. Instead, you would be better off keeping the letters in various folders organized logically, perhaps by date, recipient, or subject.

Storing data on a computer is the same way; it's much better to put your files in separate directories. For example, you can put all your recipes in a directory called \RECIPES, your poems in a directory called \POEMS, and your list of enemies in a directory called \REVENGE. You can create your own directories (and delete them, too), as detailed in the next two chapters.

EXPERTS ONLY

Read this if you're curious to know why all those directories that you didn't create are on your disk.

Directories aren't just for your files. Programs like to have their own directories, too; a typical program comes with dozens, or even hundreds, of support files. A lot of programs won't run unless all those support files are right there, in the same directory. That's why the SETUP or INSTALL utilities you use to install a program usually create a new directory to store the program in. (Flip to Chapter 18 if you want to know more about installing new programs.) For example, the DOS SETUP program creates a directory called—you guessed it—\DOS. (That funny backslash tells DOS that the next word is the name of the directory—but more about that later.)

Why Do They Call It a "Tree"?

A tree has a root, a trunk, and branches. You can think of DOS directories this way, too—although you have to turn the tree upside down, with the root at the top, as the following illustration suggests:

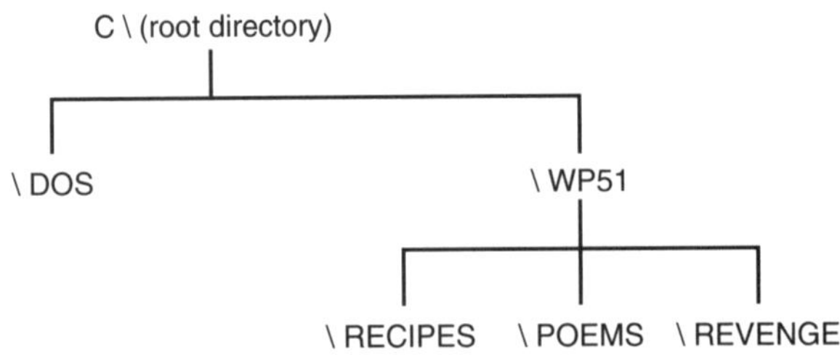

Basic facts about directories

- ✔ The root directory provides the "trunk" from which all the other directories branch out. The root directory, poor thing, doesn't get to have a name; it's indicated only by a solitary backslash (\).
- ✔ Every directory can have directories within it. In this tree, the root directory has two directories: \DOS and \WP51 (the WordPerfect directory). \WP51, in turn, contains three directories: \RECIPES, \POEMS, and \REVENGE.
- ✔ Note that every directory name must have a backslash in front of it—and that's true even if you string together two or more directory names (\WP51\POEMS).
- ✔ What are subdirectories? A directory within a directory. When you view a directory with the DIR command, you see a list of files and any subdirectories that the directory contains.

SUBDIRECTORY

A directory within a directory. C:\DOCS\REVENGE is a subdirectory of C:\DOCS.

One Directory at a Time

Why, you may still be wondering, must I learn about directories? The short answer: You need to understand directories so that you can tell your programs where to find files. To elaborate on that concept a little, consider that only one directory is current at a time. (This directory is called the *current directory*.)

What is the "Current Directory"?

Here, "current" doesn't mean up-to-date. It doesn't have anything to do with electricity. What it means is that DOS or Windows will assume that your file-related command affects the current directory, unless you tell it otherwise.

This simple fact has a number of discouraging implications, all of which add up to not being able to find files on your disk. Let's examine a very common one.

Suppose that you're using a program, and you choose a command that says to the computer, in effect, "Nuke the file called JUNK.DOC." Well, the computer goes hunting in the current directory for JUNK.DOC—but what if it's not there? You get a message like `File not found`. You might conclude, unhappily, that the file doesn't exist. But that's not true; the file does exist! It's just located in another directory.

This concept is like trying to find a love letter that you have stored in the Love Letters manila folder by looking for it in the Insurance folder. Even though the letter does exist, you'll never in a million years find it in the Insurance folder. Likewise, for your program to be able to find a file, you must type the correct path name, and you may even have to type a drive specification. The following section goes into these tedious subjects. Cheer up, this will all be over soon.

Path Names

(Is this the road to Rome?)

By using path names, you can tell your program to look for stuff outside the current directory. Path names are really important.

Let's say you've created a file called IQUIT.DOC, and it's located in the directory C:\MEMOS\BOSS. The current directory, though, is C:\WP51. When you try to retrieve the file, you get a message like `File not found`.

In such situations, you need to supply the path name. The path name tells the computer how to navigate through your disk's directory structure in order to arrive at the desired location. Here's the path name you'd need to supply in order to retrieve IQUIT.DOC:

C:\MEMOS\BOSS\IQUIT.DOC

That ought to do the trick.

Basic facts about path names

- ✔ In the path name C:\MEMOS\BOSS\IQUIT.DOC, the C: part indicates the drive. A *drive specification* is a letter (like A, B, C, and so on) that refers to a disk drive in your system, followed by a colon (:). The colon is necessary. There's never a space after the colon. A complete drive specification looks like this: A: or B:.
- ✔ The first backslash indicates the root directory.
- ✔ MEMOS is the first directory; BOSS is a subdirectory within that directory. You use backslashes to separate the directory names. You also use a backslash between the last directory name and the file name.
- ✔ No spaces, please, anywhere in a path name.
- ✔ Don't confuse the backslash (\) with the foreslash (/). Or with

backlash, which is what PC designers ought to get for forcing millions of innocent people to have to read boring technical stuff like this.

- ✔ When you combine a drive specification, a path name, and a file name, you get a *filespec*—short for *file specification*—which is a complete statement of a file's location.

Those Wacky Wild Cards

(Deal me in)

There's just one more piece of knowledge you need in order to deal with your hard disk effectively: wild cards.

In poker, you can agree to play with a wild card, so that the Joker or the deuce (2) stands for any other card. If you have three aces, for example, you would want the deuce to stand for an ace so you would have four aces—that should win it for you.

You can use *wild cards* the same way in DOS and Windows—to match characters in a file name. Doing so enables you to group files. You can type commands that say, in effect, "Show me all the files that have the extension DOC." If you type DIR *.DOC, you'll see a list something like this (assuming there are some *.DOC files in the current directory, of course):

```
LETTER1.DOC
LETTER2.DOC
LOVELTR.DOC
WILL.DOC
```

Being able to group certain files in this way is really convenient. So, wild cards are frequently used when retrieving files, copying files, moving files, and—with caution—deleting files.

You can do a lot of damage with the DOS command **DEL *.***, which says, "Delete everything in the current directory." Be careful when using wild cards with DEL. If you try using this command, DOS steps in to ask, `All files in the directory will be deleted! Are you sure (Y/N)?` If you're not sure, press N for No and press Enter.

In DOS and Windows, you can use two wild cards: ? and *. The ? matches any single character. The * matches any number of characters.

Using wild cards

- ✔ The wild card expression LETTER?.DOC groups all of the following: LETTER1.DOC, LETTER2.DOC, LETTER3.DOC, and so on, up to LETTER9.DOC. But, it won't include LETTER10.DOC in the group because the ? wild card only stands for *one* character.
- ✔ The wild card expression LET*.DOC groups all the files just mentioned—including LETTER10. That's because the * wild card stands for any number of characters.
- ✔ The wild card expression LETTER.* finds any files with the file name LETTER, no matter what extension they have. This would retrieve LETTER.DOC, LETTER.TXT, and LETTER.BAK.
- ✔ The wild card expression ???.??? finds any files with a three-letter file name and a three-letter extension (such as SIN.DOC, FUN.TXT, or TOI.JON).
- ✔ The wild card expression *.* (pronounced "star-dot-star") stands for all files.

The Horror of System Files

"You have to modify your system files," the technical support person tells you. Otherwise applications won't run, sound boards won't work, and printers go mad. What gives?

When DOS starts, it automatically checks the root directory of your hard disk for two optional files, called AUTOEXEC.BAT and CONFIG.SYS. These are short files that contain lists of commands, one on each line. These commands look like DOS commands because they *are* DOS commands. These are the commands that must be given at the beginning of every session if your computer is to work correctly.

Do you really have to modify the system files yourself? Unfortunately, you do, sometimes. You can do this using a *text editor*, a simple word processing program that doesn't do any fancy formatting. (This is good, since fancy formatting would mess up the system files so that DOS couldn't read them.) Examples of text editors are the Notebook accessory in Windows and the MS-EDIT utility provided with DOS.

You can tell when you need to make a modification to a system file—an application won't start, and you get a message such as, `To run such-and-such, your CONFIG.SYS file must contain the statement BUFFERS=15`. If you're adventurous, you can try opening CONFIG.SYS with a text editor and adding the line itself (this must be on a separate line)—but take my advice and get someone knowledgeable to help you.

Most often, though, your applications will automatically make the needed changes to your system files when you install them. Many installation utilities are so polite that they ask for permission before they do this—by all means, type **Yes**. For more information on installing programs, including dealing with system files, see Chapter 18.

TIP

A favorite game among computer hobbyists is to try to free up the maximum amount of conventional memory by making modifications to their system files. In fact, you'll see entire books on this subject in the bookstores. But there's no need to learn how to do this. DOS 6.0 and 6.2 come with a memory management program called MEMMAKER that maximizes memory automatically.

Where Do I Go From Here?

If you're going to use DOS and run DOS programs, flip to the next chapter, which contains the basic stuff you need to know to use DOS on a day-to-day basis.

If you're going to run Windows and use Windows programs, count your blessings, skip the next chapter and go on to Chapter 16. This gives you the stuff you need to know to use Windows on a day-to-day basis.

TRASH

Top Ten
Ways to Make DOS More Fun

10. Create secret codes to disguise tasteless jokes in file names

9. Use UNDELETE to see if there are any files someone thought they'd better get rid of

8. Figure out ways to use keyboard to make sideways funny faces, like :) (happy), :((sad), ;-() (wink and grin)

7. Search entire disk automatically to find files containing naughty words

6. Set DOS manuals and disks on fence for target practice with .45 sidearm

5. Have contest at office for the Most Destructive DOS Command

4. Find out how much abuse a disk can take before DOS finally can't read it anymore

3. Redefine DOS prompt so that it says, `What is thy bidding?` instead of `C:\>`

2. See if you can think of even more ambiguous wordings for DOS error messages, such as `warning, this is` *`hard`*

1. Start three-hour disk fragmentation process just before appointment with boss, in case she asks you to get something done "right away"

CHAPTER 15

All You Really Need To Know About DOS (You Learned at the C:\> Prompt)

IN A NUTSHELL

- What a command-line interface is
- The lowdown on typing DOS commands
- How to change drives
- How to tell which version of DOS you're using
- How to clear the screen
- How to look at the contents of a file
- How to create directories
- How to delete files
- How to "undelete" files you shouldn't have deleted
- How to copy, move, and rename files
- How to find a missing file

This chapter is for anyone who's using DOS. (Turn to the next chapter if Windows starts automatically when you switch on your computer.)

Why would you or anyone else use DOS? The major reason is not because you want to run DOS applications. That's not a good reason to learn all this stuff. You can run DOS applications from within Windows.

Some people run DOS because they actually like it better than Windows. They think it's faster. Plus, knowing all that technical stuff (like the difference between an *argument* and a *parameter*) gives them a charge. Big deal.

The only really good reason for running DOS, in my humble opinion, is that you *can't* run Windows because (a) You don't have Windows yet; (b) Your computer can't run Windows because it's an ancient old thing that probably belongs in a museum; (c) You have a good computer (i.e., a 386 or better), but you don't have enough memory to run Windows; or (d) You want to run a DOS program at full speed instead of the molasses-like way it runs under Windows.

All of these reasons could be remedied by spending some money, but not everyone has money to spend on computer junk. So, if you're stuck with DOS, read on. In this chapter, you learn basic DOS file maintenance—looking at files, copying files, moving files, and deleting files. Anytime you have a question about how DOS handles any of this file maintenance stuff, just refer to this chapter.

What Is a "Command-Line Operating System?"

It's an old-fashioned operating system, dating back to the days (not long ago) when memory was scarce. To give *commands* to the computer, you have to type a *line* of weird stuff (like **copy c:\docs\mystory.doc a:\mystory.bak**) and press Enter. DOS, heaven help us, is a command-line operating system.

CHAPTER 15

ALL YOU REALLY NEED TO KNOW ABOUT DOS

Basic facts about DOS

- ✔ DOS has had lots of revisions since its first appearance in 1982. The latest version at this writing is 6.2. But, almost everything in this chapter applies to every version of DOS since 4.0.

- ✔ To find out which version of DOS you're using, type **VER** at the DOS prompt and press Enter.

- ✔ You have to type a DOS command exactly right—everything must be in the correct order, and where there are supposed to be spaces, there must be spaces. Microsoft calls this *syntax*. Most people call it a *pain*.

- ✔ As you're typing the command, you can press Backspace to rub out a mistake.

- ✔ It doesn't matter whether you type uppercase or lowercase. It's all the same to DOS.

- ✔ When you're finished typing the command, press Enter to confirm it and initiate the action you've requested.

- ✔ If DOS can't understand what you've typed, you get an error message—which you probably won't be able to decipher. For quick help, flip to "12 Most Common DOS Error Messages," in the Quick and Dirty Dozens section.

- ✔ The most frequently-used DOS commands are *resident*, which means that they're in your computer's memory (RAM), and *available at all times*. But, less-frequently used commands (such as DISKCOPY or FORMAT) are actually utility programs that are kept on disk. If you try to use one of these commands and see the message `Bad command or file name`, you have to switch to the DOS directory in order to use these commands.

Changing Drives

Only one drive can be current (*active*) at a time. When a disk drive is *current*, DOS assumes that this is the drive you want to work with. For example, if you type **DIR** while drive C is current, DOS lists for you all the files and directories on drive C. If you want to look at something on another drive, you need to make *that* drive current.

How Do I Access The Disk In My Floppy Drive?

To make a floppy drive current, insert a disk into the drive. Then just type the drive letter, type a colon, and press Enter. To make drive A current, for example, type **A:** and press Enter. The prompt then shows the current drive:

```
A:\>
```

To get back to drive C, you type **C:** and press Enter.

I Can't Access This Drive!

When you activate drive A, you may see the following message:

```
Not ready reading drive A
Abort, Retry, Fail?
```

What's wrong? There's no disk in the drive, or the drive door isn't latched. DOS cannot look at floppy drives unless there's a disk in them. Insert a disk into the drive, close the latch (if the drive has a latch), and press **R** to retry the command.

I've Had a General Failure!

You also might see this cheerful message:

```
General failure reading drive A
Abort, Retry, Fail?
```

This means that the disk is not formatted, or you've put a high-density disk in a drive that can only handle low-density disks. The mystery of formatting is revealed in Chapter 6. For now, press A to abort the command. Insert a formatted (or, if necessary, a low-density) disk into the drive, and try again.

Changing Directories

The previous chapter made the compelling point that only one directory can be current at a time. If you want to do something (like erase a file) that's in a directory other than the one that's current, you need to change directories. Fortunately, there's a command you can type to do just that: **CD** (you can also type **CHDIR**).

To change to a directory, just type **CD** and a space, followed by the directory name. For instance, to change to C:\WP51 from C:\, type **CD WP51** and press Enter.

TIP

If you see the `Invalid directory` message, check your typing. You probably forgot the space after CD or mistyped the directory or path name.

To change to a subdirectory of the current directory, just type the directory name without the backslash. For example, to change to C:\WP51\POEMS\CATTLE from the C:\WP51\POEMS directory, just type **CD CATTLE** and press Enter.

To get back to the parent directory, type **CD..** and press Enter. Those two little dots, incidentally, stand for the parent directory. That's why there are two dots. One stands for Momma, and the other stands for Papa.

To change to the root directory, type **CD** and press Enter.

TIP

You can't use CD to change to a directory on another drive. You must change drives first.

Clearing the Screen of Inflammatory or Embarrassing Messages

Sometimes you'll try the same command over and over, and the results of your efforts (such as `Bad command or file name`) will be clearly displayed on-screen for everyone to see. To erase any embarrassing on-screen back talk, type **CLS** and press Enter.

Peeking at a File's Contents

When hunting for a file, you may not be able to tell by the cryptic name whether you've got the file you want. The TYPE command lets you take a little peek at the file's contents.

To peek at a file's contents, type **TYPE,** followed by a space and the name of the file. For example, to peek at the POEM1.DOC document, type **TYPE POEM1.DOC** and press Enter.

Things to remember about the TYPE command (DOS)

- ✔ If you created the file by using an application program, such as WordPerfect or Lotus 1-2-3, don't count on seeing your document the way it last looked on-screen. DOS can display only *text.* It can't display formatting changes such as bold, italic, and so on. If you open such a file with DOS by accident, you may see lots of ridiculous-looking symbols, such as happy faces, staves, knives, Greek symbols, and card suits (clubs, hearts, and so on). You're looking into the internal world of computer information, a world of happy warriors and gamblers who speak Greek. The file might contain enough recognizable text—if you're lucky—for you to tell whether you've indeed found the document that you want.

- ✔ If the file doesn't exist in the current directory, you see the `File not found` message. Remember that the file might exist in *another* directory. You can change directories and try again, or type the path name, as explained in the next section.

- ✔ If you hear a beep when DOS displays the file, the file contains funny computer stuff in addition to text. Don't worry; you haven't hurt the file or your computer. To stop the display, hold down the Ctrl key and press Break. (Break is also labeled *Pause*.)

More Rather Painful Information about Path Names

Path names were introduced in the previous chapter. With DOS, you have to type them, which can be a real hassle. A lot can go wrong.

Here's an example. Suppose the current directory is \NOVELS, and you want to peek at a file called POEM1.DOC that's in the directory, on the same drive, called \POEMS. You type the following:

```
TYPE \POEMS\POEM1.DOC
```

Note that there's a space after TYPE, but no other spaces. There's a backslash before and after the directory name (POEMS). Leave any of this stuff out, and you get an error message.

If the file is on another disk, you need to add drive names to the file name, as in this example:

```
TYPE A:\OLDJUNK\VAPID.DOC
```

This command tells DOS, "Let me peek at the file called VAPID.DOC that's in the directory called OLDJUNK, which you'll find on the disk in drive A."

Making Directories

With all this talk of directories, you're probably wondering how they're created. To create a directory, change to the directory where you want the new directory to be housed. For example, to create a subdirectory called PIGEONS within the POEMS directory, you change to the POEMS directory.

To create the PIGEONS subdirectory, type **MD PIGEONS** and press Enter. Note that there's a space between MD and the directory name.

TIP

To remember the command to use (MD), think of *Make Directory.*

Things to remember about making directories with DOS

- ✔ You also can type **MKDIR**, instead of just **MD**, if typing unnecessary characters at the DOS prompt really turns you on.
- ✔ If you see the message `Bad command or file name`, check your typing. You probably forgot the space after MD.
- ✔ Directory names obey the same structure as DOS file names: 8-character first name, period, 3-character last name *(extension)*. Extensions are optional. I wouldn't recommend adding extensions to directory names; it makes path names even more laborious to type. Also, when you use DIR, you'll have a tougher time telling the difference between files and directories.

Deleting a File

Disks fill up all too quickly. When you're sure you no longer need an old file that contains one of your documents, delete it. (Then, according to Murphy's Law, you will immediately and desperately need that file.)

Don't delete any files associated with a program, even ones that *look like* they're not all that special. Appearances can be deceiving. Many programs won't run unless dozens, or even hundreds, of innocent-looking, but vital, files are present.

TIP

If you're unsure whether you'll need a file, copy it to a floppy disk. Then delete the file from the hard disk. (The corollary to the previous Murphy's Law states that making a backup of files assures that the files will never again be needed.)

To delete a file, you change to the directory that contains the file, and then use the **DEL** command. Type the command, a space, and then the file name. Then press Enter. To delete the STICKIT.DOC file from the current directory, for example, you type **DEL STICKIT.DOC** and press Enter.

Things to remember about deleting files

- ✔ If the file isn't in the current drive or directory, you have to add the drive and path information so that you've typed a complete filespec—for instance:

```
DEL A:\MEMOS\STICKIT.DOC
```

- ✔ When you use DEL, it does its thing without giving you any confirmation, which is a little disturbing. You'd think you'd see a message such as `Uh-oh. You just deleted a file. I hope you were sure that you didn't need it.` But there's nothing. Zip. The file's gone, and that's that.

- ✔ If you would like a second chance to think through the deletion, use the /p switch, like this:

```
DEL STICKIT.DOC /p
```

continues

Things to remember about deleting files, continued

The /p switch with the DEL command turns on an option that tells DOS to ask you to confirm that you want to delete a file. When you see the message, `Delete (Y/N)?`, press Y to confirm the deletion, or N to forget the whole thing and leave the file undisturbed. (The /p switch only works with DOS 6.0 and higher.)

BUZZWORDS

SWITCH

In DOS, a *switch* is an option that you add to a command by typing a space and a slash mark (/), followed by a letter, such as /p.

Deleting a Group of Files

You can use the DOS wild cards to delete more than one file at a time. (If you're wild about learning more, flip back to Chapter 14.) Use caution when you use wild cards with DEL, however. This command can really wipe out a lot of files, and if you haven't thought through what you're doing, you could lose a lot of your data! Here are some examples:

Command	What the Command Does
DEL *.YOU	This command deletes every file that has the extension YOU, such as LOVE.YOU, HATE.YOU, and DANG.YOU. As you can imagine, a command like this one can cause a lot of grief. What if one of those DOC files contains the Great American Novel?
DEL POEM.*	This command deletes any file named POEM, no matter what the extension. (POEM.DOC, POEM.TXT, and POEM.BAD will all fall prey.)

Command	What the Command Does
DEL *.*	This command deletes all files in the current directory.

If you type **DEL *.***, you're doing something pretty drastic: deleting all the files in the current directory. After you press Enter, you see a message asking you to confirm the deletion. Press Y to proceed or N to cancel the command, and press Enter. Be careful!

Recovering from an Accidental Deletion

(Get help fast!)

Sooner or later, you will accidentally delete a very, very precious file—one that would take hours, days, or even weeks of work to re-create. You will regret ever having used the computer. Chin up. You may be able to recover the deleted files. All that DOS has really erased is the first letter of the file name. As long as the space the file occupies hasn't been used for something else, you can recover the file. The key lies in the UNDELETE command.

There's one catch to the happy news about UNDELETE: you must be using Version 5 of DOS, or later.

To undelete a file, type **UNDELETE**, a space, and then the file name you want to undelete. For example, to undelete PRECIOUS.DOC, type **UNDELETE PRECIOUS.DOC** and press Enter.

You'll see a file name like this:

```
?RECIOUS.DOC
```

DOS then prompts you, `Undelete (Y/N)?` Press Y. Then type the first character of the file name, which DOS has managed to lose. (Everything else in the file should be OK.)

If DOS can undelete the file, you see the message `File successfully undeleted`. If DOS can't undelete the file, you see a message such as `The data contained in the first cluster of this directory has been overwritten or corrupted.`

Things to remember about undeleting files

- ✔ Undelete the file right away. If you delay, DOS may overwrite the file with new data, and then it's gone for good.
- ✔ If you can't remember the name of the file, type **UNDELETE** and press Enter. DOS will go through each file that has been deleted. Press N until the file you want to undelete is listed. Then press Y. You are prompted for the first character of the file name. Type it, and the file is undeleted.

Making a Copy of a File

Copying comes in handy when you want to give a file to someone else, or when you want to keep an extra copy for yourself. It's easy to copy a file. Suppose that you want to make a copy of the first chapter of your path-breaking first novel, NOVEL01.DOC. You type the following:

```
COPY NOVEL01.DOC NOVEL01.BAK
```

This command creates a copy of the file NOVEL01.DOC and names it NOVEL01.BAK. The copy of the file is located within the same directory as the original. The next section tells you how to copy the file to a different directory or drive.

Things to remember about copying files

- ✔ You list two file names when you use the COPY command. The first file is the *source file*—the one you're copying from. The second file is the *copy* (also called the *destination*, just to make things a little more obscure).

- ✔ There's a space after COPY, and after the first file name. Nowhere else.
- ✔ When you name the copy, you must follow DOS regulations about valid file names. (Chapter 14 explains all the DOS rules for naming files.)
- ✔ If you don't include drive or path information in the filespecs, DOS makes the copy in the same directory.
- ✔ If you do include the drive and path information and you are copying to another directory, you don't have to type the file name. DOS will use the same file name.
- ✔ When DOS finishes copying the file, you see a message, such as: `1 file(s) copied.`

Copying a File to a Different Drive or Directory

Most of the time, people copy files to a different disk drive. Why? Two words: backup security. If a disk goes bad, you lose all the files on it, including copies you've made to the same disk. It's a good idea to make lots of copies of very important files. Place them on two or three floppy disks that you keep in separate places. That way, when your 72-oz. Big Gulp of Coke gushes out over your desk, there's a chance that at least one copy will escape the flood.

To copy a file to another drive or directory, include filespec information in the destination file name, as in this example:

```
COPY NOVEL01.DOC A:NOVEL01.BAK
```

This command tells DOS, "Make a copy of the file NOVEL01.DOC, name the copy NOVEL01.BAK, and store it on the disk in drive A."

Even more things to remember about copying files

- ✔ When you copy a file to a different drive or directory, you can use the same file name. However, it's a good idea to use a different name so that you don't lose track of which is the original and which is the copy.

- ✔ To copy a file that isn't in the current directory or on the same drive, include the filespec stuff, as in this example:

```
COPY C:\DOCS\NOVEL01.DOC A:NOVEL01.BAK
```

This command tells DOS to go to the directory called C:\DOCS and copy the file NOVEL01.DOC to the disk in drive A.

Copying a Group of Files

You can use DOS wild cards to copy a group of files. To copy all the files in the C:\DOCS directory to drive A, type **COPY C:\DOCS*.* A:** and press Enter.

To copy only the files with the name NOVEL01 (NOVEL01.DOC, NOVEL01.BAK, NOVEL01.BAD) to drive A, type **COPY NOVEL01.* A:** and press Enter.

To copy all the files with the extension YOU (including LOVE.YOU, HATE.YOU, and DANG.YOU) to drive A:, type **COPY *.YOU A:** and press Enter.

Moving Files

Sometimes it's nice to *move* files—change their current residence from one disk or directory to another.

If you have DOS 6.0 or 6.2, you can move files with the neat new MOVE command. To move JUNK.DOC to drive A, for example, type **MOVE JUNK.DOC A:** and press Enter.

Older versions of DOS don't have a MOVE command that lets you move files in one step. However, you can move files by copying them to the new location and then deleting them from the old location. Here's how you would move all the *.DOC files in a directory to a floppy disk:

1. Type **COPY *.DOC A:**.

   This command makes a copy of all the DOC files and puts the copy on the disk in the A drive.

2. Type **DELETE *.DOC**.

   This command deletes the DOC files from the current directory.

Before you delete the files from the old location, check the new location to make sure that all the files were copied!

Renaming Files

After you get used to the 8-character limit on file names, you may decide to rename some files. LETTER, MEMO, and REPORT aren't going to cut it when you have several hundred letters, memos, and reports. To rename files, DOS provides the appropriately named RENAME command. The following command renames JUNK.DOC with the new name PRECIOUS.DOC:

```
REN JUNK.DOC PRECIOUS.DOC
```

Things to remember about moving files

✔ Note that the old name comes first, followed by the new name, with a space between the two names.

continues

Things to remember about moving files, continued

- ✔ For those who prefer to use full names instead of nicknames, you can type **RENAME** instead of **REN**.
- ✔ REN isn't a way of getting around DOS's file name restrictions. The new name must also obey the rules.

The Quest for the Missing File

Sooner or later, you'll exclaim, "Heck! I can't find my file! It was there yesterday!" Don't panic—yet. Chances are, the file *is* on the disk. Somewhere. You probably saved it to a different directory.

Try the following extremely clever DOS command, which tries to find files by matching the name you specify. The location of the file doesn't matter. If it's on the disk, this command will find it.

Let's assume you're looking for JUNK.DOC. To search your entire C drive for any copies of JUNK.DOC, type **DIR C:\JUNK.DOC /s /b** and press Enter. DOS then lists each occurrence of the file, indicating the directory in which it was found.

TIP

Put those wild cards to work. DIR C:*.DOC /s /b will list all files with the extension DOC, wherever they might be found. DIR C:\JUNK.* /s /b will list all the JUNK files, no matter what extension you used.

Copying a Whole Disk

If you want to make an exact copy of an entire floppy disk, there's a command that's designed to do just that: DISKCOPY. It's not a resident command, though. If you get the message `Bad command or file name` after trying DISKCOPY, type **CD \DOS**, press Enter, and type DISKCOPY again. That should do the trick.

To copy a disk with DISKCOPY, make sure you know which disk you're copying *from* (the *source* disk), and the blank (but formatted) disk you're copying *to* (the *target* disk). Insert the source disk in drive A, the destination in drive B, and type **DISKCOPY A: B:** (this means "copy disk A to disk B"). This only works if both drives are the same type. More commonly, you'll have just one floppy disk drive—but don't worry, you can still copy disks, as the next section explains.

I Only Have One Drive!

OK, no problem. Put the source disk in drive A, and type **DISKCOPY A: A:**. This tells DOS to make a copy of a disk using just one disk drive, which involves swapping the source and destination disks in and out of the drive. DOS will tell you when to swap disks. (By the way, if this seems to take forever, upgrade to DOS 6.2. DOS 6.2 stores the source disk data on drive C so that you don't have to swap disks in and out all day.)

It Says "Write Protect Error!"

If you see this message, it means that the target disk is write-protected (see Chapter 6 for more information on *write protection*, which prevents the computer from erasing any existing information on the disk or writing new information to it). Are you really sure you want to erase all the data on this disk? That's what's going to happen. Rather than guessing, get a different disk. If you're absolutely sure there's nothing on this disk you want to keep, tear off the aluminum write-protect tape (on 5.25-inch disks), or flip the disk over and move the write-protect tab so that it covers the hole (on 3.5-inch disks).

My File! My File! It's Gone! (Sob!)

Don't panic (yet). Suppose the file GRTNOVEL.DOC cannot be found in the usual locations on your hard disk. Try these diabolically clever commands:

```
CD\
DIR GRTNOVEL.* /s /b
```

and press Enter. This is real DOS, heavy stuff; it switches to the root directory and then searches the *entire disk*, including all subdirectories, for files that match this pattern (including backup files). Probably, you'll find that the missing file was accidentally saved to the wrong directory.

Learning More About DOS

(At your own risk)

You can do lots more with DOS 6 or 6.2, which includes some great system utilities (disk compression, backup, and antivirus, to name a few). For more information on these, check out this book's companion volume, *I Hate DOS*, by yours truly.

TIP

Can't get to the bookstore? Get help at the DOS prompt by typing **HELP** followed by the name of the command you're having trouble with (for help on DISKCOPY, for instance, type **HELP DISKCOPY** and press Enter). You'll see lots of information about this command. It's fairly technical, but you should be able to glean the information you want from all the verbiage. To exit DOS HELP, press Alt+F,X.

THIS BEEPING PILE
OF PLASTIC JUST
AIN'T A TYPEWRITER.

Top Ten

Destructive Acts Committed after Unrecoverable File Loss (followed by estimated average repair costs)

10. Revolver emptied into computer screen ($409, not including $175 fine and 30 days for possession of unregistered firearm).

9. Attempted to connect computer to high-voltage circuit to "zap its brains out" ($1,487, not including loss of building due to fire).

8. Computer system unit struck repeatedly with baseball bat ($1,219, plus $16 for a new bat)

7. Computer system unit thrown through plate glass window ($2,676).

6. Local self-styled "DOS expert" thrown through plate glass window ($2.8 million, assuming out-of-court settlement).

5. Foreign object thrust into floppy disk drive (dry object, $95; food or other moist objects, $387; explosives, $1,653).

4. Attempted to immerse computer's chips in Drano to "teach them a lesson" ($211, not including charge for emergency room care).

3. Fist through monitor ($13,421, including average medical care and disability).

2. Disk torn to pieces with bare hands and teeth ($0.62/disk, $1,288 for oral surgery).

1. Mouse thrown to ground and cruelly stomped to death ($72).

CHAPTER 16

Picture Yourself in a World Full of Icons (Managing Files with File Manager)

IN A NUTSHELL

- How to start File Manager
- How to view files and directories
- Ways to select files
- Getting rid of files
- How to copy and move files
- How to rename files
- Steps for finding a missing file
- Using File Manager to run programs
- Undeleting a file…Yes! You can!
- How to create a directory
- How to remove a directory
- How to exit File Manager with a minimum amount of frustration and anguish

YOU COULD POUND THE KEYS HARDER WHEN YOU WERE MAD...
@★!#

You've already met Windows; Chapter 4 helped you get going if Program Manager showed its face when you turned on your computer. Program Manager helps you launch—yes, you guessed it—programs, except that they're called *applications* in the Windows world. This chapter deals with another face of Windows, the *File Manager*. The File Manager helps you manage—yes! Files!

File Manager is one of Windows' most important utility programs; it helps you do all that DOS stuff—like copying and deleting files—without those horrible DOS commands, which were examined in the previous chapter. True, some people prefer managing files with DOS, particularly if they've already spent ten years doing it that way. (You can tell who these people are because they tend to talk to themselves in computer languages.) If you're just getting started with your computer and Windows, though, don't listen to these people. The File Manager gives you quick, easy, and comprehensible ways to deal with file management tasks. Hey, it isn't as much fun as watching Jay Leno, but it gets the job done.

Why You Can't Completely Ignore DOS Yet

Because Windows is based on DOS, you still need to understand basic DOS concepts, like all that vexing "directory" business. (Flip to Chapter 14 for an explanation of crucial concepts like files and directories.)

Why? It's because Windows isn't really an operating system. It's actually a kind of glorified DOS application. Underneath Windows, DOS lurks. Occasionally it roars out at you and reminds you of its existence—for example, when you want to name or retrieve a file.

Taking a Look at File Manager

(Warm up your mouse)

To start File Manager, you begin in Program Manager (see Chapter 4). Open the Main program group, and double-click on the File Manager icon. (This icon looks like a two-drawer file unit, and is helpfully labeled File Manager.)

PICTURE YOURSELF IN A WORLD FULL OF ICONS

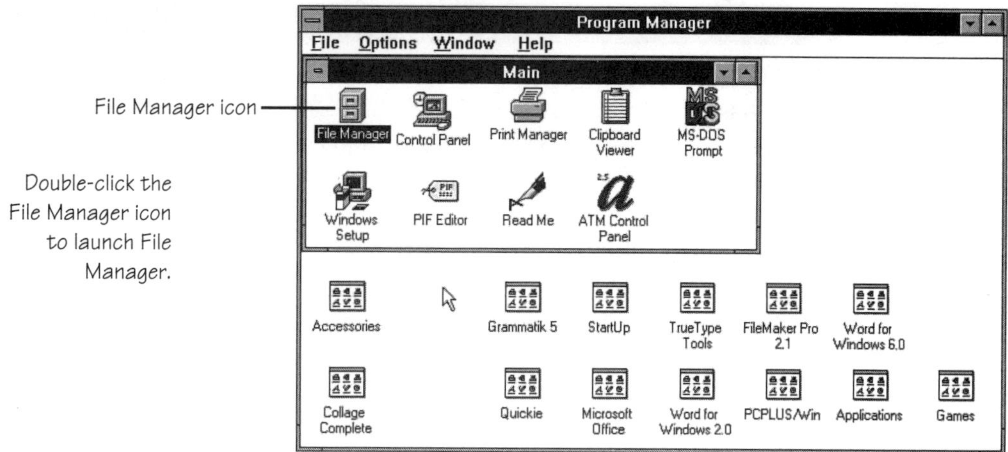

Double-click the File Manager icon to launch File Manager.

After a good deal of disk-access business, you see File Manager on-screen. File Manager uses graphics to let you see what's on your disk. Take a look, for example, at the graphic rendition of the directory tree.

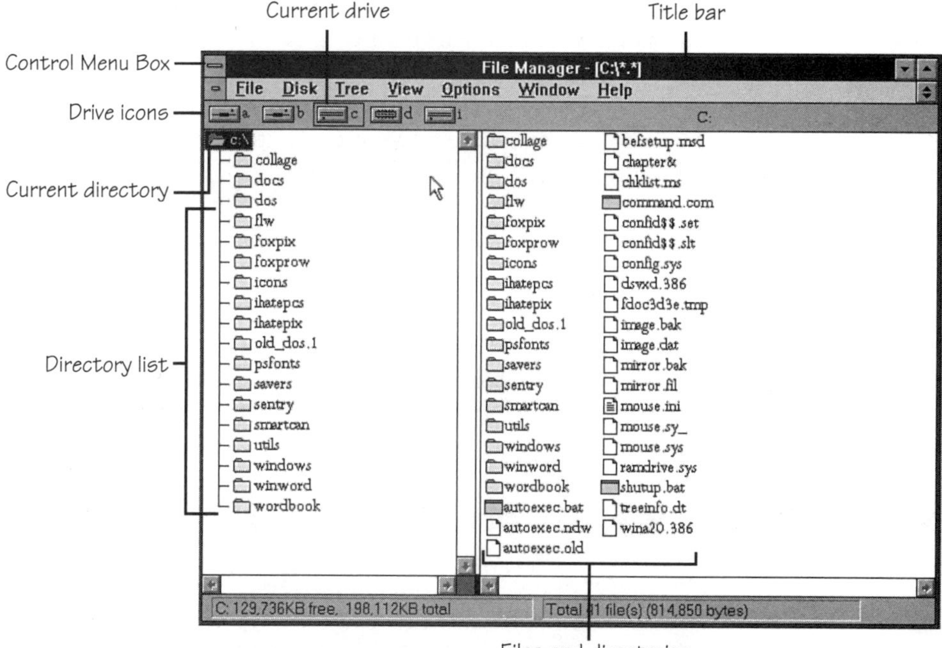

File Manager (Windows) basics

- ✔ File Manager is a typical Windows application, which means that it has all the usual windows stuff: the Control menu box, the title bar, the menu bar, the scroll bars, and all the rest. Chapter 4 introduces these features.
- ✔ You might find the window easier to read if you *maximize* it, if it isn't already. To do so, click on the Maximize button in the upper right corner of the File Manager window. This maximizes the File Manager window, but not the drive window (the one that shows the files on the currently-selected drive). To see more of this window, maximize it too.
- ✔ The title bar lists the name of the current directory (probably `C:\`, the root directory). If someone previously used File Manager, you see the directory that was last displayed.
- ✔ When the Drive window is maximized, there's one title bar. When the Drive window is not maximized, you can move and resize it. This window will have its own title bar.
- ✔ Below the menu bar are the drive icons, which tell you the disk drives that are available on your computer. The current drive is highlighted with a little box around it.
- ✔ The Drive window has two parts. The left part, called the *Directory Tree window*, shows the names of all the directories on your hard disk. Each directory is symbolized by a folder. (The open folder is the current directory.) The right part, the *Files list*, lists the files and directories that are contained in the current directory.

Displaying the Files Stored on a Floppy Disk

To display files that are stored on a floppy disk, insert a disk into the drive, point to the A or B drive icons at the top of screen, then click the left mouse button. Or, hold down the Ctrl key, press A (for drive A) or B (for drive B), and release both keys. File Manager displays the files which are on the drive that you indicate. You can then do things to these files—copy, move, delete, cut, clip, or curl.

Change back to drive C by clicking on [C:] or pressing Ctrl+C.

It Says Error Selecting Drive!

If you didn't put a disk into the drive, there is a very long interval in which absolutely nothing happens. Finally, you get a stern alert box with a big exclamation point, which seems to say "Achtung!" This subtle reminder indicates that you forgot to put a disk into the drive. Put a disk into the drive and press Enter. The box disappears and the correct drive information appears on-screen.

TIP

> If you remove a disk from one of the floppy disk drives and insert another disk, File Manager doesn't automatically update the Directory Tree or Files List for that drive. To refresh the list, press F5.

Displaying Directories

(The directory in the directory in the directory)

Think of directories as folders. You can store folders inside folders inside folders, and so on. You can't see any folders that are hiding inside other folders unless they've been opened to reveal their hidden contents.

Dancing through directories with File Manager

- ✔ To see the directories within a directory, double-click on the directory folder. The listing opens (*expands*, in Windows talk) to show the next level of directories. The icon is now an open folder.
- ✔ If you don't see any directories at all besides the root directory icon, double-click the root directory icon. The directories should

continues

Dancing through directories with File Manager, continued

then appear. If not, someone has reformatted your hard disk. I recommend a brief plea for a six-figure monetary compensation, followed by threats of violence against their favorite stuffed animal.

- ✔ To hide nested directories in the directory window (called *collapsing a directory*), double-click on an open folder icon; the folder now becomes closed and the directories within the directories do a disappearing act.
- ✔ How do you know whether a closed directory icon contains subdirectories? Here's how you can tell. Open the Tree menu, and see whether there's a check mark besides the Indicate Expandable Branches option. If so, just click back in the File Manager window to close the menu. If not, click this option. Now look at the folder icons. The ones that have hidden subdirectories have little plus signs.

Displaying Files

(What's in this folder?)

The Files list always displays the files that are in the current directory—the one with the open folder. But suppose that you want to display files in another directory. No problem. Just click on the directory folder.

Managing files with File Manager

- ✔ To see the files in a directory, just click on the directory's folder. Fwoosh! The file names appear. This is so fun, you'll probably want to click on several other directory folders to see this file fwooshing.
- ✔ If the list of directories in the Directory Tree window is so long that you don't see the directory you want, click on the little down arrow on the right border of the Directory Tree panel. (If you go too far down the list, click on the little up arrow.)
- ✔ If you don't see the directory that you want, don't despair. The directory might be hidden within another directory. You need to expand the listing; the preceding section tells you how to perform this mystical task.

There's Too Many Files! I Can't Find My Novel!

By default, File Manager displays all the files in a directory. But, you don't really need to see all of them. So, here's a neat trick. To restrict the display of files to just your documents and applications, open the View menu and choose By File Type. In the By File Type dialog box, deselect the Other Files and Directories options so that the "X" mark disappears next to these options.

Where's That File I Saved Yesterday?

This might be the beginning of a much more serious problem—The Tragedy of the Lost File. But, before saying good-bye to the file forever, try this: open the View menu, and choose Sort by Date. This puts the files in reverse chronological order, which is an extremely fancy way of saying that the most recent files are at the top of the list. Has a nice ring to it, doesn't it?

Try the other options—Sort by Type (documents and applications are distinguished), and Sort by Size (the jumbo files come first). Who knows, these might come in handy for something besides exercising your mouse. Suppose, for example, you're looking for a really, really BIG file that you've created. If you choose Sort by Size, you'll find it at or near the top of the files list.

I Want MORE Information!

Miss those cool DIR displays in DOS, which show all kinds of information about the file—the size, the date of creation, etc.? Well, File Manager can do that, too. Open the View menu, and choose All File Details to see everything that DOS knows about your files. If that's too much, open the View menu again, choose Partial Details, and click away at the boxes until there's an "X" beside only those details you want thrown in your face. Personally, I like to choose Size and Last Modification Date. It makes me think that, if I have made lots of big files and modified them recently, I may actually meet my publication deadline.

I Want My Pretty Fonts!

After all, this is Windows, isn't it? Well, if you'd really like to see your file names in Desdemona Pathetique 14 Script, you can. Open the **O**ptions menu and choose **F**ont. In the Font dialog box, you can choose the font and font size you want File Manager to use when it displays file and directory names. Click OK when you've made your choice.

Using File Manager's Windows

You probably already knew that every Windows application lives in its own window. But, did you know that it also has *application windows* within its workspace? You can do some pretty neat things with File Manager's application windows.

The following trick comes in handy when you're copying files between your hard disk and your floppy disk drive. Try it.

Put a disk in your floppy disk drive. Then, click open the **W**indow menu in File Manager. Choose the **N**ew Window option. You'll see a new window of the same drive (the hard drive). In the new window, click the drive icon for the floppy drive you put the disk in (A or B). This shows the files that are on your floppy disk.

The problem here is that the new window is covering the window that shows your hard disk files. But, help is on the way. Click open the **W**indow menu again, and choose **T**ile. File Manager automatically sizes the two windows so that they each take up exactly half the screen. Is this cool, or what? You'll find this really helpful when you're copying files from one disk to another.

Selecting Files

To do something to a file, you first select the file in the Files list. A selected file appears in a different color (if you are lucky enough to have a color monitor) or in reverse video (black-on-white becomes white-on-black, and vice versa). You can select more than one file, which lets you do things to lots of files at once. After you've selected one or more files, they're sitting ducks, just waiting for the things you want to do to them—like copy them, move them, or wipe them out.

Basics of selecting files with File Manager

- ✔ To select a file by using the mouse, click on the file. When the file's highlighted, that means it's selected.
- ✔ To select a group of files in a row, click on the first file. Then press and hold down the Shift key and click on the last file. All the files in between are selected.
- ✔ To select files that are not in a row, click on the first file you want to select. Then press and hold down the Ctrl key and click on the second file. Do this until you select all the files you want.
- ✔ To select all files, choose File in the menu bar; then choose Select Files. When the Select Files dialog box appears, choose Select, and then choose Close.
- ✔ To deselect a file, click on another file. To deselect all files, open the File menu; then choose Select Files. When the Select Files dialog box appears, choose Deselect. Then choose Close.

Deleting Files

After you have selected one or more files, it's easy to do things to them, like deleting, copying, tickling, drowning, or moving them. (Note, however, that the subjects of tickling and drowning files is beyond the scope of this book.) In this section, you learn how to delete files that you no longer need. (Of course, you will inevitably need them once you delete them, but that's beside the point.) Here's how:

1. Select the file or files that you want to delete.

2. Press Del. You see a Delete dialog box. The computer suspects that you are about to do something foolish, and wants confirmation before proceeding with this rash act.

3. If you're really serious about continuing, click on OK or just press Enter. If not, just click on Cancel or press Esc.

If you selected more than one file, you see a Confirm File Delete dialog box for each file. Choose **Y**es to delete the file, Yes to **A**ll to delete all the files, **N**o to skip this file and continue, or Cancel to give up the whole idea.

TIP

> If you deleted the wrong file, use Undelete immediately, as described in the section "Undeleting Files," later in this chapter.

Copying and Moving Files

You copy files with the mouse by doing something called *drag and drop*, which is what the cat does when it carts in those dead things. (Don't get mad, they're a present.)

To drag and drop, here's what you do. Move the pointer to the file you want to move. Then hold down the left mouse button and, while you're still holding down the button, move the mouse across the surface of the desk. That's dragging. Then let go of the mouse button. That's dropping.

Copying Files by Using the Mouse

This is how you use drag and drop to copy files:

1. Select one or more files in the Files List window.

2. Move the mouse pointer to the selected file's name (or names).

To copy the files to another drive, drag them to the drive icon [A:] or [B:]. To copy the files to another directory, hold down the Ctrl key and drag the files to that directory. You must hold down the Ctrl key. Otherwise, File Manager thinks that you want to move the files.

3. When you reach the drive or directory that you want to copy the files to, let go of the mouse button.

   After you release the mouse button, you see a Confirm Mouse Operation dialog box. The computer demands to know whether or not you're really serious.

4. If so, click on **Y**es or press Enter. If not, click on **N**o. If you're thinking, "Maybe," you'll have to just sit there, because there is no Maybe button.

Moving Files by Using the Mouse

To move files by using drag and drop, you use nearly the same set of steps, with one small twist: You hold down the Alt key while you're dragging.

1. Select one or more files in the Files List window.

2. Move the pointer to the selected file's name (or names). Press and hold down Alt, click and hold down the mouse button, and then drag to the drive icon that you want to move the files to (for example, [A:] or [B:]). You can also drag to another directory in the Directory Tree window.

3. When you reach the drive or directory to which you want to move the files, release the mouse button and the Alt key.

   After you let go of the mouse button, you see a Confirm Mouse Operation dialog box. The computer demands to know whether or not you're really serious.

4. If so, click on **Y**es. If not, click on **N**o. If you're thinking, "Maybe," throw the mouse to the ground and smash it to bits with your feet.

Duplicate File Name? Huh?

If a file with the same name is in the disk or directory to which you're copying or moving the file, you see a warning box that asks you for confirmation. Unless you're sure that you know what you're doing, press Esc or click on **N**o to cancel the operation. Why? Sometimes people accidentally give two different files the same name. If you proceed, you might overwrite a file that contains different data. If you do that, not even Undelete can get it back for you.

Renaming Files

If you don't pay close attention to file names, you may end up with file names such as UBORJXC.DOC, GRFDRG.SUK, or FMBDBBB.SIP. Pretty soon—when you're frantically searching for that letter that proves you wrote to the IRS when you said you did—you'll realize that this isn't the best naming scheme. Fortunately, you aren't stuck with the file name you chose when you named the file; you can rename it. Here's how:

1. In the File List window, select the file you want to rename.

2. From the **F**ile menu, choose Re**n**ame. You see the Rename dialog box.

3. Type the new name in the **T**o box, and then press Enter (or click on OK) to confirm your choice.

Finding a Missing File

Sooner or later, you yourself will say: "Heck! My file's gone! Oh, Darn!" (The language has been cleaned up so that we adults can imagine we are keeping younger readers in a prolonged state of naiveté—which they aren't, but what the h***. Don't ask *me* where they learned *that* language.)

Chances are, the file isn't really gone. It was probably saved to some weird directory. (This is pretty easy to do. I have a directory called C:\WEIRD for precisely this purpose.) With File Manager, you can search your whole hard disk to find the file, and in all probability, it will turn up—provided your luck is good that day.

Here's how to search your whole hard disk to find a missing file:

1. From the **F**ile menu, choose Searc**h**. You see the Search dialog box.

2. In the **S**earch For text box, type the name of the file you're trying to find. If you're trying to find JUNK.DOC, type **JUNK.DOC** (no spaces, please).

3. Press Tab to move the highlight to the next box, Start **F**rom. Then type **C:**.

4. Make sure there's an "X" in the little check box next to Search All Subdirectories. If there isn't, click on this box so that an "X" appears.

5. Choose OK.

If Search finds one or more files matching the name you typed, you see a Search Results window that lists these files.

Understanding File Manager's Search Results window

- ✔ The file name includes all that path junk (like C:\DOCS\PROSE\TIMELESS.DOC), so that you can tell where the file is located.

- ✔ You can do stuff to the file—right in this Search Results window. All the commands in the File and other menus are available for doing stuff like copying, moving, or deleting the file. But, you

continues

Understanding File Manager's Search Results window, continued

wouldn't want to delete it, would you? You just went through all this trouble to find it!

✔ If all you wanted to do was discover the file's location, just double-click on the Search Results window Control menu box (not the File Manager's Control menu box) to close this window and return to the File Manager. Be sure that you remember where that file was!

It says `No matching files were found!`

Don't give up hope. Maybe you typed the extension or file name incorrectly when you saved the file, so it's really living somewhere on your hard disk under an assumed name. Try using wild cards in the Search For box (for example, JUNK.* will retrieve JUNK.DCC, JUNK.OCC, and JUNK.OC). For more information on wild cards (which work here just like they do in DOS), flip to Chapter 14.

Running Programs by Using File Manager

You can also launch applications with File Manager. File Manager can launch an application that doesn't show up in Program Manager's group windows.

To launch an application, begin in the Directory Tree window. Select the directory that contains the application, then move the pointer to the Files list and double-click on the application's file name. You can tell which files are applications: the file icon is a rectangle with a band across the top. (It's supposed to look like a window, get it?)

Undeleting Files

Sooner or later, you will accidentally delete a file that you need. A utility called Undelete can restore the file, provided that you use this utility *immediately* after performing the deletion. The restoration of a deleted file isn't a miracle; when you delete a file, DOS (which is lurking under Windows at all times) doesn't actually erase the file, it just removes its name from a file list that's stored on the disk. You can recover the file by putting the name back in DOS's list.

If you are using DOS 6 or 6.2, the latest versions of DOS, you can use Microsoft Undelete—assuming that whoever installed these versions of DOS chose to install the Windows version of the Undelete utility. (If you have Version 5 of DOS, flip to Chapter 14 to learn how to undelete files using the DOS version of Undelete. To access DOS, quit Windows by choosing E**x**it Windows from the Program Manager's **F**ile menu.)

TIP

I've got an earlier version of DOS! What do I do?

If you don't have versions 5, 6, or 6.2 of DOS, stop working immediately and go get help from your local DOS wizard. Chances are, this resourceful person will have an industrial-strength undelete program that can recover your file. But, it's really important that you don't create and save any new files with your computer until the file is undeleted. If you do, your drive may overwrite the deleted file, and then it will be gone for good.

Here's how to undelete a file:

1. From the **F**ile menu in File Manager, choose **U**ndelete. If you don't see this command, too bad—whoever installed DOS 6.0 or 6.2 didn't install Windows Undelete. Don't install it now, though, or you won't be able to get your file back. Instead, exit Windows and use the DOS version of Undelete, as described in Chapter 14.

   You see Microsoft Undelete, with its big, funny buttons. (Hard to miss, aren't they?) Notice that Microsoft Undelete is displaying the deleted files for the current drive and directory.

2. Click on the **Drive/Dir** button, if necessary, to change to the drive or directory which contains the file that you accidentally deleted.

   After you click on this button, you see the Change Drive and Directory dialog box. You can type the directory name in the **Change to Directory** box, or you can click the drive or directory names in the **Directories** list box. (The [..] symbol refers to the parent directory, the one above the current directory. If you see this symbol, click on it until you see the names of all the directories in your hard disk's root directory.) When you've typed or displayed the drive and directory you want in the **Change to Directory** box, click on OK or press Enter.

3. To undelete a file, highlight its name and click on the **Undelete** button. (If Undelete can't find any files to undelete, you see the message, `No deleted files found`.)

   You see the Enter First Character dialog box. This dialog box asks you to supply the first letter of the file's name, which was the only information actually removed by DOS when you "erased" the file.

4. Type the letter; then, click on OK or press Enter.

   If Microsoft Undelete is able to recover the file, the Condition column displays `Recovered`.

5. To exit Undelete, double-click on the Control menu box (if you've forgotten what this is, it's the big dash thingie in the left edge of the title bar).

It Says, File Destroyed!

Too bad. Undelete can't help you. Here's what happened. After you deleted the file, you performed other actions that caused your disk drive to write new information to the disk. This new information has overwritten the file you were trying to recover. It's too late, baby, now it's too late. Moral: Use Microsoft Undelete *immediately* if you've deleted a file that you actually want to keep.

TIP

This is kind of important, so get out your highlighter. By default, Undelete is set up to use its weakest file-protection technique. You'll be very wise to choose one of the better methods, called Delete Sentry and Delete Tracker. To choose one of these, click open the **O**ptions menu and choose **C**onfigure Delete Protection. I won't go into what all the options mean, but I like Delete **S**entry. After you select it and then choose OK, you see a dialog box that lets you specify which deleted files Undelete should safeguard; select Only Selected Files. In the Include box, type wild card masks corresponding to the extensions you normally use for your most important documents (such as ***.doc**, ***.txt**, ***.wks**, ***.ppt**, etc.). Then click OK.

Creating a New Directory

It's a good idea to organize your data files into separate directories. You don't want your program and data files mingling. It's not kosher. Keeping all your data files in separate directories makes it easier to find and work with files.

Here's how you create a directory from File Manager:

1. In the Directory Tree window, click on the directory that you want to put the new directory in. If you want the new directory to be in the root directory, click on C:\.

2. From the **F**ile menu, choose Create Directory.

3. Type the name of the directory and click on OK. You can type up to 8 characters. It's a good idea to stick to characters and numbers only. Try to keep the name simple, but make it descriptive enough so that you'll be able to identify it later.

After you create a new directory, you can put stuff in it. See the earlier sections in this chapter for help on moving files.

If you have no idea what a directory is, turn quickly to Chapter 14 and get the scoop.

Deleting a Directory

If you no longer need a directory, delete it to free up the disk space that the directory and its files take. If you need any of the files in the doomed directory, move them to a different directory before deleting the one they're currently in. Then delete the directory. When you delete a directory, you also send all the files that are in that directory to the great beyond.

In the Directory Tree window, click on the directory you want to delete and press Delete. Windows displays a Delete dialog box, in essence saying, "Hey! You're gonna delete a directory. Are you sure?" Click on OK. Then, at the Confirm Directory Delete dialog box, click on **Y**es. If the directory contains files, Windows makes doubly sure you want to delete the directory. It goes through each file, one by one, and asks whether it's okay to delete the file. Click on **Y**es to delete that file. Click on Yes to **A**ll to delete all the files and the directory.

Exiting File Manager

To quit File Manager, just double-click on the File Manager's Control menu box. (Remember, it's the big dash thingie jammed all the way up in the left edge of the title bar.) Voilà! You see Program Manager again.

TIP

That darned window won't close!

Be sure to double-click on the Control menu box for the File Manager window—not the Directory window. Double-clicking on the Control menu box for the Directory window closes that window, if you have more than one open. If you have just one Directory window open, double-clicking on it does nothing. You have to have at least one window open.

SHOE
By Jeff MacNelly
HEY, COMPUTER!!

GET WITH THE PROGRAM!!

NOW WHAT? THIS STUPID COMPUTER IS STILL FREAKING OUT!!
BLEEB BLEEB...

TIME FOR DRASTIC MEASURES.

LIKE READING THE INSTRUCTIONS.

If you are experiencing difficulty in starting up your computer,

there are three basic remedies:

1. Try turning it off for a minute, and turning it on again.

2. Hit it with Something.

3. Ask a twelve-year-old kid.

Top Ten

Rejected Application Software Ideas

10. Generates numbers that "look right" for IRS Form 1040 and Schedule A

9. Faces of Hungry Animals (CD-ROM)

8. Tracks verified Elvis sightings; uses secret formula to predict location of next appearance

7. Figures out all possible Mr. Potato Head configurations

6. Suggests the best way to sort your laundry (based on your own personal list of dirty clothes) and indicates prime water-temperature settings

5. For the paranoid: Calculates weighted probability that people really *are* out to get you

4. Creates fictitious but plausible genealogy demonstrating roots back to the *Mayflower*

3. For the worrier: from user-supplied data, automatically constructs worst-case scenarios for a variety of family, work, and health problems

2. Database of processed cheese recipes

1. Screen saver with pictures of hazardous waste dumps to raise your ecological consciousness

CHAPTER 17

Finally, Programs That Actually Do Things for You (Application Software)

IN A NUTSHELL

- What an application is
- Why we can't get over our paper hang-up
- What people do with application programs
- Other cool programs you can use
- Computers, kids, and software for learning
- Games!
- What shareware is and why it's so cheap

BUT THE COMPUTER MAKES WRITING A LOT EASIER, I'LL SAY THAT.

PCs!

After several chapters on the programs, such as DOS and Windows, that you must use to keep your *computer* happy, you may have given up hope that you'd ever get to do *your* work with the computer. Don't worry, you're not alone: This is a nagging fear known to millions.

But, you're here! Those disks are formatted, you know how to change directories and stuff, and you don't even blink unknowingly anymore when someone mentions "system files!" You've come a long way! Now it's time to move to a whole new level of confusion—application programs.

BUZZWORDS

APPLICATION

This just means program, although it suggests that you can apply the computer to something. Sometimes, I'd like to apply it rather forcefully to a brick wall.

An *application* is the use of the computer for some creative or apparently productive purpose, such as printing mailing labels, composing prize-winning poetry, or designing a community newsletter.

An *application program*, then, is a computer program that helps you do one of these things. In common use, any single term or combination of these terms—application, program, software—works. Take your pick: application program, program, software program, software application, and so on. You could probably mix them up a bit and people wouldn't even notice. (My favorites, one of which sounds vaguely obscene: softplication, soft proplication, and applisoft.)

About Application Software

(Revenge of the dead trees)

It's a new age. The Computer Age. The Information Age. Or, maybe, The Age of Bewilderment. And, you'd think that people would be communicating electronically, with no intervening paper. But, it hasn't happened. What's more, it's clear that every single successful PC application has given people a computer way of pounding out the same old paper documents they used to create by other means. Application software is pretty easy to understand if you just keep this in mind.

It used to be done on paper

- **Writing and editing** innumerable, lengthy documents that no one will ever read—Ph.D. dissertations, EPA compliance reports, etc.—plus some that might actually get read, such as letters, proposals, and memos. These are the missions of the best-selling of all application software, *word processing programs*. Their five-year mission? To take over the market. Right now, WordPerfect, Ami Pro, and Word for Windows are neck and neck.

- **Number-crunching.** By this, I don't mean statistics. Rather, it's more like dealing with huge columns of numbers, and the numbing pain that comes from realizing, after you've added them all up with a calculator, that you wrote one of them down incorrectly. With a spreadsheet program, you just make the change and the whole thing recalculates automatically. It's a simple, great idea. The market leaders are Lotus 1-2-3 for Windows, Excel, and Quattro Pro for Windows.

- **Keeping index cards in alphabetical order.** Doesn't sound very glorious, does it? Well, that's basically what database management programs do. (They do all sorts of fancy stuff too, but that's the gist of it.) The market for these programs is divided into fancy programs that database professionals use, such as dBASE, Paradox for Windows, and FoxPro for Windows. These programs really aren't intended for *end-users* (that is, non-programmers) until they've been worked over and customized by a pro. Programs for end-users fall into two categories—those designed to help you use the data in gigantic corporate databases (such as Microsoft Access) or make your very own PC database (Filemaker Pro).

- **Taxes.** A big seller. Why? Ever find that you left out a valid deduction, but were too tired of recopying and recalculating all 97 forms

continues

It used to be done on paper, continued

to put it in? These programs do it instantly and print out the results in a way that mimics the distinguished, artistic appearance of real IRS forms. The market leaders are TurboTax, Simply Tax, and reputedly the best of the lot, Andrew Tobias' Tax Cut—although I don't see what good it's going to do *me* to cut Andrew's taxes.

- ✔ **Getting brochures, price lists, forms, and flyers typeset.** This is something small (and large) businesses can now do for themselves with *desktop publishing software*. There are professional programs, such as PageMaker and Ventura Publisher, but you'll be better off with an easy-to-use program such as Microsoft Publisher. These programs let you add text to ready-to-use page designs that have areas for text columns, graphics, and headlines.
- ✔ **Balancing the ol' checkbook.** One of life's really fun jobs. It's a bit easier with programs such as Quicken and Microsoft Money. On-screen, you see something that looks just like a check register. You can also write and print checks using special computer checks that you order by mail. This is only good for paying bills, though, unless you like taking your computer system and printer with you to the grocery store.
- ✔ **Making handouts, slides, and transparencies for oral presentations.** You can do a great job of this with presentation graphics programs, such as Lotus Freelance Graphics for Windows, PowerPoint for Windows, and Harvard Graphics for Windows.

TIP

DOS or Windows? For application software, folks, we're talking about Windows. You can still get DOS programs, but be forewarned—very few software companies are still developing DOS programs. If you go the DOS route, you can look forward to a pretty bleak future—few new programs, and diminished

TIP

support for new equipment (printers and video). The following sections focus on Windows applications because that's where the action is. Windows applications are easier to use and that's what people want.

Word Processing Programs

(The village wordsmith)

With word processing software, you can create, edit, format, and print all kinds of text documents. (*Formatting* refers to making the document look good on the page.) You can create memos, letters, resumes, newsletters, manuals, dissertations, and books. If text is your thing, get a word processing program. Actually, even if it isn't your thing, you should have one. Lots of people who hate to write still have to crank out letters, memos, and reports; word processing makes this wearisome task easier.

What makes word processors nifty

- ✔ Adding text with a word processor is easy. You just move the cursor to where you want the text and type away. As you're typing, you can press the Backspace key to correct mistakes as you go.
- ✔ To edit your text, you select the text using the mouse or keyboard. After you select text, you can edit it, delete it, copy it, or move it somewhere else. In this way, you can quickly restructure and rework a document, without having to retype the whole thing.
- ✔ You can also format the text you've selected. You can change fonts (typefaces), font sizes, style (like bold or italic), line spacing, alignment (right, left, centered, or justified), and indents.
- ✔ As a finishing touch, you can add page formats, such as margins, page numbers, headers (those short titles that appear on every page), and even footnotes.

continues

What makes word processors nifty, continued

- ✔ Are you a lousy speller? A lousy typist? Most word processors have a speller program that will check your spelling. Although a speller can't catch all your errors (it won't flag an error if you use *their* when you mean *there*), it will point out many of the problems.

- ✔ Can't find the right word? Lots of word processing programs come with a built-in thesaurus that helps you spice up your writing.

Spreadsheet Programs

(I've got your number)

A close second in popularity is the electronic spreadsheet program. The term *spreadsheet* refers to the lined worksheet that accountants use. Spreadsheet programs deal with numbers; you can create budgets, financial plans, and profit and loss statements. Spreadsheet programs may sound as if they are only for businesses, but you can also use them to balance your checkbook, figure out your taxes, and perform a multitude of other mundane number-crunching tasks. If you need to fiddle with figures, use a spreadsheet program.

What's cool about spreadsheet software?

- ✔ A spreadsheet program begins with a blank worksheet, which has *rows* and *columns*. Where a row and column intersect, you have a *cell*. A cell just looks like a small rectangle on-screen and is referred to by its row and column—A2, for example.

- ✔ Now for the interesting part. In any blank cell, you can create formulas to calculate totals. You can type numbers directly into a formula, like this: **2+2**. But, the hottest stuff happens when you type *cell references (cell addresses)*, like **A2+A3**. After you finish typing the formula, you don't see the formula—you see the result. Let's say you put the formula A2+A3 in cell A4, for example. If A2 contains 5, and A3 contains 10, cell A4 would add these two numbers and display the result: 15.

- ✔ You can copy formulas to different locations. When you do, the copied formulas automatically adjust so that they calculate correctly in their new location. Don't ask me how this works—just take it on faith.

- ✔ Spreadsheets aren't just for calculating a total. After you've typed in all those numbers and formulas, you can also plug in some new numbers "just to see what happens." This is called *what-if analysis* by those in the know. By typing a much larger number in the Net Income cell, you can fantasize about how much sooner you'd be able to buy that beach condo.

- ✔ Most spreadsheet programs can make cool-looking graphs of the numbers you enter, showing you that your entertainment budget makes up 44 percent of your income this month. Are you having a little too much fun this month or what?

Database Programs

In third place, and not likely to zoom any further up the charts, are database management programs.

A *database management program* is, essentially, a computerized version of a library card catalog. In a library card catalog, each individual card is a data record; it holds one unit of information about one item—often a book. On the card are data fields, where certain types of information appear, such as the author's name and the title.

Nifty things about databases

- ✔ The basic unit of data storage is a *data record*. A data record contains information about one of the things you're tracking—one book, compact disc, employee, homing pigeon, or whatever. On the record are *data fields*, which contain more specific information about the data record—Beak Type, Plumage Color, Last Seen, and the like.

continues

Nifty things about databases, continued

- ✔ It's easy to edit and update the information. Suppose a homing pigeon named Bernard suddenly reappears. You display the record for Bernard, and type today's date in the Return Date field.
- ✔ You can sort the information in various ways. In seconds, you can put your database in alphabetical or numerical order by Pigeon's Name, Date Released, Plumage Color, Number of Times It Soiled My Coat—anything you want.
- ✔ The best thing about database management programs is that you can analyze the stored data, basically, by asking questions about it. This is called *querying*. For example, you could ask, "What is the average age of pigeons who survived the last release?" Or "What percentage of pigeons with speckled grey plumage returned within 5 days of release?" Just imagine the possibilities!
- ✔ You can print the information in your database. The printout is called a *report*.

A Suite Deal

(Read this before buying an application program)

Thinking of buying some application software? Check out the "office suites" offered by Microsoft (Microsoft Office), Lotus (Lotus SmartSuite), and Borland/WordPerfect (Borland Office). For what you used to have to pay for a single application, you'll get a word processor, spreadsheet, database, presentation graphics, and more. Microsoft gives you Word, Excel, PowerPoint, and Access. Lotus gives you 1-2-3, Ami Pro, Approach, Freelance, and Lotus Organizer, a personal organizer program. Borland and WordPerfect give you WordPerfect for Windows, Quattro Pro for Windows, and Paradox for Windows.

FINALLY, PROGRAMS THAT ACTUALLY DO THINGS FOR YOU

Is Software Integration for You?

Computing beginners—or experienced users who just don't want the hassle of big, full-featured programs—are flocking to the stores to buy ClarisWorks, an *integrated* program. Instead of giving you separate packages that are difficult to learn, ClarisWorks lets you apply a variety of tools to your document—word processing, spreadsheet, and database operations, as well as charting and graphics. It's easy to learn, too. Generally, one drawback of integrated packages is that the individual modules don't offer as many features as programs such as WordPerfect or Lotus 1-2-3; before buying an integrated program, make sure it has the features you need.

Beyond the Big Three

Besides the "Big Three" general applications—word processors, spreadsheets, and databases—there are hundreds and hundreds of other, more specialized programs, such as Adobe Illustrator, CorelDRAW!, etc. Many of these programs are designed to do stuff that you could do with one of the Big Three—if you're willing to spend lots of time customizing the Big Three applications and preparing the documents. These programs do all that work for you.

Fun and Games

(Finally!)

Sega and Nintendo. They've conquered the American pre-teen—and quite a few teens and adults, too. But, they're pretty primitive, as computer systems go. Your PC has more memory, better graphics, and faster processing. That's why game-playing aficionados know that the PC is the game-playing platform of choice.

We're not talking about Windows, here—this is the one area in which DOS is likely to survive. Windows is just too slow for shoot-'em-up arcade action (or fantasy role-playing graphics).

TIP

Today's PC games require prodigious amounts of computing horsepower. I'd recommend the following *minimal* system: a 486DX2-50 with at least 4MB of memory (see Chapter 5), a SoundBlaster or SoundBlaster-compatible sound card (see Chapter 10), and a double-speed CD-ROM drive (Chapter 10 again). In addition, you'll need to clear up as much conventional memory as you can, or the game won't run. So run—don't walk—to the software store at the Mall, and pick up a copy of QEMM 7.0 (Quarterdeck Systems), a memory-management program (see Chapter 13).

What's "Shareware?"

Programs for $4 a disk? It couldn't be worth bothering with, could it? Well, maybe. *Shareware programs*, also called *user-supported programs*, are distributed by mail-order companies that sell the disks crammed with programs at ridiculously low prices. Here's the idea: you try the programs on your computer, and if you like one of them, you send the program's author a registration fee. This might be as little as $10, although the typical fee ranges from $35 to $75.

Why is shareware so cheap? Low expenses. The manual is probably written in unedited techno-speak, and there is no telephone technical support. The author hasn't spent a dime on promotion, advertising, distribution, transportation, dealer incentives, or the like.

There's an important distinction between *shareware* and *freeware*. Shareware programs run on the "try-before-you-buy" system; if you decide to use the program, you send in the registration fee. Freeware programs are sometimes copyrighted, but there's no charge for their use. Programs that are neither shareware or copyrighted freeware are in the public domain, which means you can do anything with them you please.

GLORP!

Top Ten

Least Popular Messages during Software Installation

10. Insufficient disk space; other applications removed.
9. Virus found; adding virus code to original program disks.
8. Not able to coexist peacefully with other applications; installation terminated.
7. Plenty of disk space for multiple installation; installing 5 copies to fill all available space.
6. Deleting system configuration files that conflict with application; press any key when ready.
5. Installation completed (elapsed time: 4 hrs, 43 min); repeating whole process backward just for fun.
4. Wrong disk inserted; restarting entire installation process from beginning. Insert Disk #1 and press any key when ready.
3. User configuration error; intelligent life form at keyboard not found, installation terminated.
2. Choose a dominant screen scheme: M=Military Green, H=Hot Pink.
1. Installation complete. Press Ctrl+Alt+Del and run for cover.

CHAPTER 18

Buying, Installing, and Starting Programs

IN A NUTSHELL

- How to buy software (and save big bucks)
- Why software piracy is bad
- How to tell whether a program will run on your computer
- How to conserve disk space in an age of fatware
- Installing a program with DOS
- Installing a Windows application
- Software installation tips
- How to start your newly installed program
- Learn how to use your new program
- How to keep your software happy
- When to upgrade to new versions of your program

OK, you're ready to buy and install some software. But, you have a lot of questions. How do I get the best price? Will it run on my computer? How do I get the program from that box to my hard disk? How do I learn how to use this program? Should I upgrade to the new version? This chapter recounts my own hard-won experience. I hope I can save you some of the money and time I've needlessly wasted by making every mistake in the book.

Buying Software

(Don't Get Snookered)

It's easy to pay too much for computer software. The Big Three application programs—word processing, database management, and spreadsheet software—have had list prices of up to $795, but prices are eroding fast and appear to be stabilizing around $100 or less. But, you may not get this price unless you're clever.

Clever strategies to save $$$ on software

- ✔ Don't buy software at your local computer hardware store. That's not their main line of business, and you'll pay too much. And don't believe the line about providing service and support. Does anyone who works there really know anything about the software you're buying? Maybe, maybe not.

- ✔ Don't buy a word processing, spreadsheet, or database program without checking out a suite (such as Lotus Suite, Microsoft Office, or Borland Office). In a recent magazine, PowerPoint 4.0 for Windows (Microsoft) was selling for $300 in one ad—and in the same ad, it turned out you could get the same program for $189 if you bought Microsoft Office—and you'd also get Word and Excel!

- ✔ The best mail-order companies offer overnight Federal Express delivery for a nominal charge, a humongous selection of software (PC Connection offers over 3,500 products), and great catalogues.

- ✔ Check out your local mall. Chances are there's a software chain such as Babbage's. These stores specialize in Sega and Nintendo games, but they also have a good selection of PC games and some PC application programs.

- ✔ Software specialty stores, such as Egghead Software, offer great prices—and what's more, they participate in manufacturers' rebate and upgrade programs, which can save you money and time.

- ✔ The big office supply chains (such as Office America) offer a good selection of PC programs (including games!) and good prices.

- ✔ Be sure you really want the program before you buy it. You'll run into a lot of resistance if you try to return a program after opening the shrink-wrapped cover.

Why Shouldn't I Just Copy My Friend's Program?

You mean, other than the fact that it's illegal and morally wrong? Application programs come with densely-worded software licenses, which boil down to this: The registered owner of a program can use one copy of the program on one machine; anything else violates the agreement and renders the offender liable to prosecution under Federal law.

There must be very few American homes in which a police raid would not turn up pirated computer programs, illegal cassette copies of best-selling compact disks, and other nightmarish indications of a general collapse in moral values. That doesn't make it right, though. A computer program is an intellectual product and the authors deserve compensation. And for your job's sake, don't use pirated software at work; it just isn't worth the risk to your company—not to mention your job.

Virtue, we are told, is its own reward, and this might just be true where software is concerned. Buy and register a legal copy of an application program, and you qualify for technical support, as well as low prices for program upgrades.

Will It Run on My Computer?

A good question, and one worth answering before you tear open the package. Look on the program's box for a section called "System Requirements." (This is almost always printed on the outside of the box—often on the back of the box.)

Before You Open the Package...

Most computer stores and mail-order outfits will let you return the program if you haven't opened the box. But, if you rip open everything, including the little envelope that contains the disks, some stores won't take the program back, out of fear that you ordered it with the dishonest intention of copying the disks and then getting a refund.

Also, before you tear open the package, make sure that you get a program that has the correct size of floppy disks for your computer. Most programs are available in two versions: one with 5.25-inch disks, and the other with 3.5-inch disks. If you have both drive sizes, don't worry.

If you only have one drive size, check the box to find out whether you purchased the right size; the box usually says something like, "Includes 3.5-inch disks." What if you didn't get the right size? Take back the unopened package and exchange it for the version that contains the correct disk size. Otherwise, you'll have to write to the software publisher to get the disks in the other size, and on top of having to wait, they'll probably hit you up for 10 or 20 bucks.

Listing Your Computer's Capabilities

Before you can know whether a program will run on your computer, you need to know what kind of computer and software you have. Use this handy checklist. (This information will also come in handy when you are installing the program.) To fill this out, check the manuals that came with your computer, call the shop that sold you the computer, or get a computer-knowledgeable friend to help you.

BUYING, INSTALLING, AND STARTING PROGRAMS

My system has...

- ✔ My computer has version ______ of DOS. (If you're not sure what version you have, type **VER** at the DOS prompt, and then press Enter.)
- ✔ My computer has a ________ microprocessor. (8088, 8086, 80286, 80386, 80486, Pentium)
- ✔ My computer has ______KB of conventional (base) memory, and ________MB of extended (XMS) memory. (If you're not sure how much memory you have and you're using DOS 5.0 or later, type **MEM** at the DOS prompt, and then press Enter.) Hint: All 386 and 486 computers come with at least 1MB of RAM, and more likely 4MB. Pentiums come with at least 4MB.
- ✔ My computer has a ________ floppy disk drive. (3.5-inch, 5.25-inch) It is a ________ (high-density, double-density) drive.
- ✔ My hard disk has _______MB of free disk space. (If you're not sure now much free disk space you have, type **DIR** at the DOS prompt, and then press Enter; look at the number of bytes free, shown at the bottom of the directory list.)
- ✔ My computer has a ________ display adapter. (CGA, MDA, HGA, EGA, VGA, or SVGA) Hint: If you're using DOS 5 or 6, you can type **MSD** at the DOS prompt, and then press Enter. The text next to the Video button tells you the kind of display adapter you have.
- ✔ My computer does/doesn't have Microsoft Windows. (circle one)
- ✔ I have a color/monochrome monitor. (circle one)
- ✔ My printer is made by ____________________. Its model name or number is _______________. (Be sure that you include all numbers or Roman numerals, like DeskJet 500 or LaserJet IIsi.)

What the Program Needs

The software box usually lists the program's *minimum requirements*—the things it needs to run at all.

TIP

"Minimum requirements" means just that—minimum. A lot of Windows programs just barely run with the minimum requirements. Often, you'll need twice as much memory (8MB instead of 4MB) or a much faster microprocessor (a 486DX-33 instead of a 386SX-25) to get acceptable performance. Beware!

This software requires...

- ✔ If the systems requirement stuff reads "MS-DOS Version 2.11 or later," it's referring to the DOS version number. DOS 4 is later than DOS 3; DOS 6 is later than DOS 5. The requirement really should read, "MS-DOS Version 2.11 or any higher version number."
- ✔ The same goes with microprocessor numbers; you'll see something like "386 or higher." 486 is higher than 386; "Pentium" is higher than 486. If you're curious about these numbers and what they mean, flip back to Chapter 5.
- ✔ Does the program require Microsoft Windows? If so, you must have Windows installed on your system before you can even install this program, let alone run it.
- ✔ The systems requirement stuff might read, "5.25-inch or 3.5-inch low-density floppy disk drive." Don't let this one get to you. If you have high-density drives, they can read low-density disks just fine. If you're cloudy about the differences between a high-density and low-density floppy disk drive, take a look at Chapter 6, which explains a bit more about this subject.
- ✔ The memory requirement might read something like "4MB of RAM required." This really means "4MB or more." 4MB is the absolute minimum you need to run this program. Chapter 5 explains more about memory.

Help! This Program Needs 51MB of Disk Space!

It's called *fatware*, and the truth is, it's our fault. We've demanded ever-more-impressive software features—graphics programs with 800 fonts, presentation graphics programs with 5,000 clip art images—and software publishers have responded with big font and graphics packages that take up huge amounts of hard disk space.

You won't believe how fast that hard drive fills up. At major corporations, technical support personnel know that computer users will come hunting for bigger hard drives and more memory within a couple of weeks after they get new programs.

Coping with fatware

- ✔ When you're buying a new computer, think of the maximum amount of hard disk space and memory (RAM) you could possibly need. Then, double it—or even better, triple it.
- ✔ Consider getting an integrated program such as Claris Works instead of three full-featured applications.
- ✔ Get a CD-ROM drive and get the CD-ROM version of infrequently-accessed graphics and fonts rather than installing them on your hard disk.
- ✔ Get a disk-compression utility program, such as Stacker (Stac Electronics) and compress your hard drive.

Installing a Program with DOS

(Insert disk #27 and press any key when ready)

This section details the installation procedure for installing DOS programs. Skip this section if you're a Windows user.

TIP

If you're running Windows, but want to install a DOS application (which is perfectly OK), quit Windows by choosing E**x**it Windows from the **F**ile menu in Program Manager. Then click on OK, or press Enter, to end the session.

Now you're ready. Note that the exact procedure varies from program to program, so be sure that you read the program's installation instructions. This is the general procedure that you follow to install a program:

1. Look for a disk labeled "Setup" or "Install," and stick it into the floppy disk drive. If you can't find a Setup or Install disk, look for Disk #1, which probably contains the installation software.

2. Make the floppy drive current. To do so, type **A:** at the DOS prompt and press Enter to make drive A current. Or, type **B:** and press Enter to make drive B current.

3. Look at the installation sheet or manual to find out what to type to start the installation program. You probably type **INSTALL** or **SETUP**. If there's no installation sheet or manual, look in the manual for a section titled "Installing Your Program," or something of that nature.

TIP

To find the installation program, you can use the DIR command. Type **DIR *.EXE** and press Enter. Most program files have the extension EXE. When you type this command, all files with the EXE extension are displayed on-screen. Look for a file named something similar to INSTALL or SETUP.

4. Type the installation command and press Enter. You'll probably type **INSTALL** or **SETUP**.

TIP

There's no setup or install program!

If there isn't an automatic installation program, you'll have to wade through the manual to figure out how to install the program. Check the manual for the exact instructions and try to get a computer-savvy friend to help.

5. You are now in your computer's hands. You must do what you are told to do. You must sit attentively, waiting for screen messages, and attempt to answer all questions to the best of your ability, and as truthfully as possible. Hedging, little white lies, hesitation, or lack of complete faith in the computer will be electronically reported to the authorities.

TIP

If you see an option for a Quick, Express, Easy, First-Time, or Handy-Dandy All-in-One installation, choose it!

6. Eventually, you'll be told to remove and insert disks. Do so carefully, being sure that the number on the disk you're inserting matches the number on the screen.

After a lengthy and grueling session of inserting and removing disks, you'll finally see a message informing you that the installation is complete. You may be told to *reboot* (restart your system). If so, follow the on-screen instructions. Your computer restarts, and you see the good old DOS prompt again. (You might see Windows or the DOS Shell, depending on how your computer is set up.)

If you want to know more about installation, see the section "What Might Happen during Installation," later in this chapter.

Installing a Windows Application

This section details the installation procedure for installing a Windows application. Note that the exact procedure varies from application to application, so be sure that you read the application installation instructions. This is the general procedure that you follow to install a Windows application:

1. Look for a disk labeled "Setup" or "Install," and stick it into the floppy disk drive. If you can't find a Setup or Install disk, look for Disk #1, which probably contains the installation software.

2. Exit any applications that might be running—only Program Manager should remain active.

3. In Program Manager, open the **F**ile menu, and then choose **R**un. You see the Run dialog box.

4. In the Run dialog box, type **A:** (if your Install or Setup disk is in drive A) or **B:** (if your disk is in drive B), followed by the name of the installation program. If the program is called INSTALL, for example, type **A:INSTALL** or **B:INSTALL**.

5. You see an initial screen informing you that the installation program is copying stuff to your hard disk. After a while, things start to happen. You are now in your computer's hands. You must do what you are told to do. You must sit attentively, waiting for screen messages, and attempt to answer all questions to the best of your ability, and as truthfully as possible.

TIP

If you see an option for a Quick, Express, Easy, First-Time, or Handy-Dandy All-in-One installation, choose it!

6. Eventually, you'll be told to remove and insert disks. Do so carefully, making sure the number on the disk you're inserting matches the number on the screen.

After a lengthy and grueling session of inserting and removing disks, you finally see a message informing you that the installation is complete. You may be told to reboot (restart your system). If so, just follow the instructions on-screen.

What Might Happen during Installation

Chances are, all will go smoothly—unless you don't have enough disk space for the installation. If you don't, you see an error message saying something like `Insufficient Disk Space`, and the installation utility just gives up. You'll need to move some files off your hard disk—or, better yet, get one of those disk compression programs discussed in Chapter 13.

Software installation tips

- ✔ You'll probably be asked where you want to install your software. The program wants to know exactly where to place the program—that is, in which directory. The installation software might propose to make its own, new directory for the program. That's just fine. Let it.

- ✔ If the installation program doesn't propose a directory name, don't install the program in the root directory (C:\). You want to keep this directory uncluttered. When the installation program prompts you to do so, type the name of a new directory. For instance, if you're installing WordPerfect, you can put the program into a directory **C:\WP** (this is a subdirectory of the root directory). Chances are that the installation program will propose a directory name, and if you approve it (which you should), it will create the directory for you.

- ✔ You may be subjected to a grueling list of questions, such as: What printer are you using? What display adapter are you using? What was your mother's maiden name? Usually, you're shown a list of options, and can choose your printer or display adapter from this list. Use the arrow keys to scroll this list, if necessary. The installation program generally gives on-screen instructions for selecting printers and such, and often it is able to guess what kind of equipment you have (it does this by performing various tests on your equipment).

Software installation tips, continued

✔ The installation program may ask you whether it's OK to modify your system configuration files (AUTOEXEC.BAT and CONFIG.SYS). Let it. Otherwise, the program won't run unless you modify these files yourself, and this can be an ordeal.

Starting the Program

After you've installed your program successfully, give it a whirl.

Starting a Program by Using DOS

If the installation program is worth its salt, you should be able to start the program from any directory, just by typing its file name and pressing Enter. (Leave off the EXE or COM extension.) Look in the program's manual to find out exactly what to type. For example, to start WordPerfect, you type **WP** and press Enter.

TIP

I just installed SnazzyCalc, but it says `Bad command or filename` when I try to start it!

There are a couple of possibilities here. What are you supposed to type? It could be SNAZZY, SNAZ, SC, or even SZCLC. Check the program's manual, and try again. If it still doesn't work, you need help from your local DOS wizard. Chances are that the installation program is dumber than a tree and didn't add the necessary PATH statement to one of those weird DOS files in your root directory.

Ask your DOS wizard to add the necessary PATH command. In the meantime, you should be able to start your program by changing to the program's directory before typing the program's name.

Starting a Windows Program

The installation program probably created a new program group in Program Manager, and that's where you go to start the program. Open the program group (Chapter 4 tells you how), and double-click on the program's icon.

Learning How To Use Your Software

This isn't a pleasant subject for most computer users. Learning a new program can be a very challenging experience, especially if you're new at computing. Happily, it gets easier as time goes on—the programs become easier to use, and your skills and knowledge improve. Here are some suggestions to make the learning process a bit less painful.

Tips for learning how to use your software

- ✔ Learn one program at a time. You may have come back from Babbage's with 12 boxes, but you'll show up at the nuthouse if you try to learn them all at once.
- ✔ Check to see whether your program includes an on-line (electronic) tutorial. If so, by all means start it and follow all of the lessons.
- ✔ Read the "Getting Started" section of your program's manual.
- ✔ Find someone who knows how to use the program and ask them to show you the basics.
- ✔ In Windows, check out the **H**elp menu. You may find tutorials, quick previews, and sample files in addition to the usual Help screens.
- ✔ Learn how to use *context-sensitive help*, if your program offers it. This enables you to click a screen object or menu item and see a screen of helpful information about it.

Tips for learning how to use your software, continued

- ✔ If your program comes with a quick reference card, keep this by your computer. It lists helpful things, such as what all those funny icons mean and which key to press to do something.
- ✔ If you're having trouble with something, try reading the manual before you call the technical support hotline. For more information about solving problems, see Chapter 21, "Help!"

Keeping Your Software Happy

Your programs—and you—will coexist much more happily by following a few simple rules, as the following checklist indicates.

- ✔ Don't erase or "experiment" with your system files (CONFIG.SYS and AUTOEXEC.BAT). Chances are darned good that, when you installed your program, very important changes were made to these files. Don't mess with them.
- ✔ Don't move an installed program from one directory to another. Once the program is installed, it records the location of vital files; if you move it, the program may not be able to locate them. You'll get error messages or unstable performance.
- ✔ Save your work frequently—at least once every 10 minutes. If the program has an *autosave* feature which automatically saves your work at an interval that you specify, by all means use it.
- ✔ Don't just switch off the computer with a program still on-screen. You may lose important configuration choices. Save your work and exit. If you're using a Windows application, don't forget to exit Windows properly too.
- ✔ Fill out and mail your registration card. You'll get notices of *bug fixes* (maintenance upgrades that resolve problems in the software), as well as great prices on upgrades.

Should You Upgrade?

(New isn't necessarily better)

If you were a Good User and filled out your registration card, you'll probably get a notice informing you of a grand and glorious new version of the program. These new versions, called *upgrades*, fall into two categories: maintenance upgrades and major revisions.

What Do You Expect? This Is Version 1.0

Maintenance upgrades fix something that was wrong with the program or add a feature that some people really want, like an additional printer driver. If the upgrade fixes a bug, order it. If it provides new features, order the upgrade only if you really need it. (What's the use of ordering an upgrade if all it offers is a printer driver you don't need?)

BUZZWORDS

BUG

A bug is a problem with the way a program runs. As applied to computers, the term originated back when computers were the size of rooms. One computer went awry and the technical gurus traced the problem to a huge moth stuck in one of the parts. True story.

Major revisions are new versions of the program, with major features added or drastically improved. These features are probably worth having; chances are they respond to the complaints users have been making, or offer features that competing programs already have. But it's up to you. No law dictates that you must upgrade.

How Can I Tell the Difference Between a Maintenance Upgrade and a Real New Version?

If the upgrade is numbered with a decimal increase, like Version 2.0 going to Version 2.1 (or 2.01, or 2.0001), it's a maintenance upgrade.

If the upgrade is numbered with a whole number increase, like Version 2.1 going to Version 3.0, it's a major revision. Easy enough.

YEAH, I HAVE TO ADMIT IT: THIS COMPUTER ACTUALLY DOES COME IN HANDY.

Top Ten

Facts You Don't Know If You Don't Use the Internet and Read Usenet

10. Computerized jail doors frequently release prisoners due to "bugs" in controlling software

9. U.S. National Security Agency suspected of creating computer algorithm capable of scanning 50,000 Usenet postings per second for signs of terrorist drug dealer activity

8. Experimental "gigabit network" technology capable of transmitting entire text of Encyclopedia Britannica in less than one second, but current Internet file transfer dominated by exchange of digitized pornographic pictures

7. Workers at an Ames, Iowa office "retired" computer by dropping it from a height of 40 feet and attacking it with sledgehammers

6. Callers to the Virginia General Assembly "citizen's hotline" reached phone sex line due to telephone company computer switching error

5. 99% of adult films are actually unbelievably boring, not worth watching—okay, so you already knew that

4. Bug in early F-16 software caused aircraft to flip over when it crossed the equator, giving new meaning to term "down under"

3. Military early-warning computers used in the 1970s and 1980s repeatedly mistook fog banks and geese flights as incoming Soviet missile attacks, causing panic in U.S. government and armed forces

2. At height of political correctness, students at a Pennsylvania university were prohibited from sending e-mail messages "that might reasonably be expected to offend anyone"

1. Multi-user role playing game called FurryMuckers allows on-line participants to redefine their identities by acting out fantasies as a "furry cuddly animal"

CHAPTER 19

You Too Can Become a Global Village Idiot:

Electronic Mail and Internet

IN A NUTSHELL

- What the Internet is
- What you can do with the Internet
- How to get connected to the Internet
- How to send electronic mail to the Internet
- How to join a mailing list
- What you can do with Telnet, FTP, Gopher, and WWW
- How to get over an Internet addiction

This is another computer resource you can access with your modem (see Chapter 11), but it's such a big deal that I've given it its own chapter. What else would you do with a computer network that has something like 10 times as many users as CompuServe, and is growing at an estimated rate of 40 to 50 percent per month?

What Is the Internet?

(Everyone's talking about it)

The Internet is a phenomenon. It's also hard to describe. The first point to remember is that the Internet is not an on-line service, like CompuServe. Rather, it's a collection of linked networks that are set up so that messages and files can travel freely from one network to another. Connected to this network are literally tens of thousands of humongous, CompuServe-sized computers, and hundreds of thousands of smaller ones, in well over one hundred countries. Nobody knows exactly how many people are connected to the Internet; a good guess is roughly 20 million, and counting. The Internet is the fastest-growing communications system that the world has ever seen.

Why is the Internet growing so fast? As I just mentioned, the Internet isn't a physical computer network—it's a means of connecting networks, even if they're physically very different, and facilitating the flow of messages and files through them. And, there's no Internet central office or bureaucracy that new networks need to get "permission" from in order to sign up.

As long as the new network observes the Internet standards (called *protocols*), and after a few formalities, such as registering the network's name, it's part of the Internet. And because everyone wants a piece of the action, organizations everywhere—universities, nonprofit organizations and corporations—are linking their internal networks to the Internet.

YOU TOO CAN BECOME A GLOBAL VILLAGE IDIOT

BUZZWORDS

PROTOCOL

A rule or a standard which, when implemented in computer programs, allows two computers to communicate with each other and exchange files.

The Internet is a good example of how military research can benefit the public. In the 1960s, military researchers began working on a computer network design that could survive a nuclear war. If such a war occurred, some of the computers on the network would probably be destroyed. So their design emphasized decentralization—if there's no headquarters, there's nothing for the enemy to attack. Another design feature is that messages can find their way to their destinations even if a part of the network isn't functioning.

The Internet protocols were first tried out in a Defense Department network called ARPANET. This was followed by NSFNET, which continues to provide the backbone service needed to transmit Internet messages across the continental U.S. Regional and international service providers, firms that provide access to the Internet backbone, carry Internet services to thousands of organizations, millions of people, and more than 100 countries. Still, the Internet has a collegiate flavor, given that NSFNET was originally intended as a means of connecting the education and research communities. Many of the people who pop up on Usenet discussions are college student types. However, you'll also find yourself involved in discussions and exchanges with people from companies, schools, homes, and other countries.

You've probably heard that the Internet is subsidized by the U.S. federal government, and that's true—although the subsidy applies only to NSFNET, and even then accounts for only about 10 percent of NSFNET's operating costs (approximately $18 million per year at this writing). NSFNET itself is leased from commercial data communications firms. Much of the Internet's operating costs are paid by flat fees charged to service providers, who in turn pass on these costs to people who want to hook up to the system. When the U.S. government ceases its subsidies, as is currently planned, these costs may rise, and there is even talk of introducing time-based billing—a subject that horrifies current

Internet users. Still, the prospects are that the Internet will continue to experience rapid growth. Put simply, the Internet protocols are doing for computer communications what the 1922 U.S. protocols did for telephone systems: providing the basis for different networks to communicate. It's worth pointing out that in only a matter of decades, the telephone standards led to the development of a world telephone system in which a person can dial any of several billion telephones worldwide—a stunning technological achievement.

That's Great, But, What Can You Do with the Internet?

The Internet protocols provide the technical basis for the exchange of information between dissimilar computer networks. Just about everything you can do with the Internet boils down to exchanging electronic mail messages, locating files, and transferring files.

What you can do with the Internet

- ✔ **Exchange electronic mail.** The Internet has emerged as the first world-wide electronic mail (e-mail) system. Many bulletin board systems (BBS) and on-line services (see Chapter 11) can send your electronic messages to the Internet, and receive replies to these messages.

- ✔ **Join mailing lists.** A mailing list is a collection of e-mail messages shared by people with interests in a particular subject, such as sports cars, space physics, or ethnic nationalism. To participate, you subscribe, and then you start getting copies of the message in your electronic mailbox. If you want to join in, you send an e-mail message to the list manager, whose computer copies it and sends it to everyone on the mailing list.

- ✔ **Join computer conferences.** Usenet, which isn't really a part of Internet, but is often found on Internet-linked systems, is a collection of more than 4,000 computer conferences (called *newsgroups*) on every conceivable subject. These are like mailing lists, except that the messages don't go to your mailbox. This is convenient because, unlike mailing lists, newsgroups don't give you more messages than you can easily read in one sitting. You use a program called a *newsreader* to select a newsgroup and read the messages.

- ✔ **Obtain files from remote computers.** Internet lets you contact any computer that's directly connected to the Internet (more about that in a minute). With some systems, any Internet user can browse public file directories and retrieve files. Available are such resources as the KGB-CIA World Fact Book, the complete digital text of all the Shakespeare plays, bibliographies on every conceivable subject, and much more.
- ✔ **Search for information.** A great deal of useful information is available on the Internet, but it can be difficult to find. Search tools such as Veronica, WAIS, and the World-Wide Web (WWW) help you locate information of interest to you.

All the hype aside, there are some things that Internet isn't good for. Basically, the Internet protocols are designed to transfer information without loss or error, at the sacrifice (if necessary) of some delay. (Your e-mail message may take anywhere from a few minutes to an hour to reach its destination.) But voice and video communications are just the opposite; they can tolerate some loss—a little noise or fuzziness is tolerable—but they can't tolerate delay ("Aunt Wilma! Speak to me! Are you there?").

So the Internet isn't going to be the Information Superhighway that you've probably heard about. If such a thing ever comes to be, it will carry voice and video as well as computer data—but it won't use Internet technology. (Don't panic, Internet lovers. The various proposed Information Superhighway technologies would still be able to carry Internet traffic with no problem.)

Getting Connected to the Internet

As the following checklist indicates, there are lots of different ways to get connected to the Internet. Prices will drop and more options will become available as public Internet use increases.

Ways to get connected to the Internet

- ✔ *On-line services*. Several commercial on-line services, such as CompuServe, Delphi, and America Online, offer limited Internet connections, but this may be limited to e-mail. This is an inexpensive way of accessing Internet if you're already a subscriber to these services. In the future, these services will offer more complete Internet access and will probably give you easy-to-use software to do so.

- ✔ *Dial-up access*. To do this, you need an account on a computer system that has Internet access, such as your company's central computer system, a university computer system, or a commercial service provider such as PSI. You use your modem to dial in to this computer, which then gives you access to Internet e-mail and file retrieval. The bad part of this is that the mail you get and the files you retrieve go to the computer system that has the Internet access, not your PC. This can be inconvenient. For example, if you want to print your mail, you have to transfer it to your PC in a separate operation before you can print it. On the plus side, though, this service is cheap (as little as $9 per month for unlimited access)—it might even be free if your company or university offers it.

- ✔ *Dial-up IP* (*Internet Protocol,* which basically means "talking" directly to the Internet). This option is only for the technically adventurous at present, but it is expected to become more feasible in the future. It gives you direct Internet access—the mail and files come right to your PC. But you'll need special software and a high-speed (14,400 bits per second) modem. Charges are higher, too; if you're lucky, your company or university will provide this kind of linkage for free, but service providers charge $75 per month or more.

- ✔ *Direct Connections Organizations*. Direct Connections Organizations that have many people who want to use Internet can link their local area networks (LANs) to the Internet by leasing a special, high-speed data line from the local telephone company and purchasing special equipment that physically links their LAN to the Internet. This can get pretty expensive, though, with costs running from $750 to $5,000 per month (not counting the necessary equipment).

Cracking the Code: E-Mail Addresses

You're at a conference, and somebody from Alliance Plumbing Fixtures, Inc., hands you a business card. It looks pretty normal, except for one thing: At the bottom, you see something like this:

bsmith@x-wing.alliance.com

This is an Internet *e-mail address*, and it's the latest status symbol. It's also incomprehensible to the average person. Let's take it apart and see what it means.

mailbox name —bsmith@x-wing.alliance.com— host name

An Internet e-mail address has two parts: the mailbox name, and the host name. The *mailbox name*—here, bsmith—comes to the left of the @ symbol (pronounced "at"). This is the name that has been assigned to the person's electronic mailbox. (The mailbox name might be a person's name, or the person's initials, or a funny-looking code.) The *host name* comes to the right of the @ sign. Basically, it contains information that tells Internet routing computers how to find the computer on which this person has an account.

You don't really need to worry about what this information contains, but sometimes it suggests some useful information. This is particularly true of the last part, which is called the *top-level domain*. Here, it's "com."

This means "business or commercial organization," so you know this person works for a company. Within the United States, at least, you can tell at a glance whether the person works for a company (COM), a university or college (EDU), a government organization (GOV), or the military (MIL).

Outside the U.S., the right-most code is a country abbreviation, such as UK (United Kingdom) or SE (Sweden—or Sverige, as the inhabitants like to call it).

TIP

It's easy to send an e-mail message to someone on the Internet.

If you currently subscribe to an on-line service, such as CompuServe or a bulletin board system (BBS) with Internet access, you can send an e-mail message to an Internet mailbox just as easily (in most cases) as you can to another user of the same system. Just address the message using the full Internet address, such as bsmith@x-wing.alliance.com. It doesn't matter whether you type upper- or lowercase, as long as you don't use any spaces and you type everything correctly.

Beyond E-Mail: FTP, Gopher, and More

If you go the dialup access route for connecting with the Internet, you're probably in for a shock: in all likelihood, you've got an account on a UNIX system. UNIX is a particularly unfriendly computer operating system that was designed by computer geniuses for the use of other computer geniuses. They are very nice people, really—they just had no idea that anyone other than computer geniuses would use UNIX. But I can promise you, everything we have said thus far about hating PCs will pale in significance when you give UNIX a try. Even MS-DOS will seem like a warm, cuddly thing next to your average UNIX command.

Still, people are learning UNIX and accessing the Internet this way. That's a surprise to me, but it's a heck of a good thing for the computer book publishing industry. Just look at all those Internet books on the bookstore's shelves. And I can promise you, you'll need a good Internet book. Que's *The Internet QuickStart* provides a good introduction to the UNIX programs and commands you'll have to learn to access the Internet this way. I also suggest Ed Krol's *The Whole Internet* (O'Reilly & Associates).

The following checklist sums up the most popular Internet applications.

A quick guide to Internet applications

- ✔ *Telnet*. This program lets you "log on" (access) a distant computer that's connected to the Internet, and work with it as if you were there. But, often, you need an account on the distant computer to do this.

- ✔ *Finger*. If you know a person's e-mail address, you can sometimes find out more about him or her using this program. At the minimum, it will give you the person's real name (not just the mailbox name). Some people like to add extensive information about themselves, including poems, quotes, and the names of their favorite musical groups.

- ✔ *Archie*. This is a search program that can help you pinpoint the location of publicly accessible files you want to retrieve. If you're looking for a file and you know its exact name (such as information-paradise.txt), Archie can help.

- ✔ *FTP*. This is short for *"File Transfer Protocol."* It's a program for exchanging files with remote computers that are linked to the Internet. Lots of computers have directories called /pub where publicly-accessible files are made available. You can access these computers by logging in as "anonymous," and then obtaining the files. This is called *anonymous FTP*.

- ✔ *tin* or *nn*. These are newsreaders, programs that let you read Usenet news. You can subscribe to the newsgroups you want and follow the discussions.

- ✔ *Gopher*. This is easier to use than Telnet or FTP. It uses menus, so that you can choose an option by typing a number. Gopher is a program that helps you browse for information. When you start Gopher, you see the information that's available on the system that you're using. You can also use Gopher to browse for information on other computer systems.

continues

A quick guide to Internet applications, continued

This information includes files, programs, sounds, video clips, animations, and graphic files. You can select any of these, view the text (if it's a text file), and retrieve the files, if you wish.

- ✔ *Veronica*. This is a search utility that's part of Gopher. It lets you type key words (such as "hamsters" or "gerbils"), and then it searches *Gopherspace* (the world of file names accessible to Gopher) to find matches. These are presented as a Gopher menu. You can then read or retrieve the items as you please.

- ✔ *WAIS*. This is another search utility that's designed to access the databases that Internet users have made available. Hundreds, perhaps thousands, of such databases exist, on every conceivable subject.

- ✔ *WWW*. Short for *World-Wide Web*, this program is another browser like Gopher, except that it works on hypertext principles—as you read a WWW document and see an underlined word or phrase, you can choose this to see related documents. WWW automatically makes the connection to the computer that houses this document, which might be 10,000 miles away (but you'd never know it).

Of all the Internet applications, the World-Wide Web comes closest to showing you how the Internet-derived Information Superhighways of the future will operate. From your perspective as you use WWW, the whole world Internet system is just one big computer. You don't have to worry about exactly where something is located. And, the resources are incredibly rich.

There's lots more to learn about the Internet, but it's all part of the fun. My advice: Get going with Internet e-mail, join a mailing list, start exploring a UNIX system, and above all else, have a good time. See you on the Net!

PART IV

Save Me!

Includes:

20: Gosh, It's Not Working

21: Help!

SHOE
BY JEFF MACNELLY
DEADLINE!!

HURRY UP WITH THAT COLUMN!!
RIGHT! ...ALMOST FINISHED...
A FEW MORE CORRECTIONS ON THE WORD PROCESSOR...
AND NOW TO ENTER IT INTO THE MEMORY...

GLORP!

WHAT'S WRONG?
I'M HAVING SOME ELECTRONIC PROBLEMS...
© Jefferson Communications, Inc. 1983
Distributed by Tribune Company Syndicate, Inc.

WHAT'S THE MATTER WITH THE COMPUTER?

IT THREW UP.
MACNELLY

Top Ten

Sources of User-Assisted Data Loss

10. Threw entire system out of third-story window after fifteenth `Abort, retry, fail?` message

9. Jarred power cord loose while attempting to affix Garfield doll to monitor

8. Inserted Guns n' Roses CD into floppy drive "just to see what would happen"

7. Told by "helpful" colleague that Ctrl+Alt+Del is the Save Data key combination

6. Thought the manual was serious when it said, "give it a boot," and that the computer had it coming, anyway

5. Kept working during thunderstorm, having mistaken distant booming sounds for Honor Guard drum roll celebrating return of boss to building

4. Struck Reset button accidentally during flamboyant mouse maneuver

3. Sprayed floppy disk drive with WD-40 in attempt to reduce those irritating clanking noises

2. Reformatted hard disk to try to free up a bit more disk space

1. Responded to `Drive not Ready` message by shoving sandwich in drive door, and exclaiming, "Well, read this, pal!"

CHAPTER 20

Gosh, It's Not Working

IN A NUTSHELL

- What to do if your computer won't start
- How to deal with start-up error messages without resorting to violence
- How to cope with the agony of sudden power outages
- What to do if your system "crashes"
- Getting your program to start
- Getting your mouse to work
- Fixing the computer's time and date
- Dealing with error messages when copying files
- Finding a "missing" file
- How to recover an accidentally reformatted floppy or hard disk
- Handling error messages that you get while using a floppy disk
- Determining whether your hard disk is about to go bye-bye
- Making an obstinate printer print

PCs!

Problems await every computer user, even the Technically Empowered. These are, after all, pretty complex machines. There's plenty of room for Murphy (of Murphy's Law fame) to wreak havoc, bringing annoyance, pain, and even devastation to the lives of millions of innocent computer users.

If your computer or program isn't running for some reason, this is the chapter for you. This chapter also deals with problems that arise after the computer (or the program) is up and running. You should also consult Chapter 21, which tells you how to determine whether you're up against something that will need to be fixed by an expert.

TIP

Don't traumatize yourself by spending hours trying to solve a problem. If you can't find the answer in a few minutes, get help.

I Can't Turn It On!

It worked just fine yesterday, but today, you can't get your computer started. Chances are, you can solve the problem easily. Consult the following checklist to learn the tricks I use to revive a dead PC.

What to do if your computer won't start

✔ Is it plugged in? Is the power cord connected? Check the back of the computer. The power cord has two plugs, one on each end, and one of the ends has to be plugged into the back of the computer.

✔ Is the computer turned on? Locate the switch, and make sure that it's switched to 1 (which, to toolies, means On). Is there a power center (a box with lots of plugs)? Check its switch (and circuit breaker if the power center has one).

✔ Do you hear something? If the hard drive is going, maybe you just forgot to turn on the monitor. Locate the power switch, and make sure that the monitor is turned on. Press a key or move the mouse to be sure that the screen isn't being dimmed by a screen saver program. Fiddle with the brightness and contrast controls on the monitor—someone might have turned them down.

- ✔ Is the computer locked? Most computers these days have a funny round key that can be used to lock the system. To start the computer, you have to turn the key to the open position. Flip to Chapter 2 for the details.
- ✔ If you're using a power center (one of those electrical things you can plug all your equipment into) or surge protector, make sure that the power switch is turned on. Make sure that the power supply center is plugged in and check its circuit breaker too.
- ✔ If the computer still doesn't work, unplug the power cord from the power center or surge protector, and plug it directly into the wall socket. If the computer now works okay, the problem lies in the power strip or surge protector. Replace it.
- ✔ Is the wall socket working? Plug something else into it, like a lamp, and see if it works. If there's no power, check the circuit supply box to see whether any of the circuit breakers have been thrown. As a last resort, call an electrician.

Worst Case Scenario 1: Dead Power Supply

If some of the stuff (like the printer and monitor) comes on but your system unit shows no signs of life, and if you've checked the cords and power, your power supply may have gone bye-bye. Don't panic, this isn't a very expensive repair.

It Started, But I See an Error Message

If the computer starts, you're past the first hurdle. But what if you see an error message and everything shuts down? The following checklist runs down the likely culprits.

What to do if you see an error message at start-up

- ✔ Is the keyboard plugged in? (It should be plugged into the back of the computer.) If it isn't, your system won't start, and you'll see a weird message that says something like `Keyboard error`. Turn off the computer and plug in the keyboard cable. Then try again.

- ✔ Do you see the message, `Non-system disk or disk error`? You left a floppy disk in drive A. Unlatch the drive, remove the disk, and press Ctrl+Alt+Del, or press the Reset button to restart your system.

- ✔ You start your system, and you see the message, `Starting MS-DOS`...but then, zip, nada, nothing, zero. Chances are, you've made some changes to your CONFIG.SYS or AUTOEXEC.BAT files—did you change them yourself? Did you just install a program? Get your local DOS wizard to start your system by putting a bootable floppy disk in drive A. Be sure to bring along some chocolate so that you can bribe this generous, wonderful person into taking a look at your system configuration files.

TIP

DOS 6 and 6.2 contain a new feature that lets you bypass messed-up configuration files. To use this feature, press F5 when you see the message, `Starting MS-DOS`.... This tells DOS to start your system with a minimal configuration. You can use the computer, although you may have to switch directories manually to start programs, and some programs may not run. You'll still need your DOS wizard to help you check out those configuration files, but in the meantime, you'll at least be able to do something.

Worst Case Scenario 2: Your Memory Has Gone Bad

The computer starts, and things happen on-screen, but then you see a message during the memory check. This message says something like,

`Parity error checking RAM` or `memory error`. This is bad news—one of those little chips that makes up your computer's internal memory (RAM) has gone bad. Write down whatever error message you get, especially any numbers. Then call in an expert for service, and see Chapter 21.

Worst Case Scenario 3: Your Hard Disk Has Gone Bad

When you try to start your computer, the memory test goes just fine, and there's no disk in drive A. But when your computer tries to access your hard disk, you see a truly horrifying message such as `Missing operating system`, `Invalid drive specification`, or `Seek error reading Drive C`. This isn't good news. Something's wrong with your hard disk—probably something unspeakable. Turn to Chapter 21. Hope you backed up your work.

Why Does It Always Try To Read Drive A?

When your computer starts, it first tries to access drive A. This is because if your hard disk fails (horrors), you need some way to start your computer. So, DOS lets you start from drive A and assumes that you'll be starting from this drive. Even with a bum hard drive, you can stick a disk into drive A, close the latch, restart your computer, and Lo! DOS loads from the floppy. You only need to do this if your hard disk fails, though. Under any other circumstances, make sure that drive A is unlatched when you start your computer. If DOS doesn't find a disk in drive A, it tries to start from drive C, which is what you want.

The Power Just Went Off!

You're working with your computer, and everything's just fine. Except you hear a little thunder in the background. Aren't you glad you're inside, all nice and warm? But then the lights go out. The screen goes dead. The realization slowly dawns on you: you've lost your data.

What to do if you just lost your work due to a power outage

- ✔ You've lost everything up to the time you last saved. Isn't that nice? That's why we computer book authors keep badgering you about saving repeatedly, preferably every 10 minutes. That way, you won't lose more than 10 minutes of work. Try to avoid violence—you'll only regret it later.
- ✔ When the power comes back on, your computer will restart, but you won't see your program. You'll see DOS, the DOS Shell, or Windows, depending on how your computer is set up.
- ✔ Restart your program. Then immediately try to reconstruct any work that you have lost—the longer you wait, the greater the chance that you'll forget. And make an immediate resolution to save your work more often.
- ✔ If you're lucky, your program will have an automatic recovery feature that saves your work even if you don't. If so, you'll see the recovered version of your file when you restart the program.
- ✔ If you're living in an area where power outages are common, consider buying an uninterruptable power supply (UPS). See "12 More Cool Things To Get for Your Computer" in the Quick & Dirty Dozens section.

The Computer Won't Respond

You type, you click, you swear, but there's no response; your program just stares at you, frozen on-screen. Is this a system crash? Hang? Freeze? Has it bombed? (Note that there are lots of picturesque synonyms for the same thing.)

CHAPTER 20

GOSH, IT'S NOT WORKING

What to do if you think your computer has crashed

- ✔ Wait. Particularly with big Windows programs, there are some operations that take one or more minutes to complete. Go get a cup of coffee and come back; chances are everything's fine.

- ✔ Try pressing Esc. You might be in some weird mode of the program that you're not familiar with. Try pressing F1 to get help. Try pressing F10 or Alt to activate the menu bar, if there is one. Try clicking your heels and chanting "There's no place like home." If any of these methods produce results of any sort, your system's okay.

- ✔ If you have a mouse, note that you might still be able to move the pointer around the screen even though the system seems to be hung. That's a good indication that you're in some weird program mode that you don't understand. Get someone who knows the program to help you. If clicking the mouse does nothing, however, the system has crashed.

- ✔ Look at the hard disk activity light (the little light on the front of the computer). Is it blinking on or off? If it's off, you've got another indication that the system is hung. If it's blinking on and off, the program is probably carrying out some really lengthy operation; be patient. Control will probably soon return to the keyboard.

- ✔ If you're using Windows, press Ctrl+Alt+Delete to find out whether your application has crashed. If it has, you see a screen informing you that this application has stopped responding to Windows. If it hasn't, you'll see a message informing you that everything's OK, and you can press any key to return to your application.

- ✔ You should only press the Reset button (generally on the front of your computer) to restart your system if everything else fails. Unfortunately, you lose any work you haven't saved. (Reminder: Save your work, save your work, save your work, often, often, often.)

TIP

Even if you think your system has crashed, don't reset right away. When you reset the computer, you lose any work you haven't saved. If there's still a chance you're just stuck somewhere in a program you don't know very well, try getting some help from somebody who's knowledgeable about the program.

My Program Won't Start!

For months, you've been typing **WP** to start WordPerfect. Today you type it and see the message, `Bad command or file name`, if you're using DOS. (If you're using Windows, the Application Execution Error dialog box appears, informing you that apparently the Supreme Court has stayed the execution of your application.) What gives?

If you're a DOS user, did you just install a new program? The installation utility may have messed up your AUTOEXEC.BAT file, which would prevent you from starting your program. Get a DOS wizard to help you. You need to edit the PATH statement in the AUTOEXEC.BAT file. (Your friendly local DOS wizard will know exactly what this is.) In the meantime, you can start your program by changing to the program's directory. If you're using WordPerfect 5.1, for example, the program probably lives in a directory called C:\WP51. To change to this directory, type **CD \WP51** and press Enter. For more information on directories, see Chapter 14.

If you're a Windows user, check the properties of your program icon. (The *properties* are a list of specifications about the program—like where it's located.) To see this list, highlight the offending program's icon and choose **P**roperties from the **F**ile menu. (Alternatively, just press Alt+Enter.) You see the Program Item Properties dialog box. Check the **C**ommand Line box. Does it list the correct location (Path) of the program? If the program's location and name is C:\WP51\WP.EXE, and this box says something else, you've discovered why you can't start your program.

If you're not sure of the exact location or name of your program, you can click on the **B**rowse button to see a File Manager-like directory tree and file list, which you can browse through to locate your program. After you find the program, just double-click on the program's name, as if you were launching the application. Windows will place the correct filespec into the **C**ommand Line box. Click on OK to confirm. (If all this sounds like gobbley-gook, get some Windows wizard to help you or consider a sister companion to this book, *I Hate Windows*.)

Worst Case Scenario 4: You Erased the Program

Can't start the program after changing to its directory? Congratulations. You must have erased it or one of the "helper" files associated with the main program file. Or maybe the file has become corrupt, probably from reading cheap comic books. You'll need to reinstall the program. Chapter 18 covers this grueling process.

Where's My Mouse?

Don't expect your mouse to show up when the DOS prompt is visible; DOS doesn't do mice. But, if the old familiar mouse pointer doesn't show up where it should (in "mousable" DOS applications or Windows), something may have happened to the mouse driver.

A mouse driver is one of those system files that has to be left alone for your system to work correctly. It's probably called something like MOUSE.SYS or MOUSE.COM, and this file must be correctly referenced in another system file, like CONFIG.SYS or AUTOEXEC.BAT. Maybe you erased one of these files by accident, or maybe the file became corrupt. In any case, you'll need expert help. See the next chapter, "Help!"

The Time and Date Are Wrong!

Almost all the computers sold these days have built-in clock/calendar circuits, which require a battery. The battery ensures that the circuits won't forget the time and date when you switch off the power. When you make a change to a file, DOS notes the date and time the file was last changed. This information can be important if you need to figure out which file is more current.

On some older computers, you have to type the date and time each time you start the computer. These computers don't have a battery.

If you're a DOS user, you can make sure that the date is correct by typing **DATE** and pressing Enter. You see something like this:

```
Current date is Mon 02-01-1993
Enter new date (mm-dd-yy):
```

If the date is off, reset it. Type the date in the MM-DD-YY format, like 6/30/93, or 3/2/94; then press Enter.

To make sure that the time is correct, type **TIME** and press Enter. You see something like this:

```
Current time is 12:07:52.68p
Enter new time:
```

If the time is correct, just press Enter. If it isn't, type the time by typing the hour, a colon, the minutes, and **a** for AM or **p** for PM. For example, to set the time to 6:09 PM, type **6:09p** and press Enter.

If you're a Windows user, you can check the time and date by double-clicking on the Control Panel icon in the Main program group. When the Control Panel group appears, double-click on the Date/Time icon. You see the Date & Time dialog box, displaying what the computer thinks is the current time. To change the date or time, click on what you want to change, and then just click on the little up or down arrows to raise or lower the number. Click on OK when you're done.

TIP

You can use the Clock accessory (usually found in the Accessories group) to add a digital or dial clock to your desktop. Choosing Always on Top from the Clock's control menu (that vertical bar thing button in the upper-left corner of the Clock window) will keep the clock window on top of everything else.

Worst Case Scenario 5: The Battery Is Dead

If the date on your computer reads January 1, 1980, you've got a minor but irritating problem: your battery's dead. This minor inconvenience could become a major problem, however. Your computer's battery helps the computer remember what type of hard drive you have. If the battery goes completely dead, your computer forgets this information, and you may not be able to access your hard drive. Call for service; get that battery replaced immediately. And, while you're at it, ask the service person to reset the date and time.

TIP

To avoid having your work interrupted by a trip to the repair shop, have your computer's battery replaced every other year. They're supposed to last longer than two years, but don't bet on it. By the way, don't keep the old battery around—it contains a deadly toxic chemical (cadmium). These batteries can kill—no exaggeration—if they're swallowed.

I Can't Copy This File!

This is a pretty common problem, and an easily solved one.

What to do if you're having trouble copying a file

✔ If you see the message `File cannot be copied onto itself`, you tried to make a copy of the file in the same directory, using the same name. (If you're using File Manager, you see the Error

continues

What to do if you're having trouble copying a file, continued

Copying File dialog box when you try to do this.) You can't copy a file to the same directory using the same name. It's an impossibility. It's also unnecessary. Copy the file with a different name, or copy the file to a different directory.

- ✔ If you're trying to copy the file to a floppy disk and you see the message `Insufficient disk space`, you've run out of room on the floppy disk. Get a floppy disk with more room on it, and repeat the command; or, remove some files on the floppy disk to make more room. Windows File Manager users get the message `Destination drive full` that does something DOS does not: invites you to insert another disk to continue copying. Most agreeable.

- ✔ If you see the message `Write protect error writing drive A` or `Write protect error writing drive B` while trying to copy to a floppy disk, the disk has been write-protected, which means that you can't alter it. (Windows users see the message, `Cannot create or replace filename. Access denied.` Make sure that the disk is not full or write-protected.) If you need to unprotect the disk, flip to Chapter 6, which explains how to accomplish this feat.

- ✔ If you see the message `File not found`, use **DIR** to make sure that the source file (the one you're trying to copy) is really in the directory. Also, check your typing. You probably won't have this problem in Windows File Manager, since you can't drag a file you can't click.

- ✔ If you see the message `Path not found`, DOS can't find the directory to which you want to copy the file. Check your typing. Again, this isn't a problem with File Manager.

My File's Gone!

At one time or another, this phrase has been heard echoing throughout the halls of every company whose employees use a computer. The cry is generally followed by a string of obscenities, although the latter is optional.

Relax. Your file's probably on your disk...somewhere. Chances are good that you saved it to some weird place, like your root directory. DOS users, flip to Chapter 15 for information on hunting down the lost file; Windows users should flip to Chapter 16 for the same information in Windows terms.

If you think you might have deleted the file by accident, DOS users should immediately turn to the section "Recovering from an Accidental Deletion" in Chapter 15. Then run UNDELETE. (You must have DOS version 5 or later to use UNDELETE. If you're using an earlier copy of DOS, stop what you're doing and go get a DOS wizard to help you.) Windows users, flip to the section "Undeleting Files" in Chapter 16.

I Just Reformatted My Floppy Disk!

I'm assuming here that you just reformatted a disk containing valuable data. Don't panic! If you're using DOS Version 5 or later, there's an easy solution. These versions of DOS perform a format that enables you to recover your data. The key to this wondrous capability is a DOS utility called UNFORMAT. But you must use UNFORMAT immediately, without doing anything else that would change the disk in any way.

To unformat a floppy disk in drive A, start from the DOS prompt and type **UNFORMAT A:**. Then press Enter. You see a lot of messages, and finally a confirmation request. Press Y to unformat your floppy disk. (You might have to press Y more than once.)

If you don't have DOS version 5 or later, don't do anything else with your computer. **Don't turn it off!** Go directly to your local computer wizard and ask for help. Do not pass Go. Do not collect $200.

I Just Reformatted My Hard Disk!

This takes some real effort on your part—you had to ignore DOS's repeated warnings that this is probably a dumb thing to do. If you're using DOS Version 5 or later, you can recover your data. Just use the

UNFORMAT program. To unformat your hard drive, start from the DOS prompt (boot with a floppy disk if necessary). Then type **UNFORMAT C:** and press Enter.

TIP

> Don't try this "just to see how it works." You could lose some or all of the data on your hard disk. Use UNFORMAT on your hard disk only if you've just accidentally formatted your hard disk.

If you're using a version of DOS earlier than 5.0, don't touch your computer; don't even turn it off. Just let it be and go get help. Find your local DOS wizard, who will have an unformat utility program.

This Floppy Isn't Working!

You can tell because you're getting error messages, such as `Data error reading (or writing) drive A`. In Windows, you get a pretty specific message, which even includes instructions on what to do. DOS users, you'll have to interpret the cryptic messages in the following checklist.

What to do if you see a DOS error message while using a floppy disk

- ✔ If you see the message `Not ready reading drive A. Abort, Retry, Fail?`, you probably forgot to put the disk into the drive or to close the drive latch. Close the latch, and press R for Retry.
- ✔ If you see the message `General failure reading (or writing) drive A`, DOS can't access the drive, but it doesn't know why. (That's why you see the "general failure" message; it's the DOS equivalent of the "little technical problem" that the cockpit crew tells you about after explaining that they're going to make an unscheduled landing.) Probably, you put an unformatted disk into the drive. Try another disk, or format this one.

- ✔ If you see the message `Data error reading (or writing) drive A`, it's bad news—something's wrong with the surface of the disk. Immediately copy from this disk all the files that you can, but don't use this disk again; either throw it away or use it as an office Frisbee.

Worst Case Scenario 6: The File Allocation Table (What?) Is Bad

You may see the message `File allocation table bad drive A`. This is really bad news—the table that keeps track of where files are located has been scrambled. Turn off your computer and seek expert help immediately. See Chapter 21, "Help!"

I Can't Access My Hard Disk!

Hard disks, unlike diamonds, are not forever. You'll be fortunate if you get three or four years of continuous use. And when the end is near, you start getting little warning signs. Let's say you're trying to copy a file, and you get the message `Read fault error reading Drive C`. You can't copy this file, but other things still work. But you start getting this, and other messages of the same sort, more often. These are pretty strong signs of impending disk death.

TIP

> If you get lots of these error messages, the end is probably near. Back up your whole hard disk using a program such as MSBACKUP (DOS) or MWBACKUP (Windows), included with DOS 6 and 6.2. If you don't have DOS 6 or 6.2, get a backup program and do a full backup of your entire disk.

When you are sure you have successfully backed up all your data, have a DOS guru reformat your hard disk, and then reinstall a program or two. Try using the computer. If it works smoothly (without error messages), the problem had to do with the surface of the hard disk. You might be able to continue using it.

If the disk still acts funny after you reformat it, forget it—you need a new drive. Do yourself a favor and get a bigger one.

TIP

I have to use my backup data. How?

If you've been forced to reformat or replace your hard disk, you can restore your data from the backup disks. The type of backup program you use determines what restore procedure you need to use. For help restoring the files, see the manual for your backup program.

My Printer Won't Print!

There are lots of likely causes here, but most of them aren't serious.

Dealing with a difficult printer

- ✔ Is the printer plugged in? Is the power on?
- ✔ Is the cable connected at both ends (computer and printer)? Check both connections to make sure they're tight and secure.
- ✔ Is the printer selected or on-line? There's usually an indicator light with a little button. If it's off, press the button so that the light is on, and try again.
- ✔ Is there paper? If not, load some.
- ✔ Is the paper jammed? Laser printers display a warning light when the paper's jammed. Clear the obstruction and try again.

Worst Case Scenario 7: The Printer Isn't Installed Correctly

TIP

Is this the first time you've tried printing with a program? If so, maybe you didn't select the printer when you installed it. Get somebody to help you determine which printer is the current printer for this program. If it's listed incorrectly, change it. (You may have to reinstall the program to do so; Chapter 18 tells you all about this agonizing process.)

Still Giving You Trouble?

If you're still having trouble, try these tricks, known to computer experts, but rarely communicated to beginners.

Tricks that might solve software problems

- ✔ If possible, save all your work and restart your system. Because this process enters fresh, correct copies of your programs into the computer's memory, this procedure will probably solve the problem.
- ✔ If you trace the problem to a particular program, try reinstalling the program from the original program disks. Once in a while, this trick fixes the problem.
- ✔ Unless you've been swapping programs with lots of people, the chances are slim that the problem's caused by a computer virus. But, you may want to run an anti-virus utility to make sure. See Chapter 13 for more information. (Note: An anti-virus utility comes with versions 6 and 6.2 of DOS.)

Are You in over Your Head?

Computer problems can be really frustrating. And, there are lots of problems users can't solve on their own. Ask yourself the following questions:

- ✔ Have I spent more than 30 minutes trying to solve this problem?
- ✔ Is the computer still dead after I make sure it's getting power?
- ✔ Does the system crash every time I start or restart it?
- ✔ Is the system more than two years old? (If so, the battery may be dead.)
- ✔ Do lots of error messages appear when the system starts?
- ✔ Could I have accidentally erased some files in the hard disk's root directory (C:\)?
- ✔ Am I unable to access my hard disk?
- ✔ Did the problem start right after I installed a new program?

Answering "yes" to any of these questions is good grounds for getting expert help. Turn to Chapter 21.

THAT'S THE GREATEST THING ABOUT ALL THIS HIGH-TECH EQUIPMENT:
HIGH-TECH EXCUSES.
3-12

Top Ten

Computer Versions of Murphy's Law

10. The worst computer failures occur when the technical support hotline is closed (Corollary: When they're open, the problem isn't serious)

9. The only printer and video drivers missing from your new program's disk are precisely the ones you need

8. The disk you need isn't here (Corollary: The disk that is here is useless)

7. The more you back up, the less likely it is that your hard disk will fail

6. The only file DOS can't read is the one you need the most

5. A printer fails just when the most critical document is due

4. The one program feature you can't figure out is the one not discussed in the manuals

3. The guy who knows how to fix this is in Bermuda this week

2. Something that isn't working right will work just fine when the technician comes to check out your system

1. The more time you spend trying to solve a computer problem, the less likely it is that you will succeed

CHAPTER 21

Help!

IN A NUTSHELL

- ▼ Try some last-minute tricks that might get your computer back on track
- ▼ Decide when you're over your head and need help
- ▼ Call technical support
- ▼ Learn how to describe your system to technical support and repair people
- ▼ Get your system repaired

I JUST DON'T UNDERSTAND THESE THINGS!!

It's not a happy sight when a computer dies. You hear the violin playing in the background as our hero gasps his last: `Parity error checking RAM`. Actually, a real computer death is often over a lot quicker. Suddenly, the screen goes blank or you see a funny interference pattern. Granted, computer demises are rare, but they do happen. And when they do, no amount of user finagling can get the computer going again. It's time to throw in the towel and get expert help.

Try These Tricks before Hitting the Panic Button

Computers heave a lot of information around, and even a tiny error can throw off the system. If your computer doesn't seem to be working correctly, try the tricks in the following checklist. Known to computer wizards, but rarely communicated to beginners, these tricks will soon become part of your working routine.

Things to try if your system isn't working right

- ✔ Chances are the problem comes from having pressed the wrong key at the wrong time. Did you accidentally press the Num Lock, Scroll Lock, or Caps Lock key? If you're using a word processing program, did you accidentally press the Insert key? This puts the program into the Typeover (also called Overtype) mode, which you may not be used to. If you're using a Windows program, did you press F10 or Alt accidentally? If so, you've activated the menu bar, and that's why you can't type anything, or why the computer decided to do some weird stuff when you did type (you might have accidentally activated a command). Press Esc to return to your document.

- ✔ Maybe you're in some strange mode of the program you've never seen before. Try pressing Esc (Windows) or Ctrl+Break (DOS) to see if that takes you back to more familiar territory. As a last resort, read the manual.

- ✔ Some operations take slow computers (386s and 486-25s) a long time to complete. If the disk drive is active, leave your computer alone for five or ten minutes.

- ✔ Has it really crashed? Symptom: You hear a beep when you try to type something. This isn't very good news. (Sometimes, however, a program will beep if you press a key it doesn't like. Try a different key or two before assuming your computer has crashed.)

- ✔ If you're using Windows and you're sure that a program is comatose, press Ctrl+Alt+Del. You'll see a text screen that informs you that the program is no longer communicating with Windows. If you press Enter, Windows closes the dead program, and you lose any unsaved work. But, often you can save any work done with other programs that you may not have saved.

- ✔ Is a program crashing all the time? Maybe there's some glitch that occurred when a vital file was recopied, or maybe you accidentally messed up some important settings. To cure this, try reinstalling the program from the original program disks. Once in a while, this trick fixes the problem.

- ✔ Beginning computer users think every little problem is caused by one of those awful viruses. But, cheer up. Unless you've been swapping programs with a lot of people, the chances are slim that the problem is caused by a computer virus. Still, you may want to run an anti-virus utility to make sure. (Note: An anti-virus utility comes with Versions 6.0 and 6.2 of DOS.)

TIP

Those tiny little electronic components inside your computer are more likely to fail when they're very young (less than three months old) or very elderly (more than five years old). If you're going to have a major hardware problem, it will probably happen when your computer is brand new or decrepit—not in between. If your system has been working for six months or a year, the chances are pretty good that the problem lies in the software, not the hardware.

Describing Your System

TIP

Your first recourse is any knowledgeable user in your organization that you can drag into your office. Even if such people aren't able to solve the problem, they can probably narrow it down so that you can describe the problem more accurately to technical support or repair people.

If something is wrong with your system and you turn to an expert for help, he or she might ask you to describe the system. Use the following checklist to fill out as much information about your system as you can. You need to know the following information:

TIP

If you're using DOS Version 5 or later, you can use Microsoft System Diagnostics to get most of the information on this list. To use this program, type **MSD** at the DOS prompt and press Enter. You see a screen listing your system's current configuration. If you don't have DOS 5, 6, or 6.2, check your system's manuals and sales receipts, or call the store that sold you the computer.

- ✔ Brand name: ______________________________
- ✔ Model number: ___________________________
- ✔ Microprocessor (286, 386SX, 486DX, etc.): _________________
- ✔ Math coprocessor (if any): _____________
- ✔ DOS version: _____________
- ✔ DOS manufacturer (Microsoft, IBM, Novell, etc.) :_____________
- ✔ Total amount of RAM: ____________

- Hard disk brand name and model number: ______________
- Total hard disk space: _______________
- Video adapter type (MDA, VGA, SVGA, etc.): ______________
- Mouse brand name: ____________
- Type of mouse (serial, bus): _____________
- Mouse software version: ____________
- Software version number (if it's a software problem): _________

Describing the Problem

("It's making a funny noise...")

Remember the look on the auto mechanic's face when you said, "Well, it's kind of like a funny 'clank, gronch, bing' noise that I hear when I turn the wheel to the left"? The more you can pinpoint and accurately describe the problem, the better the chance that a technician can solve the problem.

How to describe your computer's problem to a technician

- Try to narrow down the problem so that you can describe it to the person who's helping you. "It isn't working" is hardly descriptive. Just what isn't working? The printer? The monitor? The mouse? Eliminate parts of the system that seem to be working fine until you've identified the problem component.
- Jot down any error messages you see on-screen.
- If possible, learn how to reproduce the problem. (For example, you might get a certain error message every time you try to print.) Then describe exactly what happens.

Calling the Technical Support Hotline

(Help!)

Computer companies and software publishers spend a lot of money maintaining their technical support hotlines. Probably, they'd prefer that I tell you, "Check the manual before calling technical support." But, very few manuals include a troubleshooting section that details solutions to common problems. You can check the manuals if you like, but I'll bet that you won't find the information you need. Why is this? Because manuals have to cover every aspect of the program. Often, they don't devote enough space in the manual for problem solving.

How to call a technical support hotline

- ✔ Try to call first thing in the morning. Most technical support hotlines are busy, busy, busy, and you might be placed on hold for up to an hour if you call during busy times. Mid-morning and late afternoon are generally the worst times to call.

- ✔ Keep your computer manuals, disks, and receipts handy in case the technician demands to know your serial numbers. This is sometimes done to make sure you're a bona fide, registered owner of the product.

- ✔ You'll probably have to negotiate a voice mail system. You may be asked to leave your name, telephone number, and a description of the problem. Leave this information. Most technical support people will get back with you.

- ✔ If you finally get to talk to a real live human being, you'll be asked to supply information about your system or the software that's giving you fits. (Fill out the checklist earlier in this chapter before calling.)

- ✔ Describe the problem in detail. If possible, reproduce it while you're talking to the technical support person so that you can give a blow-by-blow account.

- Be nice. Technical support people often are treated as easy targets for the frustrations and rages of upset users. Keep calm. Keep in mind that your problem wasn't caused by the person on the other end of the phone. Those people are actually nice human beings, with names like Debbie or Jeff; at home they have cute pets and children. Don't dump on them.

- If you're told something vague like, "Oh, you'll need to modify your system configuration files," ask for specifics. What exactly should you do? Carefully write down what you're told and what steps you need to take.

Getting Your System Repaired

So it's a hardware problem, after all. This happens.

What to do if your system needs to be repaired

- Is your system still on warranty? Find out how to get it serviced. Some computer firms sell their computers with vague promises of "on-site" service, which turns out to be valid only if you're located within one block of the firm's Hope, Arkansas, headquarters.

- If your computer has an expensive motherboard problem, consider replacing the motherboard with one that has a faster microprocessor, rather than paying a lot of money to fix the old one.

- You may have to pack the thing off, UPS. If so, use the original boxes all that junk came in. (You did save them, didn't you?) The original boxes are designed to protect the equipment as much as possible during shipping. Also, make sure to insure the system through the shipping company for its full value!

- Don't send anything back to a manufacturer without having obtained a "return authorization number" from the company. Otherwise, they might just bounce it right back to you.

continues

What to do if your system needs to be repaired, continued

- ✔ Did your system fail within 30 days of a "no questions asked" return policy? Consider returning the system instead of fussing with getting it repaired. Call for a return authorization number before sending the system packing.
- ✔ Not on warranty? Shop around for good repair prices. Beware of prices quoted at computer stores—they tend to be absurdly high. Check out the local garage operations advertised in local newsletters; they can fix your system cheaply just by replacing the offensive part, which is actually a better idea than trying to repair it.
- ✔ Ask the computer repair shop what you should bring with you: cables, software, monitor, keyboard, printer?
- ✔ Insist on a warranty for all repair work that's done on your system.

Shoe®
JEFF MACNELLY
OUR NEW HOME COMPUTER!!
WHERE DO WE PUT IT?

WELCOME TO THE FABULOUS '80s, SKYLER!!
MEET OUR NEW HOME COMPUTER.
COMPUTER? WHY DO WE NEED A COMPUTER?
IT'S A FANTASTIC TOOL.

FOR ONE THING, IT HELPS WITH MY HOUSEHOLD BUDGET.

I'VE FED IN ALL MY EXPENSES, MY DEPOSITS, MY CHECKS, MY INVESTMENTS...
© Jefferson Communications, Inc. 1983
Distributed by Tribune Company Syndicate, Inc.

AND THE COMPUTER MAKES THE DECISIONS ON HOW TO MANAGE MY MONEY, SEE?...

WHAT'S IT SAYING?
"SELL THE HOME COMPUTER."
MACNELLY 3/20

PART V

Quick & Dirty Dozens

Includes:

12 Minor But Embarrassing Beginner's Boo-Boos

12 Good Things You Should Always Do

12 Acronyms People Expect You To Know

12 Most Common DOS Error Messages

12 More Cool Things To Get for Your Computer

SHOE
By Jeff MacNelly
TOMORROW IS THE START OF A WHOLE NEW WEEK.

I BETTER GET MY EXCUSES ORGANIZED.

WELL, NO, I DIDN'T GET TO IT BECAUSE THE COPIER WENT DOWN YESTERDAY.

NOPE. DIDN'T GET THE MESSAGE... THERE'S SOMETHING WRONG WITH MY MACHINE.

SORRY... I MEANT TO GET IT TO YOU YESTERDAY...

BUT MY FAX IS ON THE BLINK.

I TRIED TO CALL IN FROM THE ROAD, BUT MY CAR PHONE'S IN THE SHOP.

© 1991 Tribune Media Services, Inc.
All Rights Reserved
I WOULD HAVE FINISHED IT YESTERDAY, BUT THE COMPUTER WENT DOWN...

WELL, THIS MORNING THE LASER PRINTER CRASHED,...

AND I COULDN'T GET MY MODEM ON LINE.

THAT'S THE GREATEST THING ABOUT ALL THIS HIGH-TECH EQUIPMENT:
3-12

HIGH-TECH EXCUSES.
MACNELLY

I HATE PCs

Quick & Dirty Dozens

IN A NUTSHELL

- ▼ 12 Minor But Embarrassing Beginner's Boo-Boos
- ▼ 12 Good Things You Should Always Do
- ▼ 12 Acronyms People Expect You To Know
- ▼ 12 Most Common DOS Error Messages
- ▼ 12 More Cool Things To Get for Your Computer

NOW WHAT DOES IT WANT ME TO DO?

12 Minor But Embarrassing Beginner's Boo-Boos

1. **Leaving a disk in drive A when you shut down the system.**

   When you start or reboot your computer, it goes a-hunting for DOS. First, it looks on drive A. And if it finds a floppy disk there, it tries to read DOS from the floppy disk. But, DOS isn't on this disk. And so you get that inspiring message, `Non-system disk or disk error`.

   When you see this message, remove the disk and press any key to restart your system.

2. **tYPING wITH cAPS lOCK oN.**

   The Caps Lock key is one of those irritating toggle keys. When you press it once, you engage the Caps Lock mode. This is sort of like a typewriter's Caps Lock key, in that the letters you type are in uppercase. But just to be different, any letters you type with the Shift key depressed are in lowercase, resulting in a strange pattern of capitalization unique to the computer world. Press the Caps Lock key again to turn off Caps Lock.

3. **Dumping your coffee into the keyboard.**

   Sooner or later, it will happen to you. Believe it or not, most keyboards can take an inundation of this sort—if you remedy the problem immediately. Save your work, if you can, and turn off the computer. Disconnect the keyboard. Over a pile of newspapers, turn the keyboard upside down and burp it gently. Coffee will fall like rain from the keys.

   Put the keyboard face down on a pile of tissues, and let it dry out. When it's dry, spray 409 or Windex onto a paper towel (don't spray directly on the keyboard), and carefully clean off the coffee stains.

4. **Inserting 5.25-inch disks the wrong way.**

You can insert a 5.25-inch disk into a disk drive several different ways, but as you've no doubt discovered, only one way is correct.

To insert a 5.25-inch disk correctly, make sure that the disk's label is on the side of the disk that's facing up. Now rotate the disk (without flipping it upside down) until the text on the label is upside down, from your perspective. The business end of the disk—the hole that shows the disk's surface—should face away from you. The label should be closest to you. Put the disk into the drive. Close the latch on the floppy disk drive. Then just recite the following ancient Vedic mantra, and you should be fine: "Ah-oh-eh-DAHS-ah."

5. **Inserting disks between the drives.**

This happens more often than you'd think. To remove the disk, you may need tweezers. If you can't reach the disk, get your local DOS wizard to remove the computer's case.

6. **Mispronouncing computer terms everyone else seems to know.**

A quick pronunciation guide:

386	Three eighty-six (not "Three hundred eighty-six")
ASCII	Ask-ee
CPU	See-pea-you
DOS	Dahss, as in "floss" (not "dose")
GUI	Gooey (no lie)
KHz	Kilohertz

YOU COULD POUND THE KEYS HARDER WHEN YOU WERE MAD...

KB	Kay-bee, like that neat toy store at the mall. You ought to see the latest Lego Technic sets they have.
MB	Meh-guh bite
MS-DOS	Em-ess dahs (not "Ms. DOS")
RAM	Ram, as in "Spam" (not "arr-ay-emm")
user	Rhymes with "loser." Is that an omen? Northeast of New Jersey, and intensifying in Boston, however, this is pronounced "use-ah," thus rhyming with "vigor" (vig-ah).
VGA	Vee-gee-ay
WYSIWYG	Whiz-ee-whig. Is this the dumbest acronym you've ever seen, or what?

7. Logging onto the wrong drive or directory.

When you change drives, you log onto the drive you've indicated. From that point on, DOS assumes that you want your commands carried out on that drive, unless you specifically tell DOS otherwise. Let's say you are logged onto drive A, and you want to delete the file JUNK.DOC. You type the following:

DEL JUNK.DOC

But, you get the message `File not found.` Should you assume that JUNK.DOC doesn't exist? By no means! You're simply logged onto the wrong drive. JUNK.DOC is on drive C, in the directory called C:\DOCS\TRASH.

You have two options. You can override the default disk or directory by including all that nasty path information in the command. Or, switch to drive C by typing **C:** and pressing Enter. Then change to the directory.

8. **Thinking your computer has crashed when it really hasn't.**

This is pretty common. Possibilities:

- ✔ You hit the Num Lock accidentally. Now you're trying to move the cursor, but all you get are weird numbers. Just press the Num Lock key again.
- ✔ You forgot to turn on the computer or the monitor.
- ✔ You didn't close the latch on the drive door (5.25-inch disks only).
- ✔ You're using a new program and you've gotten into something that you can't get out of. Try pressing Esc ("Get Me Out Of This") or F1 ("Help!").
- ✔ You're using DOS, but you pressed the Esc key. The DOS prompt is gone and all you see is a funny little slash mark. This is OK; DOS is waiting for you to type another command.
- ✔ The mouse or keyboard cable came loose.
- ✔ The program you're using is taking its own sweet time to do something. Give it a chance.

9. **Buying software that doesn't meet your needs.**

Only one kind of program is worth buying: one right for your needs. Unfortunately, it's not very easy to determine your needs, and it's even harder to get salespeople to understand them. But, give it a shot. If you need to print mailing labels, ask yourself questions such as: "Self, how many people are on my mailing list? Do I want the labels to look really cool, with neat fonts and stuff? Do I want to sort the mailing labels by zip code (something the Post Office will appreciate)? Do I want to record other information besides name and address?" The better you summarize your needs, the better the chance that you'll buy a useful program. And here's a tip—get some mail order computer software catalogs and study the product descriptions.

Also, be sure that you get a program that your computer can run. Chapter 18 provides clues on decoding the requirement list you find on software boxes. Read the requirements before you tear off the cellophane.

10. Starting Program Manager and then getting upset because you can't find Windows.

Program Manager is Windows—at least, the part of it that helps you launch programs.

11. Using your computer with the monitor facing a big, bright window.

You could go blind doing this. The glare from the window makes it close to impossible to see what's on-screen. You can get an accessory called a *nonglare filter*, but it's best to move your computer so that the glare goes away.

12. Not backing up.

OK, OK, I know, you've already had this lecture. But you can really get into trouble by not backing up. Right now, it's a minor boo-boo—but it could turn into a major catastrophe. Back up your work.

12 Good Things You Should Always Do

1. Save, save, and save some more.

When you're working with an application, your work is in the computer's memory. It's volatile. If the power goes to lunch, so does your work. To be on the safe side, save your work every ten minutes.

2. Keep your UNINSTALL disk safe.

When you or someone else installed DOS 5, 6, or 6.2 on your system, the DOS SETUP program created something called an UNINSTALL disk. This disk is really important. In the event of a serious hard disk problem, this disk could hold the key to regaining access to all the data on your hard disk. Put it away where it can't be messed up by dust, coffee spills, or rampaging children armed with magnets.

3. Keep your distance from the monitor.

The jury's still out about the health effects of the low-level electromagnetic radiation (EMR) produced by computer monitors, but why take chances? A careful study by *PC* Magazine indicates that the level of this radiation falls off to undetectable levels about 28 inches from the screen. If you keep your face and body that far away from the screen's surface, you've eliminated the risk. Or better yet, get a monitor that meets the Swedish MPR II standards for low EMR emissions.

4. Protect yourself from repetitive strain injury.

Repetitive strain injuries (RSI) represent one of the fastest-growing causes of occupational disability, and computers are clearly to blame. Sitting at the keyboard all day, performing the same hand and wrist movements over and over again can contribute to RSI maladies such as *Carpal Tunnel Syndrome*, an injury to the nerves of the wrist caused by scar tissue forming in a narrow bone channel. RSI injuries can be extremely painful and disabling. To reduce your chance of injuring yourself while using the computer, follow these guidelines:

- ✔ Make sure that your keyboard is positioned slightly below the level of your elbows so that you don't have to hold your forearms up to peck at those keys.
- ✔ Get a wrist rest. This pad sits in front of your computer and takes the strain off your arms and wrists.
- ✔ Don't work more than two hours without taking a break.

5. Win prizes!

The registration cards that come packaged with software are valuable to you. When a new version of the program comes out, registered users can order the upgrade at a bargain-basement price, compared to what new buyers will have to fork over. You'll also get notices of maintenance upgrades—minor revisions that fix annoying bugs or add certain new features—which may be of great value to you.

6. Do your housekeeping.

Spend some time organizing your hard disk; don't just add files and programs willy-nilly. Most important of all, create directories for your data files so that they aren't mixed up with your program files. And periodically go through your files; delete the ones you're done with and don't need, and move the other ones to floppy disks.

7. Label backup disks clearly.

When you back up your work, be sure to write **BACKUP DISK** in big, bold letters. Also write today's date, as well as the names of the files contained on the disk. Keep your backup disks up high somewhere, far away from coffee and Pepsi inundations.

8. Learn to archive.

There's another angle on backing up, called *archiving*. Here's the difference between backing up and archiving. When you back up your disk, you create an up-to-date backup copy of your disk as it is now, including all files you're currently working with. If your disk fails, you can restore these files—that's why you back up. When you archive a file, you just move a finished file, one you're done with, from your hard disk to a floppy, and put it away. You're finished with it. You've printed it. You gave the report to your boss. Your boss turned it down. You don't need it on your hard disk. You probably wouldn't miss it if your disk failed. But who knows? Better archive it just to make sure.

9. **Out with the old! In with the new!**

That big, behemoth program is taking up 12MB of disk space, and what are you getting out of it? Nada. Zip. Zero. If you don't use a program, archive any data files you created, and delete the program from your hard disk. (If you later change your mind, you still have the original program disks, so you can reinstall it.)

10. **Keep your root directory clean.**

Your root directory (C:\) should contain nothing but the files DOS placed there when you installed the program, together with the names of the subdirectories created by installation programs and by you. Don't use this directory to store other kinds of files—put them in subdirectories.

11. **If at first you don't succeed, look it up.**

I've seen a lot of beginning users just sitting at the computer for hours trying to get something to work. Believe me, it's not worth it. Chances are pretty good that there's just one little thing you don't know, or you forgot, and no matter how you try, you're just not going to get anywhere. If you run into a wall like this, don't torture yourself. Get help. Look in this book. Get your local computer wizard to stop by. Ask coworkers. Call technical support. Flag down the paper boy. Do something.

12. **Don't get sucked into "computer envy."**

OK, the guy in the next office just got a Pentium-90 with 16 megabytes of RAM, a 1 gigabyte hard drive, a triple-speed CD-ROM disk, and a wave-form synthesis sound board. Does this mean your 486 is no good any more? Nope. If your computer system helps you do your work (and doesn't get in the way by running too slowly), it's just fine the way it is. But if you think it's not up to par in the performance department, you don't need to plunk down five grand for a new system—you may be able to upgrade more inexpensively by changing your microprocessor or adding more memory.

12 Acronyms People Expect You To Know

1. ASCII

This is short for American Standard Code for Information Interchange. Basically, it's a set of numerical codes that corresponds to the standard keys on a computer keyboard. An ASCII file contains nothing but the standard ASCII text characters—no fancy extra stuff, like the junk that programs add to deal with extras like boldface or page numbers.

2. DOS

Yes, DOS is itself an acronym; it stands for Disk Operating System. According to one theory, this acronym stems from the fact that MS-DOS and other early PC operating systems (such as CP/M) were provided on disk, rather than being stored on a ROM chip inside the computer. According to another theory, it stems from the fact that, so far as the user is concerned, MS-DOS mostly controls disks. These days, there's a tendency to drop the old-fashioned-sounding "disk" part in favor of OS (operating system), as in IBM's OS/2.

3. GUI

Acronym for Graphical User Interface, and pronounced "gooey." An interface is the part of the program that communicates with the user. DOS, for example, uses a command-line interface, which means that you type commands and the computer fights back with error messages. This isn't considered very friendly, so computer designers came up with this GUI stuff.

In a GUI interface, the screen is full of colorful boxes and little pictures called icons. The pictures represent computer items or procedures, like disks or printers. You can use the mouse to move stuff around on-screen and to initiate computer operations by clicking on the icons. Microsoft Windows is an example of a GUI.

4. KB (or just K)

You'll frequently run into KB when people are talking about file sizes or disk capacities. It's short for kilobyte. The *kilo* part means one thousand, and the *byte* part means one character, so the term means, basically, one thousand characters. Because computers measure everything in powers of twos rather than tens, a kilobyte is actually 1,024 bytes. But, you can forget that part; just think of 1KB as 1,000 characters.

5. MB (or just M)

This stands for megabyte, or about one million letters or numbers (characters). This measurement comes into play when people are talking about floppy or hard disk capacities and the amount of installed memory.

6. MHz

This stands for Megahertz, a measurement of how fast the computer's microprocessor runs. A Hertz is one cycle per second, and since mega means million, we're talking about one million cycles per second here—a lot. But, believe it or not, one million cycles is appallingly slow for a computer. The earliest IBM PC ran at 4.77MHz. Today's systems run at 20MHz or more, with the fastest widely available models running at 66MHz.

7. MS-DOS

The official name for Microsoft's disk operating system (DOS). Most people just shorten MS-DOS to DOS.

8. RAM

Short for Random-Access Memory. This is your computer's internal memory, which you can think of as being like the countertop in your kitchen. On the countertop, you place the items you're working with at the moment. The stuff you're not using stays down in the drawers and cabinets. In computers, RAM is like the countertop, while the drawers and cabinets are like the hard disk. RAM is measured the same way you measure disk capacity (KB and MB).

9. ROM

Short for Read-Only Memory. Every computer has some of this, and it helps the system get started when you turn it on or restart it. ROM is pretty unimportant, and you can forget about it.

10. SVGA

Refers to Super VGA. The VGA (Video Graphics Array) video standard has swept the PC world—almost all systems today are sold with VGA video adapters and monitors. Super VGA, an improvement on the older VGA standard, offers a sharper screen, more colors, and more detail.

11. TSR

Refers to Terminate-and-Stay-Resident, a type of DOS program that remains in memory, waiting for you to activate it. When you quit most programs, they leave the memory and go back quietly and harmlessly to your hard disk. TSR programs, however, remain in memory, even if you quit them. You can switch to these programs by using a special key combination called a *hot key*.

TSR programs sometimes conflict with each other, or with applications, crashing your computer and wiping out your work. If you're working with really critical documents, like a report your boss needs tomorrow morning, it's best to switch them off. Check your TSR's manual for the key that deactivates the program.

12. VGA

Short for Video Graphics Array. VGA is the standard for today's personal computer video adapters and monitors. If you're using a 386 or 486 computer, chances are good that it has a VGA adapter and monitor. The best systems today, however, come with Super VGA (SVGA) adapters and monitors.

12 Most Common DOS Error Messages

1. Bad command or file name

Cause: DOS can't find a program with that name in the current directory. Perhaps you typed a file name incorrectly. Or maybe it's not in the current directory. Or maybe it just doesn't exist.

Solution: Try typing the command again, checking your spelling carefully. If necessary, change to the directory that contains the file. If you still can't find the file, you might find some additional help in Chapter 21.

2. Duplicate file name or file not found

Cause: You tried to rename a file, but the name is already used. Or you mistyped the file name and DOS couldn't find the file.

Solution: If you typed the name of the file correctly, rename it using a different name. If you misspelled the name of the file, check your spelling and try again.

TIP

To see whether the file exists in the current directory, type **DIR** followed by the file name (as in **DIR JUNK.DOC**).

3. File cannot be copied onto itself

Cause: You're trying to copy a file, but you messed up typing the destination file name or location.

Solution: Type the **COPY** command again. If you're copying the file to the same directory, you must give the destination file a new name (for example, **COPY JUNK.DOC TRASH.DOC**). If you're copying the file to a different directory (but with the same name), you have to include path and/or drive information (for example, **COPY JUNK.DOC A:**).

4. General failure reading (or writing) Drive X. Abort, Retry, Fail?

Cause: DOS can't access the disk, but it can't figure out why.

Solution: Relax. Despite the terrifying connotations of "general failure," this probably isn't serious. You've probably just inserted an unformatted disk into the floppy disk drive. Press F to cancel the command. Then type **C:** and press Enter to make drive C current. If you want to format the disk, you can format it now. (Chapter 6, "Disks and Disk Drives" contains the dirt on formatting disks.)

5. Insufficient disk space

Cause: At last! A DOS message that's actually understandable. Simply put, you have no more room on this disk.

Solution: If you're trying to copy something to a floppy disk, remove the disk and get another one that has more room. If you get this message while using a hard disk, delete unwanted files.

6. Invalid directory

Cause: You tried to change to a directory, but something went wrong. There are two possibilities. First, you may have mistyped the directory name, or left out some of those important backslashes. Second, the directory may not exist—maybe you deleted it or never created it.

Solution: Try typing the command again, and type the full path name, including all those backslashes. If you haven't created the directory, or you deleted it, create it again.

TIP

The only time you can leave out the backslashes is when you're changing to a subdirectory of the current directory. For example, suppose you're in C:\DOCS. You can change to C:\DOCS\JUNK by typing **CD JUNK** and pressing Enter. But, you can't change from C:\ to C:\WORK\BORING by typing **CD BORING**.

7. **Invalid drive specification**

Cause: You typed a drive letter in a DOS command, but DOS doesn't think there's any such drive. If you have drives A, B, and C, but refer to a drive D in a command, for example, you get this message.

Solution: Retype the command, using valid drive letters.

8. **Invalid file name or file not found**

Cause: You tried to rename a file, but you used illegal characters in the new file name.

Solution: Type a new name that uses legal characters (stick to the letters A through Z, and the numbers 0 through 9).

9. **Invalid number of parameters, Invalid parameter**

Cause: DOS can't understand the command you typed.

Solution: Look up the command again to make sure you're typing it correctly.

10. **Non-system disk or disk error**

Cause: Stay calm. Don't panic. This problem is minor. A floppy disk was in drive A when you turned on or restarted your computer, and this disk does not contain DOS.

Solution: Remove the disk and press any key to restart the computer. If you get the same message again, it's bad news—something's wrong with your hard drive. Time to call the repair shop.

11. **Not ready reading Drive X. Abort, Retry, Fail?**

Cause: The floppy disk drive doesn't contain a disk, or the drive door is unlatched.

Solution: Put a disk in the drive, latch the door, and press R for Retry.

- ✔ If you get the much-beloved `Abort, Retry, Fail` message when trying to access a hard disk, it's very bad news. Get your local DOS wizard immediately, and don't forget to tell the wizard to bring disk recovery software.
- ✔ Don't press F for Fail. If you do, you get the message Current drive is no longer valid, which sounds worse than it is. (If this happens, type **C:** and press Enter to make drive C the new current drive.

12. **Write protect error writing Drive X; Abort, Retry, Fail?**

Cause: You tried to delete a file on a write-protected disk. Or you tried to copy a file to a write-protected disk.

Solution: If you're using a 3.5-inch disk, turn the disk over, and move the little write-protect tab down so that it covers the hole on the upper-left corner of the disk. If you're using a 5.25-inch disk, remove the tape that covers the write-protect notch. Then reinsert the disk and press R to retry the command. If you get this message while using a hard disk, get expert help.

TIP

Before you unprotect a disk, make sure that there isn't a compelling reason to keep the disk protected. One of your coworkers is going to be pretty miffed if you write over the only copy of an important file on a protected disk.

12 More Cool Things To Get for Your Computer

1. Surge Protector

It's not a pretty subject. But, that innocent-looking power receptacle might just be the death of your computer. Everyday current fluctuations (like the ones that cause the lights to flicker when your refrigerator starts) are commonplace, and they can cause your system to crash. What's worse, lightning can cause a massive power surge capable of frying just about anything that's plugged in—even stuff that's turned off. You may see cheap power centers (boxes with several plugs) that include "surge protection," but don't bet on it. Expect to pay more—up to $100—for decent surge protection. It's worth it. While you're at it, look for a surge protector that includes a power control center, which lets you turn on your computer and all the peripherals (such as printer and modem) with just one flick of the switch.

2. Joystick

A joystick is another kind of pointing device and is a must for arcade-action games. It plugs into a game port, which your computer might not have. If your computer doesn't have a game port, consider buying a sound board that includes a game port—lots do (for more information on sound boards, see Chapter 10).

3. Uninterruptable Power Supplies (UPS)

If you use your computer for a business, think seriously about getting an uninterruptable power supply (UPS). A UPS includes surge suppression, plus it offers so much more: a battery that automatically charges itself. When the power goes out the window, the battery steps in. All the lights go off and the stereo suddenly goes quiet, but you're still in business. You then have about 10 or 15 minutes to save everything, shut down, go get a brewski, and thank your lucky stars.

Uninterruptable power supplies used to cost a lot of money ($300-$500), but the price has gone down considerably. I'm seeing good units selling for as little as $129.

4. Tape Backup Drive

A *tape backup system* is like the difference between night and day when it comes to backup convenience. Also known as a *tape cartridge drive*, this thing is about the size of a floppy disk drive, and fits in one of your computer's empty drive bays. (A *drive bay* is a place where you can stick a floppy disk drive.) A tape backup system uses removable tape cartridges, which can store up to 250MB of information per tape. To back up your system with a cartridge tape, you stick in the cartridge,

NOW WHAT
DOES IT WANT
ME TO DO?

use your backup software, and just forget about it. The tape backup system copies your hard disk's contents to the tape. You take out the tape and put it away, hoping never to use it. But, if your disk crashes, you put in a new disk, and then "play back" your tape. Lo! Your hard disk is restored, at least up to the moment that you last backed up. But for business, professional, and creative users, that can mean the difference between being in business or being out of business.

Tape backup systems used to be expensive ($400-$600), but recently there's been a dramatic price drop. You can get a pretty good tape drive for as little as $150, and cartridges only run you $25 or so.

5. Copy Holder

Probably the only really cheap accessory you can get, this thing clamps onto your monitor and holds up paper so that you can see it (maybe a handwritten report that you are typing into the computer).

6. Keyboard Drawer

If your keyboard is positioned too high, you risk developing a repetitive strain injury. The keyboard should be low enough so that your elbows are at right angles to your upper arms—or even slanting a little downwards. Getting a keyboard drawer is one way to lower the keyboard. Make sure there's room for your mouse!

7. Dust Covers

These really aren't necessary, but if you'd like to keep your system covered up when not in use I'd recommend canvas rather than plastic. Canvas dust covers don't develop static electricity, which can zap your computer's memory.

8. Keyboard Cover

If your kids leave peanut butter on your keyboard like mine do, consider getting a flexible plastic keyboard cover. This fits over the keys and protects them, but lets you type almost as if the thing wasn't there. A plus: Coffee washes right off these things like water off a duck's back. The truth is, though, that these things make typing a bit more difficult and are generally used only for keyboards that will be accessed by the public. Consider it only if you've wiped out two or three keyboards already with coffee inundations.

9. Microprocessor cooling fan

Got a 486 or a Pentium system? These chips run hot. And if they get too hot, they get damaged. This microprocessor cooling fan plugs into an unused disk drive connector. It keeps your microprocessor running cooler than it would without the fan.

10. Mouse pad

Not really necessary, this pad nevertheless gives you better tracking. Get a big one so you don't run out of mouse maneuvering room.

11. Keyboard wrist pad

To avoid repetitive strain injuries, you shouldn't type with your hands angled up from your wrists. A good way to avoid doing this is to equip your keyboard with a wrist pad.

12. Glare Filter

If you must position your PC so that it reflects light, a glare filter can reduce the strain on your eyes. But the best solution (as well as the cheapest) is to position your monitor so that it's facing away from light sources.

Symbols

* (asterisk) wild card, 256
/ (slash) in DOS commands, 270
? (question mark) wild card, 256
\ (backslash) in directory names, 252
286 microprocessor, 90
3.5-inch disks, 113-114
386 microprocessor, 90
486 microprocessor, 91
5.25-inch disks, 113, 378
8088 microprocessor, 89-90

A

accessing floppy disk drives, 264
active windows, 63
addresses (e-mail), 337-338
All File Details command (Windows View menu), 287
America Online, 205
American Standard Code for Information Interchange (ASCII), 385
analog monitors, 136
applications, 18, 28, 302-305
 databases, 307-308
 DOS
  exiting, 55-56
  installing, 319-321
  starting, 49-50, 324
 games, 309-310
 integrated applications, 308-309
 Internet, 338-340
 networks, 212
 specialty applications, 309
 spreadsheets, 306-307
 troubleshooting, 352-353
 Windows
  exiting, 77-79
  File Manager, starting, 294
  installing, 322-323
  starting, 75-76, 325
  switching applications, 240
  uninstalling, 241
 word processing, 305-306
Archie, 339
archiving, 383
ARPANET, 333
ASCII (American Standard Code for Information Interchange), 385
asterisk (*) wild card, 256
audio CDs, 194
AUTOEXEC.BAT file, 257-258

B

backing up files, 273-274, 381
  tape backup systems, 392
backslash (\) in directory names, 252
Backspace key, 50
backup utilities, 234-235
Bad command or file name message, 49
basic input-output system (BIOS), 41-42
batteries
  notebook computers, 224-225
  troubleshooting, 355
BBSs (bulletin board systems), 206-208
BIOS (basic input-output system), 41-42, 86
booting, 39-41, 44-45
  BIOS message, 41-42
  floppy disks, 377
  hard disks, 43
  loading DOS, 43-44
  memory check, 42
  restarting, 57
brightness (monitors), 139
bugs (software), 327
bulletin board systems (BBSs), 206-208
busses, 87
buying
  floppy disks, 115-116
  software, 314-315, 380
By File Type command (Windows View menu), 287
bytes, 98

C

C:\> prompt, 48-49
caching software, 238
capacity
  floppy disks, 111-112
  hard disks, 98-99
Caps Lock key, 146, 377
Cascade command (Windows Window menu), 74
cascading windows, 73-74
CD (Change Directory) command (DOS), 51, 265
CD-ROM, 185-188
  audio CDs, 194
  caddies, 194
  drives, 192-193
  muliple disks, 194
  Photo CD, 196-197
central processing units, *see* CPUs
CGA (Color Graphics Adapter), 130, 134
Change Drive and Directory dialog box, 296
check boxes (Windows), 70
clicking mouse, 65, 155
clock speed, 93-96
clones, 17-18
closing windows, 66
CLS command (DOS), 266
cold booting, 39
Color Graphics Adapter (CGA), 130, 134
color monitors, 138-139
color printers, 168
command-line operating systems, 262-263
commands
  Disk menu (Windows), 122
  DOS
    / (slash), 270
    CD, 51, 265
    CLS, 266
    COPY, 272
    DEL, 256, 269
    DIR, 53-54, 276
    DISKCOPY, 276-277

guidelines, 263
MD, 268
MOVE, 274
REN, 275
TYPE, 266-267
UNDELETE, 271
File menu (Windows)
Create Directory, 297
Exit Windows, 79
Properties, 352
Rename, 292
Run, 322
Search, 293
Select Files, 289
Undelete, 295
Options menu (Windows)
Configure Delete Protection, 297
Font, 288
Tree menu (Windows), 286
View menu (Windows), 287
Window menu (Windows)
Cascade, 74
Main, 122
New Window, 288
Tile, 74
communication software, 203
compressing disks, 99-100, 236, 240
CompuServe, 205
CONFIG.SYS file, 257-258
Configure Delete Protection command (Windows Options menu), 297
configuring systems, 44
Confirm Directory Delete dialog box, 298
Confirm File Delete dialog box, 290
Confirm Mouse Operation dialog box, 291
connecting mouse, 158-159
connecting to Internet, 335-337
contrast (monitors), 139
conventional memory, 102
COPY command (DOS), 272
copying
disks, 276-277
files
back ups, 273-274
file groups, 274
File Manager (Windows), 291
troubleshooting, 355-356
cordless mouse, 158
correcting errors, 50
CPUs (central processing units), 85, 88-89
286, 90
386, 90
486, 91
8088, 89-90
cooling fans, 394
math coprocessors, 92
Pentium, 91-92
PowerPC, 92-93
speed, 93-96
upgrading, 96
crashed computers, 350-352, 367, 380
Create Directory command (Windows File menu), 297
current directory, 51, 253
cursor-movement keys, 145, 148

D

database applications, 307-308
dates, 354-355
DD (double-density) disks, 112
default fonts, 175
defragmenting hard disks, 236
DEL command (DOS), 256, 269

Delete dialog box, 290
deleting
directories (Windows), 298
files, 268-271
File Manager (Windows), 289-290
recovering files, 271-272
File Manager (Windows), 295-297
Delphi (on-line service), 205
density (floppy disks), 111-112
desktop (windows), 64
dial-up access to Internet, 336
dialog boxes, 69-70
Change Drive and Directory, 296
Confirm Directory Delete, 298
Confirm File Delete, 290
Confirm Mouse Operation, 291
Delete, 290
Enter First Character, 296
Error Copying File, 355
Task List, 76
digital monitors, 136
DIR command (DOS), 53-54, 276
Direct Connections Organizations (Internet), 336
directories, 250
creating, 268
current directory, 51, 253
directory tree, 251-252
File Manager (Windows)
creating directories, 297-298
deleting directories, 298
viewing directories, 285-286
listing files, 53-54
logging on, 379
path names, 254-255, 267
root directory, 54, 384
storage, 250-251
subdirectories, 252
switching, 50-52, 265-266
Disk menu commands (Windows), 122
Disk Operating System, *see* DOS
disk space (software), 319
DISKCOPY command (DOS), 276-277
disks
archiving, 383
compressing, 236, 240
copying, 276-277
disk repair utilities, 238-239
drives
caring for, 120
networks, 110
floppy disks
3.5-inch, 113-114
5.25-inch, 113, 378
accessing drives, 264
booting, 377
capacity, 111-112
density, 111-112
drives, 37, 114-115
formatting, 120-123
inserting, 116-117, 378
precautions, 119
purchasing, 115-116
reformatting, 357
removing, 116-117
requirements, 110
troubleshooting, 264, 358-359
unformatted disks, 264-265
versus hard disks, 108-110
viewing contents, 124-125
write-protecting, 118
hard disks, 85, 97-98
activity light, 37
booting, 43
capacity, 98-99
defragmenting, 236
managing space, 383
reformatting, 357-358

troubleshooting, 349, 359-360
versus floppy disks, 108-110
viruses, 236-237
DOS (Disk Operating System), 29-31, 385
applications
exiting, 55-56
installing, 319-321
starting, 49-50, 324
command-line operating systems, 262-263
commands
/ (slash), 270
CD (Change Directory), 51, 265
CLS, 266
COPY, 272
DEL, 256, 269
DIR, 53-54, 276
DISKCOPY, 276-277
guidelines, 263
MD, 268
MOVE, 274
REN, 275
TYPE, 266-267
UNDELETE, 271
directories
current directory, 51
listing files, 53-54
path names, 267
root directory, 54
switching, 50-52
EXE file extension, 54
fonts, 174
formatting floppy disks, 120-122
help, 278
loading, 43-44
prompt, 48-49
restarting computer, 57
SCANDISK utility, 239
shutting down, 56
viewing floppy disk contents, 124
Windows, 61
dot pitch measurement (monitors), 137
dot-matrix printers, 166
double-clicking mouse, 155
double-density (DD) disks, 112
Dow-Jones News/Retrieval Service, 205
dpi (dots per inch), 169
dragging and dropping files
copying, 291
moving, 291-292
dragging mouse, 65, 155
drives
caring for, 120
floppy disks, 37, 114-115
networks, 110
switching, 264-265
troubleshooting, 349
drop-down list boxes (Windows), 69

E

e-mail, 204
addresses, 337-338
Internet, 334
EGA (Enhanced Graphics Adapter), 130
electromagnetic radiation (EMR), 140
EMR (electromagnetic radiation), 140
Energy Star monitors, 141
Enhanced Graphics Adapter (EGA), 130
Enter First Character dialog box, 296
environment, 35-36
ergonomics, 35-36
Error Copying File dialog box, 355
error messages, 388-391
Bad command or file name, 49
File not found, 267
General failure reading drive __, 113
Invalid directory, 52
Non-system disk or disk error, 43

troubleshooting, 347-348
Esc key, 152
EXE file extension, 54
Exit Windows command (Windows File menu), 79
exiting
applications
DOS, 55-56
Windows, 77-79
File Manager (Windows), 298-299
Windows, 79
expanded memory, 103
expansion boards, 86
extended keyboard, 144
extended memory, 102

F

fatware, 319
fax/modems, *see* modems
faxing, 209-210
File Manager (Windows), 282-284
deleting files, 289-290
directories
creating, 297-298
deleting, 298
viewing, 285-286
exiting, 298-299
file specifications, 287-288
files
copying, 291
moving, 291-292
naming, 292
recovering, 295-297
searching, 293-294
selecting, 289
sorting, 287
viewing, 284-287
fonts, 288
starting applications, 294
windows, 288
File menu commands (Windows)
Create Directory, 297
Exit Windows, 79
Properties, 352
Rename, 292
Run, 322
Search, 293
Select Files, 289
Undelete, 295
File not found message, 267
file servers, 212
files, 248-250
backing up, 273-274, 381
tape backup systems, 392
copying, 272-274
troubleshooting, 355-356
deleting, 268-271
directories, 250
creating, 268
current directory, 253
directory tree, 251-252
logging on, 379
path names, 254-255, 267
storage, 250-251
subdirectories, 252
file extensions, 249
EXE, 54
File Manager (Windows)
copying, 291
deleting, 289-290
file specifications, 287-288
moving, 291-292
naming, 292
recovering, 295-297
searching, 293-294
selecting, 289

sorting, 287
viewing, 284-287
listing, 53-54
lost files, 356-357
moving, 274-275
naming, 249, 275-276
recovering, 271-272
searching, 276-278
system files, 257-258
viewing contents, 266-267
wild cards, 255-256
finger, 339
floppy disks
3.5-inch, 113-114
5.25-inch, 113, 378
accessing drives, 264
booting, 377
capacity, 111-112
density, 111-112
drives, 37, 114-115
formatting
DOS, 120-122
reformatting, 357
troubleshooting, 123
Windows, 122-123
inserting, 116-117, 378
precautions, 119
purchasing, 115-116
removing, 116-117
requirements, 110
troubleshooting, 264, 358-359
unformatted disks, 264-265
versus hard disks, 108-110
viewing contents, 124-125
write-protecting, 118
Font command (Windows Options menu), 288
fonts, 172-173
default fonts, 175
DOS, 174
File Manager (Windows), 288
point size, 176
printer fonts, 173
screen fonts, 173
soft fonts, 176
TrueType fonts, 174-175
Windows, 174-175
Form Feed button (printers), 172
Format Disk command (Windows Disk menu), 122
formatting floppy disks
DOS, 120-122
reformatting, 357
troubleshooting, 123
Windows, 122-123
front panel, 36-38
FTP (File Transfer Protocol), 339
function keys, 145

G

G (gigabyte), 99
game software, 309-310
General failure reading drive __ message, 113
Genie (on-line service), 206
Gopher, 207, 339
"Gray Scale" VGA, 131
GUIs (graphical user interfaces), 62, 385

H

handwriting recognition, 161
hard disks, 85, 97-98
activity light, 37

booting, 43
capacity, 98-99
defragmenting, 236
disk compression, 99-100
managing space, 383
reformatting, 357-358
troubleshooting, 349, 359-360
versus floppy disks, 108-110
viruses, 236-237

hardware, 19
buses, 87
CPUs (central processing units), 85, 88-89
286, 90
386, 90
486, 91
8088, 89-90
cooling fans, 394
math coprocessors, 92
Pentium, 91-92
PowerPC, 92-93
speed, 93-96
upgrading, 96
expansion boards, 86
front panel, 36-38
handwriting recognition, 161
hard disks, 85
capacity, 98-99
disk compression, 99-100
joysticks, 392
keyboard, 23, 144-145
caring for, 151, 377
cursor-movement keys, 148
Esc key, 152
extended keyboard, 144
guidelines, 152-153
key combinations, 150
keyboard drawers, 393
safety, 154-155
special keys, 147-150
toggle keys, 145-147
type-ahead buffers, 151
memory, 85-86
conventional memory, 102
expanded memory, 103
extended memory, 102
managing, 103
RAM (random-access memory), 100-101
system requirements, 101-102
modems, 26, 200-203
notebook computers, 227
monitors, 23
analog, 136
brightness, 139
caring for, 139
color, 138-139
contrast, 139
determining types, 134
digital, 136
dot pitch measurement, 137
Energy Star, 141
interlacing, 136
ISA busses, 133
local busses, 132-133
MCA busses, 133
monochrome, 138-139
notebook computers, 227
resolution, 137-138
safety, 140-141, 382
screen savers, 139-140
screen size, 135-136
types, 134-135
VESA, 132
video accelerators, 131-132
video adapters, 128-131
motherboards, 86

mouse, 24, 70-71, 155-158
connecting, 158-159
cordless mouse, 158
mechanical mouse, 158
mouse pads, 394
optical mouse, 158
safety, 159
software, 159
ports, 103-104
power supply, 87
printers, 25
color, 168
drivers, 170-171
fonts, 172-176
Form Feed button, 172
installing, 176-177
laser printers, 168-169
notebook computers, 227
On Line button, 172
page description languages, 171-172
testing, 178
troubleshooting, 178-180, 360-361
types, 166-168
Windows, 179
sound boards, 25
speech recognition, 161-162
systems, 22
trackballs, 160
HD (high-density) disks, 112
help
DOS, 278
repairs, 371-372
technical support, 368-371
troubleshooting, 366-367
HGA (Hercules Graphics Adapter), 130, 135
high-density (HD) disks, 112

I

IBM-compatible computers, 17
icons, 63
Indicate Expandable Branches command (Windows Tree menu), 286
inkjet printers, 167
inserting floppy disks, 116-117, 378
installing
modems, 202-203
printers, 176-177
software
DOS applications, 319-321
guidelines, 323-324
Windows applications, 322-323
uninstalling Windows applications, 241
integrated applications, 308-309
interlacing, 136
Internet, 332-334
applications, 338-340
connecting to, 335-337
e-mail addresses, 337-338
protocols, 333
uses, 334-335
Invalid directory message, 52
ISA busses, 133

J-K

joysticks, 392

K (kilobyte), 99, 386
key combinations, 150
keyboard, 23, 144-145
caring for, 151, 377
cursor-movement keys, 148
extended keyboard, 144

guidelines, 152-153
key combinations, 150
keyboard drawers, 393
safety, 154-155
special keys, 147-150
toggle keys, 145-147
type-ahead buffers, 151

L

LANs (local area networks), 211-214
laptop computers, 218
laser printers, 167-169
LED printers, 167
list boxes (Windows), 69
listing files (DOS), 53-54
literacy, 15-16
loading DOS, 43-44
local area networks (LANs), 211-214
local busses, 132-133
locking switch, 36
logging onto directories, 379
LPT1, 176-177

M

M (megabyte), 99, 386
mailing lists (Internet), 334
Main command (Windows Window menu), 122
maintenance upgrades (software), 327
managing memory, 237-238
math coprocessors, 92
maximizing windows, 66
MCA busses, 133
MD command (DOS), 268
MDA (Monochrome Display Adapter), 130, 134
mechanical mouse, 158
megabyte (M), 99, 386
Megahertz (MHz), 386
memory
conventional memory, 102
expanded memory, 103
extended memory, 102
managing, 103, 237-240
memory check, 42
RAM (random-access memory), 85, 100-101, 386
ROM (read-only memory), 42, 86, 387
system requirements, 101-102
troubleshooting, 348
menu bars (windows), 64
menus (Windows), 67-68
MHz (Megahertz), 386
microprocessors, *see* CPUs
MIDI (Musical Instrument Digital Interface), 191-192
minimized applications, 64
minimizing windows, 67
modems, 26, 200
BBSs (bulletin board systems), 206-208
communication software, 203
e-mail, 204
faxing, 209-210
guidelines, 201-202
installing, 202-203
LANs, 211-214
notebook computers, 227
on-line services, 204-206
sharing data, 204
monitors, 23
analog, 136
brightness, 139
caring for, 139
color, 138-139

contrast, 139
determining types, 134
digital, 136
dot pitch measurement, 137
Energy Star, 141
interlacing, 136
ISA busses, 133
local busses, 132-133
MCA busses, 133
monochrome, 138-139
notebook computers, 227
resolution, 137-138
safety, 140-141, 382
screen savers, 139-140, 240
screen size, 135-136
types, 134-135
VESA, 132
video accelerators, 131-132
video adapters, 128-131
Monochrome Display Adapter (MDA), 130, 134
monochrome monitors, 134, 138-139
motherboards, 86
mouse, 24, 70-71, 155-158
connecting, 158-159
cordless mouse, 158
mechanical mouse, 158
mouse pads, 394
notebook computers, 225-226
optical mouse, 158
safety, 159
software, 159
troubleshooting, 353
Windows, 65
MOVE command (DOS), 274
moving
files, 274-275
File Manager (Windows), 291-292
windows, 66
MS-DOS, 386
multimedia
CD-ROM, 185-188
audio CDs, 194
caddies, 194
drives, 192-193
muliple disks, 194
MIDI (Musical Instrument Digital Interface), 191-192
Photo CD, 196-197
sound boards, 189-192
speakers, 195
system requirements, 188-189

N

naming files, 249, 275-276
File Manager (Windows), 292
navigating Windows, 65-67
networks, 110
Internet, 332-334
applications, 338-340
connecting to, 335-337
e-mail, 337-338
protocols, 333
uses, 334-335
LANs, 211-214
New Window command (Windows Window menu), 288
newsgroups (Internet), 334
nn (Internet application), 339
Non-system disk or disk error, 43
notebook computers, 27, 218
batteries, 224-225
environmental concerns, 223
external connections, 226-228
mouse, 225-226
PCMCIA, 223

system requirements, 221-222
travel concerns, 225
Novell DOS 7 operating system, 242
NSFNET, 333
Num Lock, 146
numeric keypad, 145

O

On Line button (printers), 172
on-line services, 204-206
connecting to Internet, 336
operating systems, 28, 232-234
command-line operating systems, 262-263
Novell DOS 7, 242
OS/2, 242
PC-DOS, 241
UNIX, 243
optical mouse, 158
option buttons (Windows), 70
Options menu commands (Windows)
Configure Delete Protection, 297
Font, 288
OS/2 operating system, 242

P

page description languages, 171-172
palmtops, 219
parallel ports, 104
Partial Details command (Windows View menu), 287
path names, 254-255, 267
PC-DOS operating system, 241
PCMCIA (Personal Computer Memory Card International Association), 223
PCs (personal computers), 17-19
clones, 17-18
IBM-compatible computers, 17
notebook computers, 27
portable computers, 218-221
restarting, 57
setup, 34-35
shutting down (DOS), 56
uses, 19-21
PDAs (Personal Digital Assistants), 219, 228-229
Pentium microprocessor, 91-92
Personal Computer Memory Card International Association (PCMCIA), 223
personal computers, *see* PCs
Personal Digital Assistants (PDAs), 219, 228-229
Photo CD, 196-197
point size (fonts), 176
pointing mouse, 65, 155
portable computers, 218-221
notebook computers
batteries, 224-225
environmental concerns, 223
external connections, 226-228
mouse, 225-226
PCMCIA, 223
system requirements, 221-222
travel concerns, 225
PDAs (Personal Digital Assistants), 228-229
ports, 103-104
printers, 176
PostScript Laser printers, 167
power supply, 40, 87
notebook computers, 224-225
surge protectors, 391
troubleshooting, 347-350
UPS (uninterruptable power supply), 392

power switch, 36
PowerPC microprocessor, 92-93
printers, 25
- color, 168
- drivers, 170-171
- fonts
  - default fonts, 175
  - DOS, 174
  - point size, 176
  - printer fonts, 173
  - screen fonts, 173
  - soft fonts, 176
  - TrueType fonts, 174-175
  - Windows, 174-175
- Form Feed button, 172
- installing, 176-177
- laser printers, 168-169
- notebook computers, 227
- On Line button, 172
- page description languages, 171-172
- testing, 178
- troubleshooting, 178-180, 360-361
- types, 166-168
- Windows, 179

Prodigy (on-line service), 206
Program Manager (Windows), 60-65, 381
- program groups, 71-72
- switching to, 76-77

programs, *see* applications
Properties command (Windows File menu), 352
protocols (Internet), 333
purchasing
- floppy disks, 115-116
- software, 314-315, 380

Q-R

question mark (?) wild card, 256
quitting, *see* exiting

RAM (random-access memory), 85, 100-101, 386
read-only memory (ROM), 42, 86
recovering deleted files, 271-272
recovering files (Windows), 295-297
reformatting
- floppy disks, 357
- hard disks, 357-358

remote connections, 240
removing floppy disks, 116-117
REN command (DOS), 275
Rename command (Windows File menu), 292
renaming, *see* naming
repairs, 371-372
repetitive strain injury (RSI), 154, 382
reset button, 37
resolution (monitors), 137-138
restarting computers (DOS), 57
restoring windows, 67
RGB monitors, 134
ROM (read-only memory), 42, 86, 387
root directory, 54, 384
RSI (repetitive strain injury), 154, 382
Run command (Windows File menu), 322
running multiple applications, 76-77

S

safety
- computer accessories, 391-394
- keyboard, 154-155

monitors, 140-141, 382
mouse, 159
saving, 381
Windows, 78
SCANDISK utility, 239
scanners, 210
screen fonts, 173
screen savers, 139-140, 240
Scroll Lock, 146
scrolling windows, 67
Search command (Windows File menu), 293
searching files, 276-278
File Manager (Windows), 293-294
Select Files command (Windows File menu), 289
selecting files (Windows), 289
serial ports, 104
setup, 34-35
shareware, 206, 310
sharing data (modems), 204
shutting down computers (DOS), 56
sizing windows, 66
slash (/) in DOS commands, 270
soft fonts, 176
software, 19
application software, 28
applications, 302-305
databases, 307-308
games, 309-310
installing, 319-324
integrated applications, 308-309
specialty applications, 309
spreadsheets, 306-307
starting, 324-325
troubleshooting, 352-353
word processing, 305-306
bugs, 327
caching, 238
caring for, 326
CD-ROM, 185-188
communication software, 203
copy protection, 315
disk space, 319
DOS, 29-31
fatware, 319
learning to use, 325-326
mouse, 159
operating systems, 28, 232-234
command-line operating systems, 262-263
Novell DOS 7, 242
OS/2, 242
PC-DOS, 241
UNIX, 243
purchasing, 314-315, 380
shareware, 206, 310
system requirements
checklist, 316-317
minimum requirements, 318
system software, 27
troubleshooting, 361
upgrading, 327-328
user interfaces, 232
utilities, 28, 234
backup utilities, 234-235
caching software, 238
defragmenting hard disks, 236
disk compression, 236
disk repair, 238-239
managing memory, 237-238
Undelete (Windows), 295
undelete utilities, 238
UNFORMAT, 357
UNINSTALL, 382
vendors, 239-241
virus scans, 236-237

Windows, 29-31, 61
advantages, 62
applications, exiting, 77-79
dialog boxes, 69-70
exiting, 79
icons, 63
menus, 67-68
mouse, 65
multiple applications, 76-77
navigating, 65-67
Program Manager, 60-65
starting applications, 75-76

Sort by Date command (Windows View menu), 287
sorting files (Windows File Manager), 287
sound boards, 25, 189-192
speakers (multimedia), 195
speech recognition, 161-162
speed (microprocessors), 93-96
speed indicator, 37
spinner controls (Windows), 69
spreadsheet applications, 306-307
starting, 39-41, 44-45
applications
DOS, 324
File Manager (Windows), 294
troubleshooting, 352-353
Windows, 325
Windows applications, 75-76
BIOS message, 41-42
DOS applications, 49-50
File Manager (Windows), 282
hard disks, 43
loading DOS, 43-44
memory check, 42
troubleshooting, 346-347

subdirectories, *see* directories
subnotebook computers, 219
surge protectors, 391
SVGA (Super Video Graphics Array), 131, 135, 387
switching
applications (Windows), 240
directories, 50-52, 265-266
drives, 264-265
to Program Manager (Windows), 76-77

system files, 257-258
system requirements
memory, 101-102
multimedia, 188-189
notebook computers, 221-222
software
checklist, 316-317
minimum requirements, 318

system software, 27
systems, 22

T

tape backup systems, 392
Task List dialog box, 76
technical support, 368-371
telnet, 339
terminate-and-stay-resident (TSR) programs, 387
Tile command (Windows Window menu), 74
tiling windows, 73-74, 288
times, 354-355
tin (Internet application), 339
title bars (windows), 63, 66
toggle keys, 145-147
trackballs, 160
Tree menu commands (Windows), 286
troubleshooting, 366-367
applications, 352-353
batteries, 355

copying files, 355-356
crashed computers, 350-352, 380
drives, 349
error messages, 347-348
floppy disks, 264, 358-359
formatting floppy disks, 123
hard disks, 349, 359-360
installing software, 323-324
lost files, 356-357
memory, 348
mouse, 353
power supply, 349-350
printers, 178-180, 360-361
refomatting
floppy disks, 357
hard disks, 357-358
repairs, 371-372
software, 361
starting PCs, 346-347
technical support, 368-371
time/date, 354-355
TrueType fonts, 174-175
TSR (terminate-and-stay-resident) programs, 387
turbo button, 37
TYPE command (DOS), 266-267
type-ahead buffers, 151

UNDELETE command (DOS), 271
Undelete command (Windows File menu), 295
undelete utilities, 238
undeleting, *see* deleting
UNFORMAT utility, 357
unformatted disks, 264-265
UNINSTALL utility, 382
uninterruptable power supply (UPS), 392
UNIX operating system, 243
upgrading
microprocessors, 96
software, 327-328
UPS (uninterruptable power supply), 392
Usenet, 208
user interfaces, 232
utilities, 28, 234
backup utilities, 234-235
caching software, 238
defragmenting hard disks, 236
disk compression, 236
disk repair, 238-239
managing memory, 237-238
Undelete (Windows), 295
undelete utilities, 238
UNFORMAT, 357
UNINSTALL, 382
vendors, 239-241
virus scans, 236-237

V

Veronica, 340
VESA (Video Electronics Standards Association), 132
VGA (Video Graphics Array), 130, 135, 387
video accelerators, 131-132
video adapters, 128-131
View menu commands (Windows), 287
viewing
directories (Windows), 285-286
file contents, 266-267
files (Windows), 284-287
floppy disk contents, 124-125
virus scans, 236-237

W-Z

WAIS, 340
warm booting, 39
wild cards, 255-256
- copying files, 274
- deleting files, 270-271

Window menu commands (Windows)
- Cascade, 74
- Main, 122
- New Window, 288
- Tile, 74

Windows, 29-31, 61
- advantages, 62
- applications
  - exiting, 77-79
  - installing, 322-323
  - starting, 75-76, 325
  - switching, 240
  - uninstalling, 241
- dialog boxes, 69-70
- exiting, 79
- File Manager, 282-284
  - copying files, 291
  - creating directories, 297-298
  - deleting directories, 298
  - deleting files, 289-290
  - exiting, 298-299
  - file specifications, 287-288
  - fonts, 288
  - moving files, 291-292
  - naming files, 292
  - recovering files, 295-297
  - searching files, 293-294
  - selecting files, 289
  - sorting files, 287
  - starting applications, 294
  - viewing directories, 285-286
  - viewing files, 284-287
  - windows, 288
- fonts, 174-175
- formatting floppy disks, 122-123
- icons, 63
- menus, 67-68
- mouse, 65, 70-71
- multiple applications, 76-77
- navigating, 65-67
- Norton Desktop utility, 240
- PC Tools for Windows utility, 240
- printers, 179
- Program Manager, 60-65, 381
  - program groups, 71-72
  - switching to, 76-77
- saving, 78
- viewing floppy disk contents, 124

windows
- active windows, 63
- cascading, 73-74
- closing, 66
- desktop, 64
- File Manager, 288
- maximizing, 66
- minimized applications, 64
- minimizing, 67
- moving, 66
- restoring, 67
- scrolling, 67
- sizing, 66
- tiling, 73-74, 288

word processing applications, 305-306
write-protecting floppy disks, 118
WWW (World-Wide Web), 207, 340
WYSIWYG, 61